THE COMPLETE IDIOT'S GUIDE® TO

Coping with Difficult People

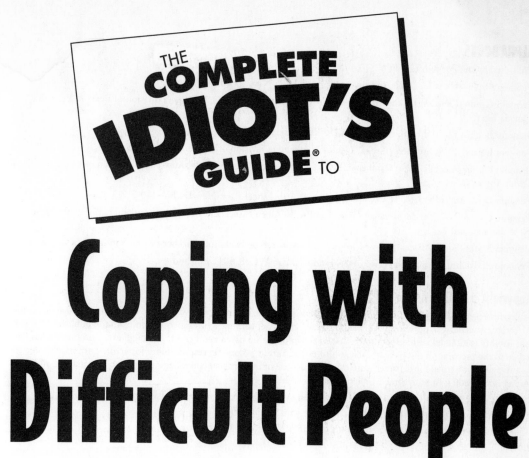

THE COMPLETE IDIOT'S GUIDE® TO

Coping with Difficult People

by Arlene Matthews Uhl

A member of Penguin Group (USA) Inc.

ALPHA BOOKS

Published by the Penguin Group

Penguin Group (USA) Inc., 375 Hudson Street, New York, New York 10014, U.S.A.

Penguin Group (Canada), 10 Alcorn Avenue, Toronto, Ontario M4P 3B2, Canada (a division of Pearson Penguin Canada Inc.)

Penguin Books Ltd, 80 Strand, London WC2R 0RL, England

Penguin Ireland, 25 St Stephen's Green, Dublin 2, Ireland (a division of Penguin Books Ltd)

Penguin Group (Australia), 250 Camberwell Road, Camberwell, Victoria 3124, Australia (a division of Pearson Australia Group Pty Ltd)

Penguin Books India Pvt Ltd, 11 Community Centre, Panchsheel Park, New Delhi—110 017, India

Penguin Group (NZ), cnr Airborne and Rosedale Roads, Albany, Auckland 1310, New Zealand (a division of Pearson New Zealand Ltd)

Penguin Books (South Africa) (Pty) Ltd, 24 Sturdee Avenue, Rosebank, Johannesburg 2196, South Africa

Penguin Books Ltd, Registered Offices: 80 Strand, London WC2R 0RL, England

Copyright © 2007 by Arlene Uhl

International Standard Book Number: 978-1-59257-578-7
Library of Congress Catalog Card Number: 2006938597

09 08 07   8 7 6 5 4 3 2 1

Printed in the United States of America

Note: This publication contains the opinions and ideas of its author. It is intended to provide helpful and informative material on the subject matter covered. It is sold with the understanding that the author and publisher are not engaged in rendering professional services in the book. If the reader requires personal assistance or advice, a competent professional should be consulted.

The author and publisher specifically disclaim any responsibility for any liability, loss, or risk, personal or otherwise, which is incurred as a consequence, directly or indirectly, of the use and application of any of the contents of this book.

Most Alpha books are available at special quantity discounts for bulk purchases for sales promotions, premiums, fundraising, or educational use. Special books, or book excerpts, can also be created to fit specific needs.

For details, write: Special Markets, Alpha Books, 375 Hudson Street, New York, NY 10014.

Publisher: *Marie Butler-Knight*
Editorial Director: *Mike Sanders*
Managing Editor: *Billy Fields*
Acquisitions Editor: *Paul Dinas*
Senior Development Editor: *Phil Kitchel*
Senior Production Editor: *Janette Lynn*
Copy Editor: *Tricia Liebig*
Cartoonist: *Richard King*
Cover Designer: *Bill Thomas*
Book Designer: *Trina Wurst*
Indexer: *Angie Bess*
Layout: *Chad Dressler*

Contents at a Glance

Appendixes

Contents

Introduction

Will Rogers, the renowned American humorist, famously said, "I never met a man I didn't like." He never would have needed a copy of this book. For the rest of us, however, it's essential to have strategies in place for dealing with people who annoy us, thwart us, and frustrate us. We say such people "drive us crazy," but the truth is they can only do so if we let them do the driving. It's time to take control of the wheel.

Ah, but what can be done with difficult people? Woody Allen suggested immersing them in warm gravy, but that sounds messy. The hero of Shakespeare's *Taming of the Shrew* used starvation and sleep deprivation—but that sounds like grounds for a lawsuit. Henry VIII simply beheaded those who displeased him, but this approach—in a rather positive development—has gone out of fashion.

As it happens, the sanest, wisest thing to do with difficult people is to learn to cope with them: the selfish and self-centered, the rude and the crude, the overtly and passively aggressive, the naysayers and nitpickers, the mean and the menacing. In whatever environments we encounter difficult people, we have to learn to respond to them rationally, rather than reacting impulsively (which usually makes the situation worse) or letting them take advantage of us (which they all too quickly turn into a habit).

That's the challenge, you see: managing our own behavior. The more we can develop and stick to a game plan for coping with tough people in tough situations, the better the results will be. The goal of this book is to help you develop that game plan—for your work life, your private life, and your general out-and-about-in-the-world life.

Difficult people are everywhere. We can't wave a magic wand and make them disappear. But we can develop the emotional skills we need so that our encounters will seem almost magically transformed from the torturous to the tolerable.

How This Book Is Organized

This book is divided into six parts. Each will assist you with different aspects of dealing with difficult people.

Part 1, "The ABCs of 'DPs'," describes our modern epidemic of difficult people, tells us how to spot a chronically difficult individual, and offers some basic self-protective strategies.

Part 2, "The Self-Absorbed," addresses the challenges of coping with self-centered people in the workplace, in personal relationships, and in public situations.

Part 3, "The Controllers," tells how to regain control from controlling types in any setting. It looks at overt, demanding controllers as well as deceptive and covert types.

Part 4, "The Obstructionists," will help you cope with the challenges of people who block your way—at work, at home, and in the world at large—with pessimism, perfectionism, irresponsibility, and indecision.

Part 5, "The Truly Toxic," offers advice for coping with people who have crossed the line from difficult to dangerous or cruel. It offers strategies for avoiding victimization across a wide range of scenarios.

Part 6, "Advanced Attitude Adjustments," will help you flex your skills by offering strategies for coping with "combination types" of difficult people as well as nice people who are having a difficult day. It also focuses on what we all can learn from the challenging people in our lives, and how we can make ourselves easier for others to get along with.

Coping Companions

Sidebars and margin notes have been placed throughout the chapters in this book to make it especially easy to begin getting a handle on managing the difficult people in your life right away. Within these text boxes, you'll find various tips and nuggets of knowledge. There are four kinds of sidebars:

DP Disarmer

These savvy strategic maneuvers will help you avoid sticky interpersonal tangles and minimize the impact of potentially difficult people.

Manhole Ahead

These alerts will help you identify signs of problematic behaviors and prevent you from provoking difficult people into being even more difficult.

Tried and True Tactics

Here you'll find anecdotes and advice from men and women who are learning to better cope with the challenging people in their lives.

def•i•ni•tion

Look here for an elaboration of terms used in the text.

Trademarks

Part 1

The ABCs of "DPs"

No doubt there have been difficult people around since prehistoric times, when we lived amidst much smaller populations. But in today's crowded, highly interconnected world it's not so easy to avoid people who test our patience. It's also inadvisable to take a caveman approach and bop them over the head with a rock. This part explains why, more than ever, we need to cultivate emotional skills to manage our people-related frustrations. It introduces the four primary types of difficult people ("DPs"), and lays down some basic rules for self-protection.

Chapter 1

They're Everywhere—
Or So It Seems!

In This Chapter

- ◆ Learning cooperative and competitive instincts
- ◆ Dealing with cities, civilization, and social stress
- ◆ The unnerving effect of technology
- ◆ Why avoidance won't solve things
- ◆ How aggression backfires
- ◆ Emotional intelligence to the rescue

"Listen to what he did to me now!"

"Can you believe she said that?"

"I can't stand that guy—he's driving me crazy!"

We overhear these sorts of comments every day. They're certainly the kind I listened to for years as a practicing psychotherapist in New York City. Complaining about other people seems to have surpassed baseball as the national pastime.

Are more people more difficult now than ever before, or does it just seem that way? To learn the somewhat complex answer to that question, it's a good idea to understand some fundamentals about human social interaction.

No Man—or Woman—Is an Island

Seventeenth-century English author John Donne is well known for these words: "*No man is an island, entire of itself; every man is a piece of the continent, a part of the main ...*"

Donne meant, of course, that none of us is entirely self-sufficient. Each of us relies on others. We are all part of an intricate social web. Think about your own day-to-day life for a moment and you'll understand how profoundly true this statement is.

If you're like most of us modern humans, you rely on other people in countless essential ways. You depend on others for your livelihood. You probably work with other people, but even if you work alone you still rely on others to use the goods or services you make or provide. You might share your home with others—spouses, partners, kids, parents, or roommates. But even if you live alone, you surely rely on friends and family for all kinds of assistance and emotional support. (It's hard to give yourself a good hug, hold your own hand, or cry on your own shoulder.)

We even rely on strangers to get us through our day: the bus driver, the weatherman, the guy who makes our coffee at Starbuck's. And we rely on professional acquaintances—doctors, tax accountants, teachers, mechanics—to help us negotiate the complexities of our lives. Without other people, life would be unmanageable—not to mention insufferably lonely.

Cooperation and Competition

If life to you feels like a cooperative endeavor, you've got the right feeling. A large part of the reason the human race has survived so far and made the progress it has is because of our propensity for helping one another out, and being helped in return. As many anthropologists, biologists, and even economists have pointed out, we appear to have an *instinct* for cooperative behavior.

From our earliest days, we traveled in groups, settled in groups, and benefited as groups from the contributions of one and all. Together we developed common languages and rituals. Together we hunted and foraged. Together we increased our odds of survival by developing group defensive strategies. (It's easier to fend off predators, for example, if some group members keep watch while others sleep.) It didn't take us long to figure out that there's safety in numbers.

But wait a minute! *Not everyone you know seems so cooperative.* You might wonder if there's more to the story, and indeed there is. Human beings are also fundamentally competitive with one another. At the most primal level, we compete to pass along our genes. This means we compete for desirable mates and for the resources necessary to procreate successfully and keep ourselves

def•i•ni•tion _____

An **instinct** can refer to a fixed, inborn behavior, but in a species as complex as humans, it is usually meant to signify a predisposition to learn a certain behavior or set of behaviors.

and our progeny healthy and strong. Our competitive instincts necessarily ignite aggression along with emotions such as jealousy. They also lead us to create social hierarchies, with some of us taking places higher up in the pecking order than others.

Striking a Delicate Balance

So, though it might seem strange, we are all wired to both cooperate and compete. (No one ever said being human was simple and straightforward.) Interacting with other people requires striking a delicate balance between our cooperative and competitive instincts. Throughout our lives, in innumerable situations and countless shifting circumstances, we all have to locate our social niche and negotiate what roles to play.

- ◆ At work, we have to agree who is the boss of whom (and, of course, most bosses also have bosses, and so on).

- ◆ In the marketplace, we have both buyers and sellers, negotiating from both vantage points.

- ◆ In our families, we decide which responsibilities fall to which family member and who provides what resources to the rest.

- ◆ In our friendships, we must form multiple bonds with diverse people, making implicit bargains about the trade-offs these alliances will yield.

Even in anonymous public settings we take on multiple roles and personae. Driving down a highway with the goal of making it to work on time requires both cooperation *and* competition. You have to drive in such a way that you won't endanger other motorists, let alone yourself. Ideally, you'd probably also like to be "humane" enough to accommodate fellow drivers' needs, such as waving them into your lane when they signal they'd like to be there. But if you happen to be running late, you're less likely to be so generous. In fact, you might—while still being cooperative enough not to cause a wreck—make some fairly aggressive maneuvers to keep ahead of the pack. Of course you have to compete with all the other drivers who are also late for work and want to get ahead.

Each day, every one of us is on that metaphorical road. We navigate between behaviors that benefit all (us included), behaviors that benefit others, and actions that serve only our own immediate needs and long-term goals. We all need to know how to co-exist with others—no matter how agreeable or disagreeable they may be—while at the same time tending to self-preservation.

But while coping with this dichotomy has always been part of the human condition, the ability to do so—and do it well—is more critical in our modern world than ever before. That's because there are just so many of us living so closely together.

Tribal Life to Modern Civilization

Humans have always lived in groups, but they used to be much smaller. Most prehistoric nomadic tribes probably consisted of a few interlinked, extended families. As the practice of agriculture began, we settled in hamlets, and later in slightly larger villages of perhaps 5 to 30 families. In these settlements, homes were situated together for sociability and defense, and the surrounding land was farmed.

Of course, even in tribal and village life, a certain amount of what we now call "people skills" was called for. And dealing with some people probably required more energy and forbearance than dealing with others. Human nature being what is, every group of cavemen or cluster of rural villagers probably had its share of the selfish, the demanding, the manipulative, and the downright unsavory. As civilizations grew, however, more people had to deal with more *other* people, of all sorts, in more and more complicated ways.

As people took on increasingly specialized livelihoods—not all of them agricultural—humans began gathering in densely populated cities. With the coming of the Industrial Age in the eighteenth century, people drawn by factory work flooded into European cities and took up residence in extremely close quarters.

This march toward crowded city life, in which the web of social dependencies grew increasingly complex, made for some knotty dilemmas. For one thing, city folk hailed from many disparate cultures and classes. People had to deal with others who had different habits and different social norms. It's often more challenging to be cooperative when there is less common ground.

In addition, increasing population density meant that everyone simply had less space. Back on the prehistoric plain it was relatively easy to find a little breathing room when your clan members were getting on your nerves. Not so in crowded modern environments. If you've ever been jostled on a subway, mobbed at the mall, or simply overwhelmed by the sheer number of fellow humans with which you share your corner of the planet, you'll understand how *crowding stress* can rapidly lower your patience threshold.

def•i•ni•tion

Crowding stress is a type of psychosocial stress induced by an increased density of population. It can induce complex behavior changes, including an increase in aggression and a decrease in the ability to learn and adapt.

Living as most of us do—amid lots of people with lots of differing priorities, practices, and personal agendas—contributes to our sense that difficult people are everywhere. After all, the odds are good that on any given day, we're going to encounter a few—and perhaps more than a few. Sometimes those encounters strain our emotions to the breaking point.

Busy, Busy: 24/7 Interactions

Complex civilizations might be viewed as astonishing human achievements, but no one has ever claimed that they offered the solution for getting along with our neighbors. The same can be said of modern technology: it's a wonder, all right, but it's no cure for interpersonal dilemmas. In fact, it tends to exacerbate them.

Long ago, if someone wanted to contact us from far away, they had to write a letter and find some sort of messenger to carry that letter. Then came the telephone, which allowed instantaneous access to whoever wanted to talk with us. If the telephone was a miracle, to some people's minds it was also a mixed blessing. Its insistent ring was hard to ignore, and people found they would interrupt just about any activity if the telephone summoned, even if they weren't in the mood to chat. Still, the intrusive nature of the telephone was limited, at first. After all, you could only answer the phone if you were at home or in your office when the call came in.

Then technology raised the ante. Along came answering machines, then voice mail, and then cell phones, the relentless miniaturization of which soon allowed them to slip into a pocket or handbag. These devices went from being a relative rarity in the 1980s to a must-have by the millennium. Before we knew it, none of us had an excuse not to answer the phone whenever it beeped, buzzed, or bleated a tune. Even if we didn't answer, it hardly mattered, because soon enough the impatient caller would no doubt send the same message via e-mail to our desktop computer, our laptop, or our Blackberry.

The capability to receive and respond to all manner of communications on a 24/7 schedule has added a number of wrinkles to our dealings with other people:

♦ We feel the pressure of having to reply, even if we'd rather not.

♦ We feel our availability leaves us no zone of privacy, no ability to retreat from our dealings with other people.

♦ Any number of difficult people are more than willing to exploit technology to try to get what they want from us—whenever and however they want it.

Now and again, that "no man is an island" trope makes us sigh wistfully. Wouldn't it be nice to be an island, or at least alone on one, just once in a while?

Why "Flight or Fight" Won't Work

Being so accessible to so many people so much of the time would be stressful even if everyone we dealt with was easy to get along with. The sheer exposure can be overwhelming. But when people are oblivious to our needs, or make a habit of obstructing our goals, or try to control us, or have outright ill will toward us, our stress level soars exponentially.

Obviously, dealing with difficult people is stressful for all of us. The question is, how do we handle that stress? The human brain evolved to respond to stressful situations by coordinating a host of simultaneous reactions in the nervous system, the muscles, and the endocrine system (which secretes hormones) that prepares us to either evade a perceived danger or rally the strength to fight against it. These reactions comprise what is known as the *fight-or-fight response*.

One can easily see the usefulness of the fight-or-flight instinct when dealing with acute primal threats. If a landslide or a tsunami is occurring, you need all that extra adrenaline that's being pumped into your system to help you run for your life. Encounter a poisonous rattlesnake and you'll need it to either make

def•i•ni•tion

The **fight-or-flight response** is the term coined by physiologist Walter Cannon to describe a reflexive sequence of internal reactions that prepare an organism to seek escape from or do battle with a stimulus that it considers a threat.

a break for it or, alternatively, hurl a heavy rock at the rapacious reptile. If someone is coming at me with a lethal weapon, I'd be grateful to my autonomic nervous system for helping me to duck, run, or perform an awesome series of karate chops that disarm my assailant.

But most of the stress we endure as a result of difficult people is not of the acute, immediately life-threatening sort. It's usually chronic, meaning that it's ongoing instead of a one-shot deal. And even though this stress can be seriously draining and debilitating, it's a more subtle, low-grade effect than, say, being hugged by a boa constrictor.

Given this, it seems logical that the fight-or-flight impulse is often not the best response when it comes to dealing with difficult people. That's not to say, however, that many of us don't try to employ it—usually without success.

The Avoidance Option

It's not surprising that many of us try to avoid interacting with difficult people as much as we can. This avoidance behavior is, after all, a manifestation of the "flight" reflex. If we can dodge difficult people, we just don't have to deal with them, right?

Well, not in most cases. Most of the difficult people you know are probably fixtures in your life. Dodge an encounter with your controlling boss or passive-aggressive co-worker today, and they'll just be back to haunt you tomorrow. Put off addressing problems with a selfish spouse or fickle lover now, and you'll only have to face them later.

As for the annoying strangers you encounter out in the world—the road hogs, the litterbugs, the controlling class moms, the tenacious telemarketers—the sad truth is that there's no way you can avoid such types unless, perhaps, you become a cave yogi or take up work as a lighthouse keeper.

Besides, even though the life of a hermit might have a certain transcendental appeal, most of us would actually suffer with too much solitude. Remember, human beings are social creatures at heart—and I don't use the term "at heart" loosely. Our social bonds are not simply practical but emotional as well. Study after study has shown that people who are socially isolated are at far greater risk of psychological and stress-related physical ailments than those who are part of various social networks.

Don't misunderstand: taking a breather from a tough interpersonal situation or "getting away from it all" now and again can be good. Doing these things can help restore your perspective. But fleeing the challenging people in your life, or shutting yourself off from other people in general, offers no permanent solution to the dilemma of difficult people.

> ### Tried and True Tactics
>
> "I used to get so fed up with my needy clients and demanding boss and complaining girlfriend that I would fantasize about living alone in a cabin in the woods. One summer I actually tried it. I took two weeks and vacationed alone, camping in the middle of nowhere. The first week was a much-needed break. The second became torturous. Even contact with the most annoying people I knew began to seem more appealing than having only my own company."—Christopher, 36

The Aggression Option

Along with taking flight, the urge to fight is deeply ingrained in our primal brains. Sometimes there's nothing more satisfying than thinking about taking a pop at someone we feel is doing us wrong or acting insufferably. But unless that person is physically endangering us, *thinking* about physical violence is really where we ought to stop.

Physical aggression only breeds more aggression and retaliation. I'll bet you can't come up with a single instance where anyone ever reacted to a physical assault—even one that was arguably deserved—by saying, "Ah, you were right. I see your point. I'll start being more reasonable right away." On the contrary, they only become more enraged and more determined to make their assailant's life miserable.

Manhole Ahead

Resist the urge to resort to physical violence. In our modern world, retaliation might not mean that someone responds with a punch in the nose: it might well mean they respond by slapping you—with a lawsuit, that is.

Of course, fighting doesn't always mean physical fighting. We can fight with words as well. We can hurl insults at those who thwart us, belittle those who provoke us, and call difficult people every name in the book. We can employ aggressive political tactics at work or in the community. But the same principle applies. A verbal barrage is likely only to engender a response in kind, or to set in motion a drive for revenge that will make a difficult person's former gambits look like the ministrations of Mother Teresa.

Despite its visceral appeal, aggressive fighting is apt to do more harm than good. That's not to say, however, that you can't stand up for yourself and defend yourself when dealing with difficult people. The trick is to use not weapons, but tools—the tools of emotional intelligence.

Emotional Intelligence: The Tools of Coping

Emotional intelligence is a phrase that has come to both embody and expand on what psychologists used to call *social intelligence*. It refers to the skills involved in understanding oneself and others and in getting along with other people. Popularized by Daniel Goleman in his 1997 book of the same name, emotional intelligence is sometimes referred to as EQ—for emotional intelligence quotient. It's an effective bit of shorthand because, as Goleman points out, EQ is as essential for functioning well in the world as are the cognitive abilities measured as IQ—arguably even more so.

Different researchers have enumerated slightly different factors that contribute to the general concept of emotional intelligence, or EQ, but they all include variants in these core abilities:

- The ability to name and identify our own emotions.

- The ability to exercise self-control and to distinguish between one's emotions, thoughts, and actions.

- The use of self-awareness to manage and, when necessary, modify one's responses to others.

- The capacity to read, interpret, and even influence other people's emotional states.

- The command of language (and nonverbal communication) related to emotional expression.

- The ability to sustain satisfactory interpersonal relationships.

- The feelings of emotional competence and strength.

The sum total of all these abilities adds up to good relationship management. The more we employ emotional intelligence, the greater the likelihood that the outcome of our interactions will be positive. Indeed, over the last decade researchers have inextricably linked measures of emotional intelligence with outcomes such as success at work and overall high relationship quality.

DP Disarmer

Cultivating emotional knowledge is critical because it helps us act consciously rather than simply reacting reflexively. Self-knowledge helps us modify the fight-or-flight response, which is based in our primal, reptilian brain, by allowing our neocortex—the seat of thought—to intervene.

Where does emotional intelligence come from? Some of these social aptitudes are most likely genetic, the result of inborn temperament. But the good news is that EQ can also be acquired and developed. What innate skills we do have can be honed.

Throughout this book, you'll be invited to up your EQ by learning ways to identify and understand the motivations of various types of difficult people, to predict what they might do, and to respond to them in ways that will not make bad situations worse but will, in fact, allow room for improvement.

Our modern world, with its lack of privacy and personal space, is a tough environment in which to practice being socially smart. But it's precisely because of this world we've created that we *must* practice. By learning to use emotional intelligence to cope with difficult people, we will lessen our stress, enhance our ability to enjoy our day-to-day lives, and begin to take pride in being more in control of ourselves and our circumstances.

The Least You Need to Know

- Human beings are predisposed to both compete and cooperate with one another, so peaceful coexistence has always required striking a delicate balance.

- As we moved toward increasingly complex societies and closer living quarters, social stress increased. We are around more people, and our odds of encountering difficult ones have increased.

- Our dealings with other people, especially challenging ones, have been strained by technology, which has made us easily accessible. It's tough to get a quiet moment alone to regroup.

- Dealing with difficult people is stressful, and under stress our reflexive response is one of fight-or-flight—but often neither fleeing nor fighting is a sound strategy.

- To counteract our primal fight-or-flight impulses, and actually manage relationships better, it's worthwhile to cultivate the skills of emotional intelligence.

Identifying a Difficult Person

In This Chapter

- ◆ The most common traits of difficult people
- ◆ The impact difficult people have on others
- ◆ The four major categories of difficult people
- ◆ The "personality disorder" factor
- ◆ The impact of personal biases
- ◆ The best way to avoid negative self-fulfilling prophecies

If someone asked you to name the difficult people in your life, you probably wouldn't have trouble making a list. Maybe it's your business partner, your sister-in-law, your next-door neighbor, your kid's school principal, your boss, your dad, your dental hygienist, your general contractor ....

What *is* it about certain people that sets you off? If you knew more about their modes of operation, you would be better able to deal with them. And if you could hone your radar when it comes to spotting certain major types of difficult people, you would be better able to enact emotionally intelligent strategies sooner rather than later.

This chapter looks at some traits that difficult people share, and at what kinds of feelings nearly all difficult people tend to evoke. It then breaks "DPs" down into four major types. Finally, it helps you sort out the truly difficult from those you might be overreacting to because of your own subjective hot buttons.

Characteristics of Difficult People

Look up "difficult" in the dictionary and you'll find numerous definitions. They include "requiring a lot of effort," "having aspects that are hard to endure," "hard to deal with," "hard to please or satisfy," and "hard to convince or persuade."

Sound like anyone you know? Well, given human nature, it probably sounds like *everyone* you've *ever* known, at one time or another. The truth is that anyone can be difficult some of the time. But if someone in your life fits some or all these definitions the vast majority of the time, it's fair to say they're difficult.

Unlike the occasionally thoughtless, stubborn, or crabby, the perennially difficult show a consistent pattern of behavior and a disinclination to be flexible. They have a set of behaviors and attitudes with little variation—behaviors that a number of people would verify. In other words, most people who know this person experience them the same way.

But the *effects* of those behaviors and attitudes are the real giveaway. The easiest way to spot a difficult person is to ask yourself how they make you feel.

How Difficult People Make Us Feel

Think about two people in your life, one of whom you define as easy to get along with and one you would call difficult. Now choose the responses that match your reaction to each of these two people:

1. **When you encounter them you feel:**

    A. Relaxed
    B. Tense

2. **When you talk with them you feel:**

    A. Natural, not self-conscious
    B. Unnatural and self-conscious

3. **After you've talked with them you feel as though you were heard and understood:**

   A. Often
   B. Rarely

4. **You share a laugh with these people:**

   A. Often
   B. Rarely

5. **You would be comfortable offering them a constructive suggestion:**

   A. Yes
   B. No

Chances are high that your answers with regard to the person you think of as easy to get along with were all, or mostly, As. That difficult person most likely had you choosing mostly Bs.

When we're around people we find difficult, we tend to feel overwrought and on edge. We may begin to act stiffly and unnaturally, for we feel it's risky to be spontaneous and let down our guard with such people.

DP Disarmer

Being in the company of a difficult person can literally make you uptight; your upper chest will feel constricted. If you pay attention to your internal state, you might find you're actually holding your breath. To begin to better manage your emotional reactions, be conscious of your breathing and try to deepen it. Getting some air into your diaphragm will actually trigger a physical relaxation response that in turn creates a calmer emotional state.

After we've spoken with a difficult person, we feel somehow less than satisfied, as if our words have been bouncing away without making an impression. We have the uneasy feeling that these people haven't really registered what we've said or acknowledged our point of view. It's not so much that they don't agree with us—even people we get along with might not always do that. It's more like they don't even hear us, they're so wrapped up in their own perspective and their own agenda.

You probably indicated that you don't share much spontaneous laughter with difficult people. We don't usually feel comfortable enough to make light of a situation around them. That's actually a shame, because laughter is one of the chief ways human beings have of bonding socially and of discovering common ground. (In the next chapter, we'll actually look at ways that your sense of humor can come in handy when dealing with certain difficult people.)

Finally, you probably indicated that you don't feel comfortable offering constructive suggestions to difficult people. You're probably afraid that whatever you say will either fall on deaf ears or set them off. Later, this book will also address some ways to make your suggestions more palatable, but for most of us this, too, is a learned skill. Our typical gut feeling about difficult people is that we don't want to "stir up a hornet's nest."

The Four Major Categories of Difficult People

All difficult people tend to consistently make us uneasy; but, of course, not all difficult people are difficult in exactly the same ways. This book will look primarily at four major types: those who are self-absorbed; those who are controlling; those who, in various ways, obstruct people around them; and those at the upper end of the difficulty spectrum who are truly toxic.

The Self-Absorbed

To be self-absorbed means to be wrapped up in oneself, preoccupied with one's own needs and desires. Now, you might be thinking, who isn't? To some extent, all of us are concerned with getting what we need, not just to survive, but also to prosper. It's only natural and healthy to keep one's well-being in mind—so long as that's not the only thing on your mind.

But several things distinguish those who are so seriously self-centered that they are consistently difficult to deal with.

- They are focused on their wants to the exclusion of almost anything else.
- They are oblivious to others' needs—and that these needs might sometimes be different from their own.
- They are not only greedy, but also emotionally needy—they expect everyone else to be as absorbed with them as they are with themselves.

It's usually easy to tell when you're in the company of a seriously self-absorbed person. They'll be so unmindful of you and your thoughts, wishes, and concerns that you'll practically feel the urge to pinch yourself to make certain that you still exist.

However, that dynamic can turn on a dime the moment such a person feels as though you can be of some use to them. If that happens, they're apt to stick to you like deer ticks—and try to suck everything they can out of you.

The Controllers

Controllers are people who want to be in charge, and who want their ideas to prevail. Of course, most of us want others to do our bidding in some situations (ask my 13-year-old about our chats regarding the laundry), but full-fledged controlling types want things to go their way just about all the time.

What gives difficult controllers away is that they will brook absolutely no resistance. If someone tries to exert opposition, they will pull out all the stops to reassert their dominance. Their controlling tactics, however, can take a number of forms:

  ◆ They might be hostile and aggressive—so volatile that others do what they want to keep the peace.

  ◆ They might assert that they know more than everyone else, and try to intimidate others into believing that they are smarter.

  ◆ They might lie, omit facts, go behind people's backs, or be otherwise deceptive to manipulate the outcome of situations.

  ◆ They might be *passive-aggressive*—agreeing with other people on the surface, but covertly controlling the situation by not acting or following through on any ideas or plans except their own.

def•i•ni•tion

> **Passive-aggressive,** a seeming contradiction in terms, refers to a style of exerting control by indirect means, for example, by intentional failure. The term was coined during World War II by a U.S. military psychiatrist who noticed certain soldiers subtly rebelling against authority by ignoring orders, feigning illness, or pretending to be incompetent.

When people use the first or second of these tactics, it's pretty easy to recognize you're in the presence of a controller. Not only do you feel like a marionette to their puppeteer, you also feel resentful and diminished. *What's the matter with my plan, my ideas? Why can't I ever be right for a change?*

But outright negative reactions to deceptive or passive-aggressive controllers take longer to come to the fore. Before you get mad, you're likely to go through a period of self-doubt and insecurity. *Are they the problem*, you'll wonder, *or is it me?* You'll know the answer when a consistent pattern of behavior becomes evident, or you start to compare notes with your fellow puppets.

The Obstructionists

Obstructionists are people who somehow always manage to stand in the way, gum up the works, and generally bring progress to a halt. There are quite a few varieties of obstructionist:

♦ Some put a damper on any project or plan by always being pessimistic—thinking of reasons why things won't work out.

♦ Some bring things to a halt by nitpicking and micromanaging every detail, or by enforcing "by the book" rules and red tape.

♦ Some can't, or won't, make up their minds.

♦ Some move so slowly you'd think they were standing still.

♦ Some never show up to do their part.

♦ Some are perennially prone to personal crises—or so they perceive them—that they derail the activity at hand.

In the company of an obstructionist, you'll feel frustrated and impatient. You'll probably also feel the urge to become secretive. You'll dread including them in anything or running anything by them for fear they'll become an impediment.

Tried and True Tactics

"There are some people in my extended family and at my job who I always think of as wanting to rain on my parade. I know there's no sense in trying to avoid them, so every time I know I'll be talking to them I always visualize myself opening an umbrella and holding it over myself. I have had to train myself not to let their attitude affect my own."—Meredith, 41

The Truly Toxic

The most difficult people are those who are truly toxic. They are the people whose behavior goes beyond irritating. It is truly and deeply hurtful. These people may be verbally derisive or dismissive, emotionally cruel, or sometimes completely craven and ruthless.

We take the actions of toxic people more personally than those of self-centered, controlling, or obstructionist types. And well we should. For on some level, even if they are not consciously aware of it, toxic people do not wish us well. In many cases, they are the kind of people who have what's referred to as *Schadenfreude*.

def•i•ni•tion

Schadenfreude means pleasure taken at the misfortunes of others. It's a German word used as a "loaner" not only by English, but by many other languages as well.

When we have encountered a toxic person, we feel far more than annoyed.

- We may feel emotionally numb, dumfounded, or even shocked.

- We may feel devalued, even totally worthless.

- We might doubt our own abilities and feel that personal failure is inevitable.

- We might feel lethargic and unmotivated—perhaps even depressed.

After a run-in with a toxic type, we might also find ourselves engaging in self-destructive behaviors. These can include such actions as overeating, drinking too much, driving too fast, spending money recklessly, and many other self-harming activities. When we do these things after contact with the same person over and over again, it can be because we have internalized what we feel is the toxic person's negative opinion of us.

Difficult or "Personality Disordered"?

From time to time, the behavior of any of the various types of difficult people might make us scratch our heads and wonder whether we're dealing with someone who has some sort of diagnosable psychological condition. In some cases, and to some extent, the beginnings of an answer might be found in the *DSM IV: The Diagnostic and Statistical Manual of Mental Disorders*.

The DSM IV lists the American Psychological Association's current criteria for mental disorders to facilitate professional diagnoses by mental health professionals. It covers the full range of clinical diagnoses, including mood disorders (such as depression), attention deficit disorders, eating disorders, and major psychotic disorders such as schizophrenia. In this manual, there is also a category known as *personality disorders*.

def•i•ni•tion

A **personality disorder** is a mental disorder signaled by an enduring and inflexible pattern of maladaptive behavior and inner experience (thoughts, feelings, perceptions) that results in dysfunction and subjective distress.

Some of the personality disorder symptoms listed in the DSM IV certainly are reminiscent of the actions and attitudes of people we might call difficult.

♦ Those with *narcissistic personality disorder* have an inflated sense of self-importance, believe they're "special," have a sense of entitlement, and can be interpersonally exploitative.

♦ Those with *obsessive compulsive personality disorder* are perfectionists, rigid, and preoccupied with details, rules, lists, and order.

♦ Those with *antisocial personality disorder* show a flagrant disregard for social norms and for the rights of others, as well as a lack of remorse.

So how will you know for sure if a self-centered person, or a perfectionist who obstructs your work, or a person who says hurtful, inappropriate things actually has a personality disorder? The answer is you won't.

Behavior traits fall on a continuum, and a certain line must be crossed to rate a clinical diagnosis. Moreover, a lot goes into making a professional diagnosis, including a thorough understanding of a person's inner world.

Besides, even if you did know, it shouldn't change how you deal with them in the day-to-day world. Although you should try to use your emotional intelligence in all situations, playing therapist when you're not one won't help you or anyone else.

Even if the difficult people you encounter don't meet the criteria for a full-fledged personality disorder, they might benefit from some form of psychotherapeutic intervention. It is well and good for you to have compassion for them and recognize that on some level they, too, may be suffering. But you will still need to cope with them wisely and skillfully while protecting and defending yourself.

Manhole Ahead _____

Never tell a difficult person "you need professional help" in a glib or insulting manner. You will only anger and humiliate them. If you have a close relationship with someone whom you feel could benefit from therapy, and if they express to you that they are in distress, you can gently ask whether they've considered confiding in a professional. If they don't respond well, table the subject for the time being. People will enter therapy when they're ready, not when *you're* ready.

Is It All in Your Mind?

One thing to take into account when you're tempted to think of someone as difficult is the impact of your own subjective opinion. We would be deluding ourselves to think that we have no personal biases at all about people. When we meet someone, we're not starting with a blank slate. It's human nature to have some preconceptions, and it helps to be cognizant of them.

Difficult or Different?

Whether we readily admit it or not, most of us at some time or another have stereotyped various people—prejudging them based on overgeneralized ideas we may have about them. Stereotypes can affect our views of people affiliated with particular cultural, ethnic, or gender groups. The phenomenon can also color our view of anyone with a distinctive characteristic—clothes, hairstyle, body decoration—about which generalizations are routinely made.

You've heard statements such as, "*Short people are control freaks—to compensate for their inferiority complex*," or, "*Young people are totally self-involved these days—only out to serve their own ambition.*" If you've heard such comments frequently enough, you might—without even being completely consciously aware of it—bring subtle biases to your relationships with the types of people in question.

We don't like to think of ourselves as prejudiced, but stereotyping can be ingrained at such a subconscious level that it's wise to be vigilant about your attitudes. If you notice that you have a lot of preconceived notions about someone before you really give them a chance, it's time to do an honest reality check and make sure you're not giving credence to broad, unfounded notions. Stereotypes are more about caricatures than character.

> **Tried and True Tactics**
>
> "In my job at a telecommunications company, I work with people from many different countries. I see that people raised in various cultures have different styles of interacting and that this sometimes leads people to make assumptions that are not true—for example, thinking that someone is unfriendly when they are just reserved. The remedy for most of these situations seems to be time. The longer we work together, the more we all see one another as individuals. That doesn't mean everyone always gets along, but it does mean we stop buying into stereotypes."—Bill, 45

Bad Reputations

Similar to the problem of stereotyping is the dynamic that can occur when we encounter someone with a so-called bad reputation. If we've heard that someone we're about to encounter is no day at the beach, we're probably going to look for telltale signs of the flaws or faults we've heard about. They might be there—but then again, they might not. It's best to form your own opinions.

There are two things you especially want to remember with regard to evaluating people based on their reputation. First, consider the source. Ask yourself if the person who told you about someone else's character might have biases of his own, or any possible ulterior motive. Does the woman who bad-mouthed someone you're about to go on a date with want to date that man herself? Is she just jealous?

Second, be wary of news that travels through the proverbial grapevine. When a gossip chain gets going, much gets lost, or grossly exaggerated, in translation. Second- and thirdhand information is usually not very reliable.

Now, if a number of diverse, trusted people with firsthand knowledge have mentioned that so-and-so is difficult, it's understandable that you might get your guard up a little bit. There's no harm in asking them if they have any good advice for dealing with so-and-so, and to keep that advice in mind. Even so, you must ultimately resolve to decide for yourself if someone has earned their reputation or gotten a bum rap.

Recreating the Past in the Present

Sometimes we encounter a person without having any preconceptions and take an almost instantaneous disliking to them. This might occur after just one conversation with them—it might even occur after only a few words. In some cases, it can happen as soon as we lay eyes on someone, without any words being exchanged at all.

When our reaction is so fast and furious, it is possible that we are in the grips of what psychotherapists call *transference*. That is, we might be transferring thoughts and feelings we have about someone in our past to a person we've only just met.

We could dislike somebody who resembles, say, a manipulative ex-spouse, or be wary of someone who resembles a domineering parent whose approval we craved. Transference can cause us to abandon realistic perspective in a heartbeat. Powerful feelings could take hold of us even if what we see (or what we sense on an unconscious level) is but a distant echo of similar mannerisms, voice inflections, or physical appearance.

def•i•ni•tion

Transference is a psychological phenomenon that involves the unconscious redirection of feelings from one person toward another. Transference was first described by Sigmund Freud, pioneer of psychoanalysis, who saw the phenomenon as a way of better understanding patients' conflicts.

Transference is such a potent force that it is hardly possible to simply ignore it. Your best bet is to be aware of it. If you have an instant, overwhelming "gut feeling" about someone whom you barely know, and if your feelings seem disproportionate to the level of contact you have had with that person, think about a significant person in your past about whom you feel similarly and ask yourself if there is a chance you are confusing one with the other. After you know you have a transference trigger, you should be better able to understand your reactions to your new acquaintance.

Loaded Relationships

Some types of relationships simply have a high innate difficulty level. In such relationships, there is a built-in wariness. This hypersensitivity can color whether we view someone as difficult. Typical loaded relationships include:

- Relationships where the connection is through a third party that both individuals care about, such as the relationship between a man and his mother-in-law (both parties are primarily bonded to the woman who is the man's wife and the mother-in-law's daughter).

- Relationships that involve a person who has taken on a replacement role of some sort, such as a stepparent.

- Relationships where there is a built-in power differential, such as employee/boss.

This is not to say that many people do not have positive, healthy relationships with in-laws, stepparents, bosses, and the like. However, it's always a good idea to make an extra effort to remain objective when a new person in any of these roles enters your life. These are excellent opportunities to practice giving someone the benefit of the doubt.

About Self-Fulfilling Prophecies

Ironically, the danger in deciding that someone is difficult before you have objective evidence is that your beliefs can actually create the reality you dread. That's because when we expect someone to be a certain way, we might act as though that expectation is already a fact. Our actions then cause others to *react* to us in a way that "proves we were right." But instead of proving we were right, all we have really done is created what's known as a self-fulfilling prophecy.

For example, if we expect someone to be critical of us, we might be very defensive with them. This might cause them to wonder what we're being so defensive about, and to respond negatively to our ideas. If we expect someone to be controlling, we might try to get control of the situation ourselves as a preemptive maneuver. But then they see *us* as controlling, and respond in kind to defend their turf.

The reverse can be true as well, however. If we go into a situation expecting the best of someone, they might well rise to our expectations. There's no guarantee that this will happen, but there's certainly nothing to lose and everything to gain by trying to approach each new relationship without personal baggage and biases.

The Least You Need to Know

◆ Although everyone can be difficult sometimes, truly difficult people display consistent behaviors across many situations, and show an inability or unwillingness to be flexible.

◆ In the presence of difficult people, we tend to feel tense and defensive, to lack spontaneity, and to feel misunderstood.

◆ Difficult people can be divided into four major categories: the self-absorbed; the controlling; those who obstruct progress; and those who are truly toxic.

◆ As much as we'd like to think otherwise, we're all capable of bringing biases to our evaluations of other people. Try to cultivate objectivity by recognizing your tendencies to stereotype, adopt others' opinions, or confuse people with significant others in your past.

◆ Be careful of beginning any relationship by acting on unfounded expectations—you could set a self-fulfilling prophecy in motion, and actually create the dynamic that you dread.

Basic Self-Protective Strategies

In This Chapter

- ◆ Honing your listening skills
- ◆ Curbing impulsive reactions
- ◆ Cultivating self-respect
- ◆ Accessing your sense of humor
- ◆ Fighting fire with fire
- ◆ Knowing what you can—and can't—control

If you've established that you're dealing with a difficult person, there are some basic things you can do to defuse potential problems and shield yourself from potential frustrations. Throughout this book, you will learn strategies for dealing with particular types of difficult people, but there are a number of basic skills you can employ in nearly any situation. This chapter helps you get your general emotional intelligence skills in gear.

Listen Carefully

Are you a good listener? Most of us would probably say "Sure!" After all, when we talk we also listen, right?

Well, not always. In fact, if you really think about it, there are probably many times when you are speaking with someone and your mind wanders into left field. You might start thinking about your to-do list, what you're going to pick up for dinner, or a conversation you had with someone else. As your brain meanders, the speaker becomes a background drone—then they stop talking, and you have to play catch-up, trying to figure out where they left off and perhaps saying something noncommittal and banal in the hopes that they won't realize you were mentally absent.

When we are speaking with difficult people, it can be especially tempting to drift off. Blocking them out can even seem like a reasonable defense; if we are effective enough, we'll reduce their speech to a meaningless *blah blah blah*.

Another thing we often do when we have a conversation with a difficult person is to plan out our response while they're talking. For example, while they're critiquing a plan we've proposed, we're busy organizing a slew of evidence to show we're 100 percent right. If they're explaining why they should be in charge of something, we're busy preparing an argument about why they shouldn't.

To someone watching, it might look as though we're taking turns talking and listening. But in fact it's more of an act than an action.

Make no mistake—in some situations it will be in your best interest to tune out what a difficult person is saying, or to employ strategies that discourage them from talking quite so much. But the problem with *never* listening is that you won't gain any useful insights into the person you're dealing with, nor any clues about how to deal with them in a more productive way. To gain such insights, you need to listen *actively*.

The Art of Active Listening

To listen actively means to listen with careful attention. It also means to be sincerely curious and engaged. No faking it! Doing so will not only give you valuable knowledge, but also make the person speaking feel more positively inclined toward you. That's because the vast majority of us—difficult or not—have an inner radar that registers whether our words are falling on receptive ears.

Understandably, you might not always feel like being genuinely engaged when some-one with whom you have a difficult time is talking, especially if they're being critical of you or going on about something you've heard a million times before.

But have you really *listened* to them lately, or were you mostly just pretending to? Could they possibly have anything new or valuable to tell you? Might they provide you with clues on how to respond to them in a noninflammatory way? Active listening will help you find out.

Active listening involves both nonverbal and verbal behaviors, each of which will let the person speaking know that you're registering and considering their comments. Moreover, these behaviors will help *you* process what's being said in an emotionally skillful way—without flying off the handle.

To listen with active attention:

♦ Assume a listening posture. Lean in slightly, unfold your arms, and make eye contact.

♦ Offer nods and encouraging noises. Nodding your head slowly from time to time makes a speaker feel understood. Offering an occasional *"Mm-hmm"* does the same.

♦ Ask for details. This lets a speaker know you are paying attention and are inter-ested and curious. It also serves to slow down a person who seems to be going off on a tangent.

♦ Agree with factual information. You certainly might not agree with every-thing they say, but when they mention a fact, let them know you agree that it's a true statement. Even the tiniest bit of agreement can break down mistrust and ease conflict.

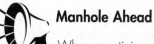 **Manhole Ahead**

When practicing active listening, never drum your fingers or your feet. These non-verbal cues indicate impatience and inattention.

Echoing

Two additional listening skills will serve you well when dealing with difficult people and defusing loaded conversations. The first is *echoing*, which is essentially a kind of paraphrasing. Echoing involves hearing the underlying *intent* behind the *content* of what's being said, and then repeating it back. This is far less inflammatory than defensive reactions.

For example, without echoing, your conversation with a difficult needy person might look like this:

> **Speaker:** You're always making plans with everyone else but you never spend any time with me.
>
> **Listener:** No I'm not. I spent time with you last Thursday. You're just too clingy. You need more friends.

From there, things can only deteriorate into more accusations and counter-accusations. But with echoing it might look like this:

> **Speaker:** You're always making plans with everyone else but you never spend any time with me.
>
> **Listener:** I understand that you're feeling neglected and that's not a pleasant feeling.
>
> **Speaker:** Yes, I am.
>
> **Listener:** We did go out last Tuesday, and I have been busy. I do understand your feelings, though. It would be all right with me if you wanted to make plans with others so you don't feel that way.

Mirroring

A second essential listening skill is *mirroring*, which involves acknowledging similarities between yourself and the speaker.

Now, wait! Don't rule out this skill because you think you could never have anything in common with the difficult people in your life. All human beings share a similar spectrum of emotions—fear, joy, love, anger, sadness, and surprise among them—even if they don't always see eye to eye. When mirroring, look for and mention common emotional ground. Frame responses that say, "I understand how you feel and have felt the same way."

Let's say you are listening to a person you think of as an irritating perfectionist:

> **Speaker:** I don't want anyone reading our committee's report until it is letter-perfect and answers every possible objection that might arise.

You could express anger at how utterly impossible you perceive this requirement to be. But you could also try mirroring the speaker's underlying feeling:

Listener: I get anxious, too, when it's time for others to comment on a project I've been working hard on. It can be hard to let go.

Now the speaker might soften their position. They might sense a bond with you, and you've given them the subtle message that despite their feelings, they need to think about letting go.

def•i•ni•tion

Echoing is a communication skill that involves understanding a speaker's emotional intent, paraphrasing it, and then repeating it back to them. It indicates: *I understand your feelings.*

Mirroring involves acknowledging to the speaker that you are capable of feelings similar to the ones they are having. It signifies: *I've felt the same way.*

Please note that neither mirroring nor echoing involves being insincere or claiming to agree with someone when you don't. But both skills are ways of making the person who is talking feel heard, and both have the added advantages of defusing negative emotions and buying you, the listener, some time to rein in any rash impulses and gather your thoughts.

DP Disarmer

You can reinforce verbal mirroring with nonverbal postural mirroring. If you arrange your body so that it mirrors that of a speaker—for example, if you lean forward with your right hand under your chin while they lean forward with their left hand under their chin—you will increase the speaker's sense of rapport with you. Experiments have shown that, although people aren't consciously aware of it, when someone deliberately mirrors their posture, they'll feel favorably about that person.

React Slowly

Why the emphasis on slowing your reactions down? Because often the first response that occurs when we're feeling frustrated isn't the wisest, sanest, or most constructive one.

How many times have you thought back on a situation that didn't turn out well and thought, "If only I'd said *this* instead of *that. What was I thinking*?" Of course the answer is that you *weren't* thinking, at least not clearly.

There is a reason why diplomatic negotiations and labor contract talks take a long time. We're all emotional beings, but emotions are not supposed to rule when there is a lot at stake. Rational thinking must prevail, and that takes time to crystallize.

Tried and True Tactics

"To slow down my reaction time when someone is making me feel frustrated I picture water running out of two faucets in my house. One faucet gives me unfiltered water. The liquid rushes out of the tap, but it contains all kinds of impurities. The other faucet filters water impurities out, though the water comes out of the tap in a slower stream. I'd rather react more slowly and have what comes out of my mouth be better for everyone."—Michael 38

See the Big Picture

To temper any tendencies to react too impetuously or speak too quickly, try to see a difficult situation as one piece of a large jigsaw puzzle. This circumstance fits into a matrix of other, interconnected pieces—all which form, yes, a big picture.

Is your overly demanding boss pushing your buttons? Think carefully before you explode, walk out the door, or do anything else that you can't undo. Take some time to consider whether you can respond in a way that challenges his excessive demands without jeopardizing your job security.

Is your tight-fisted spouse depriving you of yet another object you desire because it costs too much? You could quickly and secretly order whatever you want online. You could stomp your feet and yell at him for being a cheapskate. But either course of action could jeopardize your relationship. Mull it over. Perhaps you can convince him to want what you want, and to think it was his idea in the first place.

If a driver cuts you off, you could chase him and retaliate in kind. But wouldn't you rather get where you're going safely?

DP Disarmer

If you're having trouble seeing the big picture, try flashing forward five years. Is this encounter going to be something you'll remember? If the answer is no, it's not a significant piece of your puzzle. Consider letting it go.

Choose Your Moment

After you decide *how* you want to respond to a difficult person, you should think about *when*. Difficult people often like to dangle emotional bait and hope you'll snap it off their fishhook like a starved tuna. Sometimes they actually like to see you lose your temper, because then it makes it seem as if *you*, in fact, are the difficult one. Don't go for it.

If you're not sure yet what you want to say or how you want to say it, there are many ways to buy time:

- ◆ Slow down the conversation by asking them to give you additional information.

- ◆ Indicate you want to get more information on your own before continuing.

- ◆ Look for an opportunity to change the subject and temporarily steer a loaded conversation onto more neutral ground.

- ◆ Mention that another obligation will keep you from giving this conversation the time it deserves right now.

- ◆ Simply say, "I'd like to take some time to think about this, so let's make a plan to pick this up later."

You might meet with resistance here. If someone feels they have you on the hook, they will be reluctant to let you wriggle free. But after you announce your preference for deferring your talk until another time, stand your ground.

You can usually quiet objections by making a firm plan to talk again at another time—and this is not a bad idea in situations where you know you are dealing with an issue that, in fact, has to get resolved sooner or later. When you make a plan, you will be less tempted to simply avoid an important issue and hope it goes away.

Respect Yourself

Another important aspect of dealing with difficult people is to hold on to your sense of self-respect and protect your own integrity. Sometimes we get so consumed with thoughts about the challenging people in our lives that we lose track of what *we* want. But ultimately your life is not about them; your life is about you.

Say No to People Pleasing

One thing you will need to honestly examine about yourself is whether you are exacerbating the problems you have with certain people because—regardless of how difficult they are—you feel compelled to please them.

Some of us are actually addicted to gaining the approval of others. We devote an exorbitant amount of time, effort, and mental energy trying to ensure that people like us. Ironically, we may do this even with regard to people *we* do not especially like or hold in especially high esteem.

Are you a compulsive people-pleaser? Answer these questions and see.

1. **Do you often say "yes" when saying "no" would be better for you?**

   A. Often
   B. Sometimes
   C. Never

2. **Do you take on tedious tasks and chores that are clearly the responsibility of others—and that they are perfectly capable of doing?**

   A. Often
   B. Sometimes
   C. Never

3. **Do you feel anxious about how others will react to your decisions, even when you're sure those decisions make sense?**

   A. Often
   B. Sometimes
   C. Never

4. **Do you dread people saying negative things about you or giving you dirty looks?**

   A. Often
   B. Sometimes
   C. Never

5. **Are you hesitant to express your needs to other people?**

   A. Often
   B. Sometimes
   C. Never

6. **Do you feel reluctant to express disappointment when someone lets you down?**

   A. Often
   B. Sometimes
   C. Never

Give yourself one point for every "B" answer and two for every "A."

If your score is between four and six, you need to look at your tendencies to make approval-seeking a priority in certain situations and with certain people.

If your score is seven or more, it's time to really examine your priorities. You seem to put an unhealthy amount of effort and energy into pleasing people.

We all like to be liked, and there's nothing wrong with trying to be friendly and cooperative in most circumstances. Doing so certainly makes most interactions go more smoothly, and it makes us feel better about ourselves.

However, it's a whole other matter to cross the line into martyrdom. Addictive people-pleasing results in a loss of personal identity and a sense of worthlessness and ineffectuality. Although you race around trying to please even perpetually unpleasable people, you can risk your emotional and physical health. Moreover, you will invite difficult people to take advantage of you. They know a pushover when they see one!

Granted, many difficult people have overbearing personalities. There are times when taking the path of least resistance might serve you best. But don't make a habit of it. Keep your needs in mind. Remember your values and your priorities. Try to develop a thicker skin and don't worry so much about what everyone else thinks. In the long run, you'll deal better with everyone when you deal fairly and compassionately with yourself.

Manhole Ahead

Don't overexpose yourself to a difficult person to protect others from them. Being a human shield won't do much for you, and ultimately everyone must learn for themselves how to interact with all kinds of people.

Set Limits

One important way to respect yourself is to set limits when you're dealing with difficult types. If you're going to be with someone for whom you have limited tolerance, plan to cap the amount of time you'll be in their company.

To the best of your ability, make social and work engagements that have defined ending times. Plan a breakfast or lunch (in lieu of an open-ended dinner) and explain that you'd like to meet at such-and-such time so that you'll have time to talk *before your next appointment*. In other words, agree on a meeting that will have to end.

In addition, try to meet with difficult people on neutral ground. When you're on their turf and they're feeling comfortable, they might feel even more prone to bad behavior, and you might feel more weak and self-conscious. When they're on your turf, you could be faced with the problem of how you're going to get rid of them. (See Chapter 5.)

DP Disarmer _____

If you're dealing with someone who has a volatile temper or tends to be overly dramatic, suggest meeting in a public place, such as a restaurant or coffee shop. You'll feel safer and more comfortable, and there's a good chance that being in public view will temper outbursts or melodramatic tendencies.

Keep Your Humor Handy

In Chapter 2, I mentioned that most of us don't often share a laugh with the difficult people in our lives. Nevertheless, a sense of humor can help us cope with all kinds of stressful and frustrating interpersonal situations. Humor is an emotional safety valve—the body's way of neutralizing anxiety, aggression, fear, and anger. Socially, humor defuses tension, reduces conflict, and puts others at ease.

So how can we use humor with difficult types? First, let's separate humor into two types. There's *external*, or shared, humor, which we engage in with other people. There's also *internal* humor, the kind that we use to bolster our spirits and maintain perspective when circumstances seem absurd.

We can successfully use external humor with difficult people, but not if we use it to attack them or if we confuse sarcasm with benign humor. Never be humorous at the expense of difficult people. Instead, you can increase their goodwill toward you and lower their own level of defensiveness and anxiety when you:

- **Share a humorous anecdote.** Everyone gets a lift hearing about life's little inconveniences, annoyances, and ironies. That's because everyone experiences them at one time or another. If your golden retriever retrieved and ate your lunch, or if you just flew to San Diego while your luggage flew to Santiago, Chile, go ahead and spin an entertaining tale. It will make you feel better, and it may distract a difficult person from their usual irritating agenda.

- **Repeat a great gag.** Although originality is great, there's no harm in asking, "Hey did you hear what Leno/Letterman said last night?"

- **Use self-deprecating humor.** You won't offend anyone if you're targeting your own foibles. No, don't put yourself down—just make yourself seem like the fallible human that we all are.

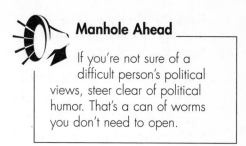

Manhole Ahead _____

If you're not sure of a difficult person's political views, steer clear of political humor. That's a can of worms you don't need to open.

Now, there may be certain difficult people that you simply do not believe have even the tiniest sliver of a sense of humor. So be it. But here's where your internal humor can come into play.

Sometimes a difficult person might make you feel as if you don't know whether to laugh or cry. When you can, choose laughter. See the absurdity of your predicament and remind yourself that it'll make a great story at the bar. You'll get a lot of mileage in imagining how you might style your tale for an appreciative audience.

Please note, laughing on the inside should be just that. You never want to laugh at the other person—and no smirking, either! Just enjoy the warm glow of internal humor.

Know When to Fight Fire with Fire

What about giving back to a difficult person exactly what you get? You know, an eye for an eye?

It's a valid question. And indeed there are times—some of which will be mentioned throughout this book—when you will have to resort to fighting fire with fire. You might have to out-manipulate a manipulator, out-control a controller, out-deceive a deceiver, and so on. But such strategies are "big guns" that you should keep in reserve. To use them all the time would be emotionally exhausting—and could turn you into a somewhat difficult person yourself.

Know What You Can and Can't Control

Finally, we come to what is essentially the golden rule of coping with difficult people, one that this book will remind you of numerous times because it is so important.

Think for a moment about all the strategies discussed in this chapter: listening actively, setting limits, slowing down your reaction time, and choosing your moments, using humor, and even fighting fire with fire. What all these coping mechanisms have in common is that they involve you controlling the ways in which you respond to difficult people. *Not a single one of them is about changing someone else!*

There's a good reason for that. The reality—like it or not—is that unless you have a magic wand, some fairy dust, and a knack for casting supernatural spells, you cannot change anyone but yourself. You can, on the other hand, always change your own behavior—and in doing so you might be able to alter the dynamics of your interactions.

Many of us find ourselves going around and around in our troubled relationships. A difficult person dangles the bait and we snap at it, acting out in some rash fashion or saying something defensive. This eggs them on, and the cycle repeats. But our response actually is the one part of this cycle that we have the ability to change.

Do people sometimes change on their own? Yes, but you cannot wait and hope. People usually reinvent themselves only when the pain of not doing so outweighs the effort involved. Focus on what you can do here and now to take control of your own actions and reactions. If you remember nothing else, you will have the most powerful tool for coping with difficult people.

The Least You Need to Know

- If we listen to difficult people, we can gain useful insights about them, and clues to dealing with them constructively.

- Choose your moment for responding to difficult people. Buy time instead of reflexively snapping at the emotional bait they dangle, and set limits with people who set you on edge.

- Humor can ease the stress and frustration of dealing with difficult people—don't use sarcasm or mock them, but do look for opportunities to laugh over something funny, and help yourself laugh on the inside by seeing the absurdity of it all.

- Sometimes nothing will do but to fight fire with fire, but save that for a last resort or you may not like the person you become.

- The golden rule of dealing with difficult people is that you can never change anyone else, you can only change your response—which may be enough to change the dynamic.

Part 2

The Self-Absorbed

It's nice to like yourself, even love yourself—but there's such a thing as going overboard. This part of the book looks at self-centered types who barely recognize that others exist unless those others can do something for them. You'll find out what makes narcissists tick and what actually lies beneath their apparent self-adoration. You'll also learn how to cope with needy, greedy narcissists at work, in your personal life, and in a number of social situations and public settings.

Chapter 4

It's All About Me

In This Chapter

- ◆ Having a sense of entitlement with narcissism
- ◆ Determining the false self of the self-absorbed
- ◆ Seeing the fickle nature of narcissists
- ◆ Learning why narcissists violate personal boundaries
- ◆ Gearing up to deal with the self-absorbed

In a well-known Greek myth, a handsome young man rejects the advances of a smitten nymph and, as punishment, is doomed to fall in love with his own reflection in a pool of water. Spellbound, he pines away—ultimately transforming into the flower that bears his name: Narcissus.

This tale, immortalized by Ovid, has survived for so long and carries so much emotional resonance because it carries the shock of familiarity. We've all encountered self-absorbed people similar to Narcissus. This chapter helps you cope with them by helping you understand them, including how they got to be that way and what lies beneath their apparent self-ardor.

I'm So Special

If we say that someone is a narcissist, we probably don't mean it as a compliment. The word is usually used pejoratively, implying that someone is conceited, egocentric, and selfish.

But self-regard, as with many character traits, falls on a continuum. In moderation, positive self-regard is an essential component of a healthy psyche. It enables us to have fulfilling relationships (if we don't care for ourselves, it's not likely others will). It also gives us self-confidence—that can-do attitude that helps us get ahead. Indeed, people without a healthy self-regard can be self-destructive and masochistic (more about masochists in Chapter 13).

Excessive, exclusive self-regard, however, is a problem. In the Greek myth, we can see how self-absorption is a problem for the person consumed with it—for they are wrapped up in illusion and insatiable longing. But if you deal with narcissists in your personal life, your work life, or in the world at large, you also know that certain people's self-absorption can be a problem for *you*.

The narcissistic people we encounter manifest obvious traits of greediness and neediness. Obvious to us, that is. They, however, believe that they are special and therefore entitled to certain things, such as recognition, flattery, and favors. They feel that rules are fine—for others—but the rules don't necessarily apply to them. They are exceptional, and therefore merit exceptions in the form of preferential treatment and blind loyalty.

In personal relationships, this *sense of entitlement* can lead narcissists to believe it's acceptable to honor commitments only when it suits them, and to remain oblivious to the legitimate needs of family, friends, and lovers. At work, it can mean they take all the credit, shirk any hard work, and point the finger at others for their own mistakes or oversights. In social situations, it can translate to all kinds of inconsiderate and disrespectful behavior. Simply put, narcissists believe that their needs take precedence in any group.

def•i•ni•tion

Narcissists' **sense of entitlement** creates a feeling of supremacy and assumptions that they deserve subservience, leniency, special treatment and favors, and special outcomes and concessions. For example, even if they break a rule or a law, they believe they should escape consequences and receive immunity.

The narcissistic sense of entitlement is a phase that all humans experience at some point. We experience it in early childhood, when it's age-appropriate to feel self-important and invincible, the center of the universe.

But as we develop and mature, that self-absorbed perspective is *supposed* to be replaced with a growing awareness that other people have thoughts, beliefs, and feelings that do not always coincide with our own but nevertheless must be taken into account.

For narcissists, however, this transformation never occurs. The bubble of specialness never pops. They are, in a sense, perpetual children—the Peter Pans of difficult people.

The Roots of Me-ness

Why do some of us develop beyond the childish phase of self-importance, while others get stuck in it? Any number of scenarios can generate narcissism, but psychological theorists generally agree that at the root of many of them lies some form of psychic damage, usually inflicted by parents or by other significant individuals in a child's environment. Narcissism can be a response to:

- **Physical or emotional abuse.** Rather than endure feelings of shame, rage, and frustration, a child may develop a façade of invulnerability in reaction to harsh punishments or criticism.

- **Too much parental pampering and indulgence.** Although pampering might not seem damaging on its face, it hurts children immensely when parents do not help them develop a realistic worldview, an ability to share, and a tolerance for frustration.

- **Self-absorbed parents.** Mothers or fathers who are themselves consummately self-involved view their children as mere extensions of themselves. Their children comply—at least on the surface—by pretending to be as "special" as their parents.

- **Unrealistic expectations.** All children, even the most gifted and talented, can be pushed well beyond their limits by over-eager adults. When nothing one does is quite good enough, it's tempting to pretend that one is profoundly exceptional in special ways.

In each of these circumstances, the child is so busy protecting themselves from feeling bad, enduring disappointment, or being perceived as inadequate that they miss out on the key step of developing *empathy*. In self-defense, they develop an aggressive sense of entitlement, envy, and arrogance.

def•i•ni•tion

Empathy is the ability to understand and relate to the feelings and perceptions of others. It doesn't necessarily entail agreeing with others, but it does entail being able to imagine how circumstances appear from their point of view.

Cultural Causes of Narcissism

However, if it seems to you—as it does to many observers of contemporary society—that there are an awful lot of narcissists around, you might wonder if troubled parent-child dynamics tell the whole story. Are we, perhaps, living in a society that encourages and even rewards narcissism?

In his bestselling 1979 book, *The Culture of Narcissism*, historian and social critic Christopher Lasch argues that American and Western society is a generator of the narcissist attitude. Lasch convincingly details how our emphasis on celebrity worship and material gain (especially in the form of displayable consumer goods—cars, electronics, designer clothes) has eclipsed our other priorities, including art, religion, and most devastatingly, our sense of family and community.

Lasch describes a social milieu in which competition to accumulate the outward signs of achievement has replaced genuine achievement for its own sake. This dynamic, most social commentators agree, has only become more extreme in the years since he first made his case. In recent times, we as a society have experienced:

- Americans taking on greater and greater debt to purchase larger and more impressive cars and homes that many of us cannot afford.

- An increased emphasis on brand labeling in everything from one's choice of morning coffee to what colleges one's children "must" apply to.

- A dot.com boom (and subsequent bust) in which so-called geniuses and visionaries created companies with illusory business models with no regard for such "mundane details" as productivity or the bottom line.

- A spate of executive ransacking of corporations without thought to the ruinous consequences for stockholders, employees, and retirees.

- An increase in frivolous lawsuits as litigants try to blame everyone but themselves for their own mistakes.

Our culture seems to be becoming more and more a powerful enabler of narcissism. Granted, these social forces do not take the same toll on all individuals—but anyone predisposed to narcissism by childhood experiences will all too easily find reinforcement for that particular bent.

So if it seems as though there are more and more needy, greedy narcissists among us—it's because there really are. The better acquainted you become with their psychological makeup, the better you'll know what to expect and how to cope with them.

 Manhole Ahead

Don't take someone's material trappings as evidence that they actually have special skills, knowledge, or expertise. It's all too easy to get sucked into a grand financial or business scheme by a narcissist who has nothing tangible with which to back it up.

Greed and Grandiosity

So let's look a little closer at the greedy aspect of narcissism. Self-centered people are obsessed with accumulating not only material things, but also intangibles such as attention, approval, praise, admiration, even reverence and veneration. This can be exhausting, for the self-absorbed have a way of always needing more no matter how much they get. Even worse, if they don't get what they want, they can become mean and spiteful.

To understand what the narcissist is really after, you'll have to remember that they have carefully constructed a cover-up self, or *false self*, to mask the real self that was initially vulnerable to disappointment, criticism, and rejection.

This false self may look coherent on the outside, but it is really akin to a balloon with a small hole in it that is constantly leaking air. Just as a leaking balloon must be kept continually inflated with a stream of air, a leaky self must be kept continually inflated with a steady stream of *narcissistic supplies*.

def•i•ni•tion

The **false self** is a grandiose construct that narcissists project as their persona, but which actually masks underlying feelings of inadequacy. **Narcissistic supplies** can be material objects (such as branded objects indicating wealth) or interpersonal reinforcements (including attention and adulation) that keep the narcissist's false self from deflating.

The narcissist can only keep painful feelings at bay by getting more and more of anything that temporarily fills a fundamental sense of emptiness and insecurity. Sadly, the narcissists in your life might just decide they have to get these things from you. They'll treat you well as long as you comply, but slip up in your role as flatterer, admirer, suck-up, or supplicant and you'll pay the price.

Need and Exploitation

Given all this, you might think narcissists are people to be steadfastly avoided. Maybe you'll encounter them at work or other settings in which you have no control, but why fraternize with them voluntarily? Yet somehow many of us end up with narcissistic lovers, spouses, and friends.

That's because narcissists need other people to validate them so desperately that they often develop ways of being—at least initially—very appealing to hang around with. In fact, they can be extremely compelling and charismatic.

To get what they need from someone—say, from you—a narcissist will often turn on the charm. They will, at first, provide you with the kind of attention and admiration they want. (For more on their *modus operandi*, see Chapter 6.)

Narcissists can be especially dogged in their quest to make a friend/lover/ally of you if they perceive you as having some of the qualities they would like others to see in them. They will redouble their seductive efforts if they are preoccupied with their physical appearance and find you good-looking, if they are preoccupied with seeming smart and find you intelligent, or if they are concerned with projecting an air of success and perceive you as successful. In other words, the more of a "catch" they think you are, the more bait they'll dangle in front of you. And they can be very hard to resist.

DP Disarmer

If you suspect someone has narcissistic tendencies and do not want a personal relationship with them, resist your inclination to reciprocate if they flatter you. Otherwise you will set up a dynamic where they come to rely on you more and more to feed their faltering ego.

At first, your relationship might seem easy and equitable. But after a while it will become exploitative. A "give and take" relationship will become strictly about you giving and them taking. They will take your time and they will take your energy, and the more you give the more they will want. Narcissists never really ask what they can do for you, only what you can do for them.

When you begin to withdraw—and at some point you'll feel as though you have little choice—hold on to your hat. They may ratchet up their level of need by invoking guilt or even creating a crisis in which you feel you must help them (and not desert them!). If nothing works, they may switch to abusive mode, belittling and bad-mouthing you with the same fervor with which they once complimented you and sought your favors.

Of course, you may not always be the first to withdraw from a relationship with a narcissist. Because of their exploitative tendencies, they might "dishonorably discharge" you from a relationship if someone whose companionship they think will reflect even better on them comes along. You might think that would be a relief, but rejection is never easy to bear. Unless you're well inured to the tricks and traits of the narcissist, chances are you'll be left feeling hurt and confused.

When a narcissist rejects you, it can happen in a flash. And if you're waiting for an explanation or apology from them, don't. They see no reason to justify their actions. More likely than not, they will pretend you no longer exist (and in their distorted view of reality, you pretty much don't).

Tried and True Tactics

"What I have learned about narcissistic types is that they are fickle. They can be entertaining companions, but you have to reconcile yourself to the fact that they can be here one moment, gone the next. Sometimes it seems that the relationships that start out with fireworks fizzle out most quickly. They can be fun, if you don't get over-invested in them. I say: easy come, easy go."—Gene, 37

Bad Boundaries

For as long as you do remain in a relationship with a narcissist, be prepared to endure a particular kind of strange sensation—a sense of being emotionally (and perhaps even physically) crowded.

Along with their grandiosity, greediness, and neediness, narcissists are renowned for having what therapists refer to as *bad boundaries*. It's as if they have difficulty distinguishing exactly where they stop and someone else begins.

Because narcissists' sense of self is flawed, they see others as extensions of themselves. What need is there for space and separateness in that case? In fact, feeling separate in what most of us would consider a healthy, mature sense only makes a narcissist feel isolated and frightened. Although all children go through a natural phase of *separation anxiety*, the narcissistic type has never fully resolved this developmental stage.

def•i•ni•tion

Separation anxiety is a psychological condition in which an individual displays excessive anxiety when faced with the prospect of separation from people to whom they have strong emotional attachments. It is often seen in early childhood, but can occur at any age.

Narcissists violate personal boundaries with regularity. Ways they can do so include …

- Talking incessantly (often in self-praise or about hatching grandiose schemes).

- Impinging on physical space (for example, standing or sitting too close or hovering over you).

- Asking too many personal questions (no topic is sacred, including your finances or your sex life).

- Offering too much personal information about themselves (which can embarrass you, although it certainly does not appear to embarrass them).

- Snooping, such as reading your mail over your shoulder, poking through whatever's atop your desk or dresser—or, in extreme cases, what's *in* your desk or dresser.

- Eavesdropping. They hate to be left out of any conversation, especially if they think it might be about them—and it's *always* about them.

- Inviting themselves along; they refuse to be excluded and can't imagine you'd rather do something alone or in the company of others.

- Getting uptight whenever you part from them or whenever they fail to hear from you.

If the narcissists in your life seem omnipresent, it is because they devote a lot of time and energy to being so. The nearer they are to you, physically and psychically, the more they feel they can influence you to keep them supplied with the admiration they require. The further you slip away, they more insecure they become.

Getting Ready to Cope with the Self-Absorbed

All in all, it's not too hard too see why dealing with the self-absorption of narcissists can be a daunting prospect. Their sense of entitlement, their grandiose posturing and preoccupation with image, their obliviousness to the needs of others, their fickleness, and their continual encroaching of boundaries can be infuriating. Moreover, the fundamental insecurity that all these behaviors mask can rear its head in baffling, even frightening, ways. Narcissists can turn on a dime in how they feel about you and can treat you horribly if they feel their admiration- and attention-seeking agenda is being thwarted or ignored.

In the next several chapters, we'll look at the specific challenges of dealing with narcissists at work, in personal relationships, and in the great, wide world. Each of those chapters will offer strategies that are specific to those circumstances. But as you get ready to deal with a narcissist in any circumstance, you should keep these general principles in mind.

Know Yourself, Control Yourself

Stay in touch with and in control of your feelings. The actions of narcissists can unleash powerful emotions in us. These may be positive (if they are in the process of courting and charming us) or negative. But because narcissists have weak personal boundaries, they are very good at "injecting" their own feelings into others.

Whose feelings are whose? It's not always easy to tell. If you sense you are in the company of a narcissist, take periodic inventory of what you're feeling and consider why you're feeling as you do. Never act impulsively on an intense feeling that seems to "overtake" you in their presence, but buy time and use it to take stock of who you are and what you need.

Conduct Reality Checks

Narcissists' belief that they are all-powerful and all-knowing can also be very infectious. The more confidence and charisma they project, the more tempting it is to believe that you are in the company of someone whose brilliance outshines yours and everyone else's.

But before you hitch your wagon to the star of someone whose capabilities seem almost too good to be true, and who never seems to manifest a shred of doubt or tolerate a moment of disagreement, step back and evaluate the circumstances objectively.

Are you about to invest in real estate or create a start-up company with an extremely charismatic, self-aggrandizing person who assures you they cannot miss? Speak to a third-party expert who has an objective perspective. Accumulate as much information from as many external sources as possible. Research the details—get granular.

Know When Enough Is Enough

If you want to temporarily satiate and neutralize a narcissist, the best way to do so is to keep them talking about themselves while you offer affirmation. But as a long-term strategy with a narcissist you encounter on a routine basis, this approach has severe drawbacks. Quite simply, it will suck time and energy out of your life.

In ongoing relationships, you'll have to learn to indicate—both verbally and non-verbally—where the limits lay. Reclaiming your time and space as your own without offending and alienating a narcissist can be tricky. Sometimes you will have to deflate their egotistical balloon a bit to protect yourself. But save yourself you must, unless you wish to lose control of your life.

Don't Interpret

Don't try to enlighten a self-absorbed person as to their "condition," or speculate on their childhood development gaps, or in any way interpret or label their behaviors as evidence of narcissism. Above all, never point out that you can see their underlying insecurities.

Narcissists are very invested in their false selves and in *magical thinking* that allows them to routinely confuse wishes and fantasies with reality. If you pull their carefully crafted rug out from under them—no matter how gently you tug—they will almost surely respond with animosity or melodramatic outrage and hurt.

Don't Think You're an Exception

If you've noticed someone consistently exploit, betray, abandon, or otherwise selfishly mistreat others, don't flatter yourself into thinking their behavior will be any different with you over the long haul. Sooner or later, narcissists will repeat their patterns.

As with all difficult people, do not imagine that you can change them. Most self-absorbed people do not want to be changed, would be appalled at the very thought, and will resist your efforts—foot, horse, and artillery. Unless you enjoy the feeling of banging your head against the wall, stick with the more rational goal of altering your responses to such people. You only have control over you.

Look for Reciprocity

All in all, the surest way to keep from getting over-involved with narcissists is to focus on cultivating relationships that have reciprocity—that is, the kind where each person gives and receives.

Obviously, all relationships go through phases, and there will be times in even the healthiest relationships when one party receives more support in one form or another. But both individuals should be entitled to avail themselves of such support in turn.

There's no need to keep score in most good relationships. Things tend to even out on their own. In fact, if you do find yourself keeping score, consider it a warning sign. On some level, you already have a glimmer that things are not as they should be. Trust those instincts!

The Least You Need to Know

- Although the roots of narcissism lie in an individual's childhood—often with abuse, pampering, or unrealistic expectations on the part of parents—we also live in an image-oriented culture that promotes and even rewards self-centered behavior.

- Narcissists construct a false self to protect a real self that is vulnerable and insecure—their fragile egos require continual bolstering.

- Narcissists can be engaging and charismatic when they want something from you, but they will abandon you in a heartbeat if you no longer give them the attention and admiration they require, or if they encounter someone else whose attentions seem more valuable.

- Seeing other people as extensions of themselves, narcissists habitually violate physical and emotional boundaries—they hover too closely, inquire too deeply, and feel anxious about separation.

- General strategies for coping with narcissists include examining intense emotions you may experience in their company, subjecting their assertions to reality checks, and resolving to maintain a degree of personal privacy.

Chapter 5

Coping with the Self-Centered at Work

In This Chapter

- ◆ Identifying self-centered personalities at work
- ◆ Handling credit-takers, blamers, and buck-passers
- ◆ Setting limits with self-centered talkers
- ◆ Coping with narcissists in meetings
- ◆ Managing a self-centered boss
- ◆ Dealing with narcissists who work for you

Are there self-absorbed people in your work environment? Well, are there bears in the woods? Whether you work in an office, a service business, a school, a store, or a factory, the answer is probably yes. Self-centeredness, also known as narcissism, is a widespread phenomenon for all the reasons discussed in the last chapter, including a culture that reinforces needy, greedy "me-ness."

But self-centered narcissists, for all their grandiose notions about themselves, still have to make a living. At work, you might find self-centered people working alongside you. You might work for one, or have one working for you. Maybe you have multiple narcissists in your work environment—all focused on their needs to the exclusion of everyone and everything else. This chapter shows you how to cope with them so that their self-promoting behavior doesn't make you feel like a cipher or, worse, truly turn you into an "invisible" employee.

Spotting the Self-Centered

When you first run into a self-centered person in the workplace, you might not realize that their agenda is strictly self-promotion. Narcissists might strike you as driven go-getters with healthy dollops of ambition. At first you might even admire their drive. After all, there's nothing wrong with wanting to get ahead, is there? But then it dawns on you. This person's drive is so single-minded that they make you feel immaterial—except perhaps as a stepping-stone to their success.

If someone you work with, work for, or supervise has a way of ignoring you except when you serve their needs, that's a certain tip-off that they are the center of their own universe. As far as they're concerned, everyone else is a distant planet. You might as well be Pluto.

Narcissistic people have a way of making those around them in the workplace feel alternately ignored or exploited. They also have a way of making you feel very, very frustrated on a daily basis. Some of the things you might notice about working with a self-centered person:

♦ Every discussion about work-related issues seems to come back to how decisions will reflect upon them.

♦ Every team activity ends up revolving around their agenda.

♦ Any good idea is portrayed as theirs, even if they had nothing to do with it.

♦ Any bad idea is cast as someone else's, even if it was theirs.

♦ Any opportunity to grab the spotlight will be seized by them.

You might think these kinds of behaviors would turn everyone against the workplace narcissist right off the bat. But that's not necessarily the case. Narcissists can be disarmingly ingratiating, and they always make sure they have people on their side. When they think you can help them, they'll act as the sweetest, most solicitous folks in the world. "*How are you, today?*" they'll ask, though they don't really care. "*Great job on that memo,*" they'll say, but only if the memo made *them* look good.

Many self-involved people learn to project a very charming demeanor, and it's easy to get sucked in. It's gratifying to feel that you have finally made it onto their radar screen. But if they're truly the self-centered sort, rest assured that their fawning attentions will last only as long as they need you. You're just a bit player in their personal drama.

Manhole Ahead

Sometimes the little things give away a person's self-centered nature. Beware the co-worker who routinely empties the coffeepot and doesn't put another on to brew.

Dealing with Grandstanders

Scratch a narcissist and you will find someone who is insecure to such a high degree that if they're not receiving positive attention they feel as though they are nonexistent. At work this translates to infuriating grandstanding, including taking credit when none is due, blaming others for their mistakes, and evading tasks they view as "beneath them."

Who Gets Credit?

Self-centered people are glory-seekers. At work, they want to bask in the reflected glow of any project that is going well, any profit that is being made, any task that is completed under budget and ahead of deadline. They want all the glory even if they had nothing to do with the work, or even if they played a limited role.

Needless to say, this presents a problem for fellow employees who have been making significant contributions to projects with good outcomes. When the boss shows up for a review, or a client shows up for a presentation, suddenly a glory-seeker who has been flying under the radar is everywhere in evidence. What's a hardworking co-worker who's been banished to the sidelines to do?

First and foremost, if you are working with a narcissistic credit thief, you must make it a habit to document everything you do. Because part of your job is to *protect* your job, you must develop a CYA (cover your, er, backside) approach. Save copies of all the work you do, and note when you do it. Note the significance of the work to the over-all project. If billable hours are an issue, be sure to keep flawless time records.

DP Disarmer

Make CYA (covering your backside) a part of every day. Never leave the workplace without making notes of the progress you've made. This might seem like an annoying chore, but if you are coping with self-centered credit thieves, it could be one of the most important self-protective measures you take. Get used to it.

But don't stop there. If your documentation only sits in your desk drawer, in your glove compartment, or on your hard drive, it won't do you much good unless and until you are specifically called upon to justify your role. There's no need to let things come to that. Instead, become an effective communicator to everyone with a stake in the work at hand.

- Fire off memos whenever you reach a new milestone or have a brainstorm.

- Ask questions to show how hard you are thinking about the situation.

- Keep people apprised of the timetable you are following, what you have accomplished to date, and what you hope to accomplish in the future.

- If you work directly with customers, let them know how you're taking care of their needs.

Unlike your self-centered co-worker, give credit to other team members and praise their contributions, but don't forget to blow your own horn. Finally, in a presentation situation where a credit thief is stealing the show with a relentless string of "I did this" and "I did that," be prepared to jump in and reframe the discussion. It's not always easy to interrupt a grandstander; they can get up quite a head of steam, like a Shakespearean actor in mid-soliloquy. Be prepared with a repertoire of polite but firm phrases you can interject. These include …

- And to add to what _____ just said, the entire team decided to take this approach.

- And just to further clarify, I'd like to note why that solution occurred to all of us.

- Not to interrupt _____ , but here's something else I've noticed.

None of these interjections are direct challenges to what Self-Centered Guy is saying. And there's a good reason for that. In most instances, direct challenges will only agitate a narcissist by stirring up his insecurities. When it comes to dealing with the self-centered, subtlety often works better than a hammer blow. Besides, although you must know your enemy, you do not want to _become_ your enemy.

Who Gets Blame?

Just as self-centered grandstanders want glory, they also want to avoid blame at all costs. When something goes wrong at work, their mode of operation is usually to shift the blame elsewhere. Worse, they might make a great show of pointing out who's at fault, so that they still get attention, while someone else gets the grief.

Suppose you get blamed when you are blameless? Again, CYA is your best defense should you really get called on the carpet. In fact, if you work with a blamer and you sense that a project is going awry, try to document not only what you are doing to correct the situation but also what Self-Centered Guy is doing—or not doing. Because self-centered folks rarely think they're anything less than wonderful, you can actually get your narcissistic colleague to help you keep records by asking them for memos detailing their "wonderful" ideas.

Be aware, though, that if you use this material to prove your innocence and your colleague's culpability, you will risk creating an ongoing feud between the two of you. When exposed, self-centered types will make every effort to pay you back in kind. Having a feud with a co-worker beats getting fired, but it certainly won't make for a happy, productive work environment. Before you point the finger at a finger-pointer, try instead to make them see how it would be in *their* best interest to avoid casting blame and focus on solving the problem.

DP Disarmer

Suggest to a narcissistic blamer that they will look like a hero if they come up with a solution rather than point fingers. If you have a solution in mind and want to get it implemented quickly, let them think it was at least partly their idea.

This subtle approach might not feel as immediately gratifying as using your documentation to stage a *gotcha* moment. But unless your *gotcha* is so good it will earn your co-worker a pink slip, remember that you'll still have to deal with them tomorrow.

Shirking the Grunt Work

Another thing that self-absorbed grandstanders like to do is stake out high-visibility tasks and roles for themselves and avoid any actual hard, painstaking work. In their opinion, grunt work is for anyone but them. They get to wine and dine a client while you stay up all night and prepare the prospectus they'll take with them. They get to chat up shoppers while you're taking inventory in the stockroom.

Why does it so often shake out this way? Unless the self-centered person in question is your boss (more about this particular situation shortly), it could be that they've simply got the nerve to make demands, while you are acquiescing too easily. Don't be a pushover. Instead, try these strategies:

- ◆ **Consult a third person.** Ask someone to whom you both report to assign roles. If a team leader or manager decides that you get the more glamorous job for a change, the narcissist will be angrier at them than you—and you will not be stuck toiling over tedious tasks until dawn.

- ◆ **Flip a coin.** If it's not appropriate to involve a third party, suggest a coin toss. Sure, you might lose, but you won't lose all the time. Besides, you'll give your co-worker the message that it's not fair to simply assume they get the desirable jobs.

- ◆ **Use the Tom Sawyer tactic.** In Mark Twain's classic novel, young Tom gets a group of kids to believe that painting a picket fence (a chore he'd rather avoid) is actually great fun. If you can get a self-centered person to believe that a certain kind of work is sure to win them lots of positive attention ("Hey, I hear that client loves lots of well-documented research") you just might get them to take it on.

Finally, look for situations where you can give self-centered colleagues enough prover-bial rope to hang themselves. Do you think they're biting off more than they can chew in taking on a particular task? If so, you don't necessarily have to point that out. If they botch their performance, they might not be so quick to take on that task again.

> **Tried and True Tactics**
>
> "One of my self-centered colleagues found out that an important professional orga-nization had asked her to give a talk. She insisted that it was her role as 'promotions director' to give such a talk. The thing is, I knew she froze whenever she had to speak before a large audience. I actually started to suggest she might be uncomfortable, but she just about bit my head off. So I smiled, shrugged, and wished her well. Right before it was time for the speech, she mysteriously developed 'laryngitis' and asked me to do it. I obligingly stepped in."—Pete, 34, marketing manager

Setting Limits with Self-Absorbed Talkers

For all their self-involvement, narcissistic types are dependent on the approval of oth-ers. They feel most validated when they are interacting with "admirers." Trouble is, even if you're not exactly an admirer of theirs, you have the potential to be one as far as they're concerned.

Because they don't have well-honed boundaries, narcissists are always apt to invade your physical and emotional space to talk about their favorite topic: themselves. This can make it very difficult to get your work done, unless you know how to set limits.

Look Out for Space Invaders

Communication in the workplace can be very constructive. It's beneficial to exchange ideas and information with co-workers, and convivial chitchat is part of a socially healthy work environment. But sometimes your workspace and your work mind-set are continually interrupted by one of the following types:

- **The Barger:** Bargers will stroll uninvited into your office, cubicle, or other personal work space, plop into a chair, maybe even put their feet up, and tell you more than you could possibly want to know about their day, their job, or their life. The fact that you are engrossed in a project, banging away at a keyboard, is immaterial to them. They can wait! (And while they do, they might just rummage through your stuff.)

- **The Lurker:** Lurkers always seem to be hanging about in communal work spaces, such as the coffeemaker alcove, the copier nook, or the restroom. When you venture into one of these spaces, they pounce—showering you with insights, opinions, and irrelevant minutiae that they're sure you find compelling.

- **The Shadow:** Wherever you go, the Shadow goes, too. They'll follow you down the hall, to the water cooler, into the lounge—yakking all the way. If you speed up, they speed up, too. You get the feeling they're going to finish what they have to tell you unless you walk off the edge of a cliff (and you're tempted to!).

 Manhole Ahead

How do you know you're speaking with a self-centered person? When you have the distinct impression that they are talking *at* you, not *with* you. The self-centered don't *interact* so much as they just *act*.

We often say such clingy attention-seekers just can't take a hint. But we need to be careful about what kinds of hints we give. As you know, one of the guiding principles of this book is that *you cannot change another person, but you can change your response to that person.* If you have been unable to discourage a self-centered co-worker from talking and talking, you need to become aware of the verbal and nonverbal messages you're sending.

Setting boundaries with a narcissist can be tricky. They are encouraged by what they take to be signs of admiration. Remember the advice about active listening in Chapter 3? Making eye contact and keeping the conversation flowing with encouraging verbal cues can be a good strategy for getting difficult people to be less hostile, but such niceties can backfire when used with a narcissist. A self-absorbed type may perceive even routine conversational niceties as an invitation to babble on endlessly.

Instead …

◆ Limit eye contact.

◆ Keep your facial expression neutral rather than smiling when they're speaking.

◆ Don't encourage them with polite questions to which you really don't want answers.

◆ Refrain from nodding as they speak.

If you are dealing with a particularly relentless type, you might have to politely but firmly explain that you are busy. To avoid an insult they'll make you pay for later, it's best to objectify—rather than personalize—your justification for cutting them short.

Don't say, *I don't have time for this right now.*

Say, *I'm sorry I can't chat, but I'm meeting a customer/crunching a printer's deadline/late to teach a class.*

Setting Boundaries in Meetings

Speaking of meetings, they're full of narcissist types as well. Meetings provide another workplace setting in which boundary issues will arise.

For narcissists, any group gathering is an opportunity to demonstrate their high opinion of themselves. Given the floor, they gush as predictably as Old Faithful unless someone sets limits on their fountain of self-adoration and personal agenda-pushing.

Needless to say, it's exasperating to be trapped in a meeting with someone who doesn't know when to stop talking. They don't just eat up valuable time, they don't give others a chance to contribute. When a meeting is being dominated by a self-absorbed filibuster, you might be tempted to do something drastic—such as call an emergency fire drill—but that's probably not the best idea.

Instead, plan ahead. If you're in a position to influence the agenda, be certain that your self-centered colleague is not scheduled to speak first or last. If they take the floor right up front, they may never relinquish it. If they take it last, your meeting might go on until everyone else in the building, including the night custodial staff, has gone home.

In addition, if you have any influence over how the meeting is run, set it up so that each person is allocated a particular amount of time to speak. Stress that this is in the interest of efficiency, and that the rule applies to all. Don't single out any one person as requiring restraint.

If you're not in a position to control the agenda or allocate time limits, practice diplomatic ways of curtailing a long-winded presentation. Thank the speaker for their insights, and then inquire: *So, what's the bottom line here?* Or: *What do you think our takeaway should be here?* Although these are interruptions, they still allow a speaker to save face by giving them a moment to make a final "important" statement.

Tried and True Tactics

"When someone is going on and on in a staff meeting at our high school, I notice our principal does a clever thing. She says, 'That is just so much valuable information that it is hard to digest in one sitting. Would you give me a thorough written memo on that?'"—Christine, 40, history teacher

The Needy, Greedy Boss

As difficult as it can be to cope with a self-centered colleague, a self-involved boss can present some special challenges. Faced with a boss who wants all the glory for himself or who makes excessive demands on your time, you might be tempted to simply "cave," because he has all the power. But there are things you can do to protect yourself and still maintain the goodwill of someone in a power position.

"Just Make Me Look Good"

What self-centered bosses want most is for everyone who works for them to make *them* look good. Be realistic and understand that this is, in fact, an essential part of your job.

If you've made a significant contribution, be sure to share the credit with your narcissistic boss. Even if he hasn't actually done anything, things will go best for you if you acknowledge his "support" or "leadership" or "great idea." It will also serve you well to ask your boss for advice at regular intervals, even if you don't actually take it.

Never do an end-run around a self-centered boss. If you are communicating with her boss, or with an important client or constituent, be sure to copy her on everything. Narcissists become suspicious if they think they're being left out of the loop.

Understandably, offering gratuitous flattery might rub you the wrong way, but as with any difficult person, you have to remember to look at the big picture. Making a self-centered boss look good actually does help you because it makes you more valuable in his eyes. What's more, the better you make him look, the better the chance he'll be promoted to a job in which he won't interact directly with you anymore!

Cell Phone Stalkers and E-mail Egomaniacs

Boundary issues with narcissistic bosses are also apt to present special problems. There will surely be times when she'll ramble on at you while you're at work. However, you can take comfort in the fact that she'll leave you alone as soon as someone more important comes along. That's because self-aggrandizing bosses are constantly *managing up*—that is, they are continually promoting themselves in the workplace hierarchy. Face time with *their* boss is more critical to them than talking with you ever will be.

def•i•ni•tion

Managing up refers to the practice of influencing those above you to recognize and reward your abilities. Although a certain amount of this is sound survival strategy, self-centered types take it to extremes by overstating their accomplishments and by fawning.

More annoying than on-the-job boundary-breaking babbling is the narcissistic boss's penchant for monopolizing your time when you are *not* at work. Unfortunately, modern technology has made it all too easy for bosses to reach employees on a 24/7 basis via cell phone or laptop or Blackberry. And rest assured, it's probably only a matter of time before they start trying to abuse the privilege.

Sure, an occasional phone call or e-mail at home is par for the course in many occupations. But when are interruptions to your home or social life truly an invasion?

- ◆ When you spend all the time during your kid's soccer game looking for a spot in the field where your cell phone has "five bar" reception.

- ◆ When your dinner routinely gets cold because you're too busy sending text messages to pick up your fork.

- ◆ When you're reluctant to turn off your Blackberry while you sleep, shower, or make love—lest you miss an "urgent" communication.

For the needy, greedy boss, of course, everything is urgent. Even trifles require immediate attention. It never occurs to them that anything you do is more important than responding to them, reassuring them, and flattering them.

This is a tough situation. A narcissistic boss is a high-maintenance boss. If you value your employment, you can't be unavailable all the time. But if you value your life, you can't be at his beck and call each minute of every day.

If you are feeling truly besieged, you have two choices. The first is to have a direct, calm discussion with your boss explaining the importance of your other commitments. Don't make it seem as though these other commitments challenge your loyalty. Avoid that kind of either/or dynamic. But do be clear about how the needs of your family and your outside obligations require attention.

As you do this, be on the lookout for common ground with your boss. Narcissists are most comfortable with other people when they feel "in synch" with them. If they have kids, for example, they're likely to relate to the demands of parenthood. If they're married, they're apt to relate to the fact that a spouse requires some proper TLC.

Instead of insisting that your boss stop contacting you outside of work, offer a reasonable compromise. Offer to check and respond to voice mails and e-mails at pre-designated intervals, and then stick to that plan even when your boss tests your resolve.

If Plan A fizzles, your second choice when dealing with an invasive boss requires a bit of, shall we say, creative technological sabotage. Instead of looking for that spot on the soccer field where cell phone reception is clear, try talking from the depths of your basement or the back of your broom closet. Narcissists have a pretty low level of frustration tolerance. If your boss is interrupted by too much static, they'll find someone else to call.

 Manhole Ahead

Avoid fraternizing with a narcissistic boss outside of work. Becoming part of your social life will further blur their boundaries and encourage them to take even greater advantage of your time.

When a Narcissist Works for You

If you have a narcissist reporting to you, you might have to deal with someone who isn't clear on just who works for whom. You might even be wondering why you hired this person in the first place! That's easy. Self-involved types often perform very well in job interviews, where it certainly does not pay to be self-effacing. (And maybe someone forgot to ask them for examples of how they work as a team player!)

Highly self-involved employees will cheerfully sap your time and energy if you let them. Without quite realizing it, you might get sucked into the psychodrama of their lives, and find yourself offering advice and assistance above and beyond the call of work-related mentoring. Sure, you want to be a good boss, but if everyone were as needy as this type of employee, you'd never get anything accomplished.

Additional problems can crop up because of a narcissistic employee's inflated sense of self-importance. These workers might shirk tasks that they consider beneath them, trying to pawn them off on other employees—perhaps even you. At the same time, they might be overly ingratiating to you trying to make them your "heir apparent." It can feel good to have someone sucking up to you, but beware! It could be akin to an actor's eager understudy who's not above seizing—or perhaps creating—opportunities to steal the show.

There's no reason to panic and fire someone simply for being self-centered. Just because someone is self-absorbed doesn't mean they might not also be very capable. But if you want them to do their job without wreaking havoc and demoralizing the rest of the staff, you will need to make your expectations and their job description clear. Remember, you are the one in charge.

Also keep in mind that all narcissists respond very well to praise. You don't have to overdo it, but rewarding them with compliments for a job well done is a surefire way to reinforce good habits.

The Least You Need to Know

- Self-centered types love to steal credit, lay blame, and shirk low-glamour tasks. Protect yourself, but avoid wounding their pride if you don't want an ongoing feud.

- The self-absorbed can disrupt your workday by invading your space and bending your ear relentlessly. Learn to set limits by subtly altering your verbal and non-verbal cues during conversation.

- Narcissists will monopolize a meeting if they're given a chance. Prepare ahead of time to contain them with time limits, self-defensive scheduling, and diplomatic interruptions.

- The self-involved boss presents special challenges—you'll need to thank them for their support (even if they gave none), ask them for advice (even if you don't take it), and diplomatically curb their tendency to contact you outside of work hours.

- When a self-centered person works *for* you, they might not be good at working *with* you, but you can reinforce good habits with judicious praise.

Chapter 6

Relating to the Self-Absorbed in Relationships

In This Chapter

◆ Learning about the perils of courtship with narcissists

◆ Living with a self-involved spouse

◆ Dealing with self-absorbed parents

◆ Tolerating self-centered siblings

◆ Having ups and downs with narcissist friends

Narcissus, the quintessential self-absorbed type, spent all his time staring with great infatuation at his own reflection. He was the love of his life. Can you imagine trying to have a close personal relationship with someone like that? Well, if you're reading this, you probably can do more than imagine it: you probably already know how tough it can be.

Don't worry, you're not alone. Nearly everyone has someone in their personal life who could be described, like Narcissus, as "stuck on themselves." This chapter looks at how to cope with being the lover, spouse, child, sibling, or friend of a self-centered person.

The Me-Me Lover

When I was a practicing psychotherapist, I often heard tales from hurt, baffled people who embarked on whirlwind romantic relationships only to find these affairs took a sudden and unexpected turn. Although the details of each situation were somewhat different, the underlying pattern was the same. Let me share one of these stories:

Belle was an attractive, bright 26-year-old who worked in the fashion industry. She was at a business–related party when she met Jack, a 33-year-old magazine editor who had recently moved to New York from California. "As soon as I saw him we just connected," she said. "He made me feel like there was no one else in the room, even though there were hundreds of people around. He told me he should have been net-working with other people, but that he wasn't going to leave my side. He said, 'I don't want you vanishing on me.'"

Jack and Belle left the party early. At Jack's suggestion, they walked a few blocks to Central Park and then rode through the park in a horse-drawn carriage. "I thought people only did that in the movies," Belle said when she recalled that evening. "It was so over-the-top romantic—and I also knew it was really expensive, but Jack did not seem to care and I remember he gave our driver an enormous tip." Later the new couple enjoyed a nightcap, snuggled at a small table at the bar of an elegant nearby hotel, deeply lost in conversation. "Jack was incredibly easy to talk to," Belle said. "He was so funny, he told great stories, and it seemed as though he was really interested in me. We seemed on the same wavelength about so many things. Sometimes, it was like he could read my mind."

Jack escorted Belle home. Before parting, Jack said that he could not believe his incred-ible luck, and declared that he had obviously moved across the country because, unbe-knownst to him, she had been waiting for him. Their meeting, he said, was destiny.

After that, Jack and Belle rapidly became inseparable. For the next two weeks, he was what she later called "a fantasy boyfriend." He showered her with attention, surprised her with thoughtful gifts, and impressed her girlfriends with his charm and his obvious adoration. Soon, Jack started talking about future plans, even broaching the prospect of renting a beach house together for part of the summer.

One weekend, however, something odd happened. Jack said he had a lead on a great summer rental and wanted to drive out to the beach to have a look. He didn't want Belle to go along, though, because he wanted to surprise her. Although Belle thought this was a little strange, she spent a Saturday catching up on work and waiting to hear about the house from Jack. He didn't call on Saturday, or Sunday, and he did not answer his phone when Belle called him.

By Sunday night, when she finally reached Jack, Belle was distraught because she feared something had happened to him. But Jack was cool and distant, saying he did not know why she was making such a fuss. He was vague in responding to questions about the summer house, and when Belle continued to ask questions, he became testy, saying he did not understand why she was so concerned about a house that *he* might or might not rent. "It was as if we had never talked about spending the summer together," Belle said. "I didn't know what to think. I started wondering whether I had misunderstood him, even whether I was crazy."

But soon Belle had something else much more confusing to deal with. For that was the very last conversation she ever had with Jack. He never called her again, and never took her calls. "He vanished into thin air," she said. "I kept going over and over it. What had I done wrong? What was the problem?"

The problem, however, had nothing to do with anything Belle did or didn't do. She was being courted by a full-fledged Narcissus—and playing the role he had scripted for her to perfection.

Seduced or Smothered?

The consummately self-centered are quite capable of becoming temporarily infatuated by another person. And the more they deem that other person desirable—portraying qualities they themselves would like to have—the more intense their campaign to win their affections will be. They will often spare no effort or expense to make a good impression. Their *modus operandi* is to overwhelm.

An infatuated narcissist is amazing to behold. Their romantic overtures happen so quickly and appear to contain so much sincere emotional conviction that the object of their desire is often swept off their feet. And why not? They are the recipients of compliments, gifts, thoughtful gestures, and—above all—statements that imply the sense of an almost mystical bond as well as an intention to preserve that bond in a future together.

If Belle could have gotten a glimpse into Jack's past, she would no doubt have found a trail of women he had treated the same way. Of course, it's not always possible to learn about a partner's romantic history. Still, there are things she could have been on the lookout for—things that might have warned her that her new boyfriend's super seduction masked an egotistical agenda. Then she might have been more cautious before giving her heart away.

DP Disarmer _____

Before things get hot and heavy, inquire about a new partner's romantic past. If they evade answering, or refer to many short-term relationships that ended because the other party "wanted more" or "was putting on pressure," be alert to the fact that they might be acting out a narcissistic pattern of instigating brief, passionate involvements and then abruptly terminating them.

Head Over Heels: Merger Madness

Some narcissists are blatant schemers, aware from the get-go that they are playing a game. On the other hand, some are actually deluding themselves for a time, feeling everything they say they do—right up until the moment they don't. Either way, despite narcissists' smooth talking, they do offer many clues about their hidden romantic intentions—of using the feelings of merging with another person to temporarily bolster their egos. These clues are available to anyone who is willing to pay attention and do some reality checking. If someone seems too good to be true, there's a good chance they are! Be on guard against heartbreak if the person romantically pursuing you:

- Assumes there will be instant exclusivity in the relationship.

- Declares their "love" after knowing you only a brief time.

- Continually dwells on similarities between the two of you.

- Monopolizes your time so that you see less of friends and family.

- Disparages others in your life or previous lovers.

- Wants to be almost constantly in contact by phone, e-mail, instant messaging, and so on.

- Maintains that they alone understand the "real you."

Manhole Ahead _____

If it seems as though your newfound love can read your mind, be careful. Their boundary-blurring approach to interpersonal relationships may have made them very good at interpreting subtle verbal and nonverbal clues. They use the insights they gain to create the illusion that a special bond is shared.

Sure, falling in love can be a heady experience for anybody, and to some extent there is always a sense of a special connection between new lovers. But in a healthy relationship, regardless of how close two people are, each individual is aware of, and respectful of, the other's separateness. If you feel as though you are being swallowed up in a relationship before you quite know what happened, that's a sure sign you should cool things off for a while. If the other person can deal with that, fine. If not, you will be saving yourself a lot of grief.

Commitment: "There's No One for Me but ... Me"

If you have fallen for narcissists in the past, or are in the midst of falling for one now, don't chastise yourself. After all, these are very charismatic and confident people, with a remarkable gift for flattery. Even the smartest among us can be fooled into thinking such intense feelings will last forever. Our society certainly idealizes and glorifies "perfect" romantic love. Isn't it tempting to think that we will find a soul mate whose every trait and action is so captivating?

But the proof of the pudding, as they say, is in the eating. The fact is, nobody's perfect, and no lasting relationship comes without its share of challenges. Only when both parties are willing to expose personal flaws and iron out conflicts can you really know if a relationship has staying power, and that you can really claim to "love."

Ultimately, most narcissists do not want to commit to anyone. How can they? They're terrified of exposing their flaws and of having to meet anyone else's needs. Committed only to themselves, they generally want only to *conquer* a lover, and then move on to the ego-inflating thrill of conquering another. If the person left behind pines over them and pursues them, they get an added bonus of feeling special because their ex-girlfriend or ex-boyfriend is carrying a great big torch.

Tried and True Tactics

"I've seen lots of friends in scenarios where a self-centered guy just up and disappears on them and they try and try to get the relationship back. I think it's because they had gotten used to how 'great' the guy used to be and also because it all ended so fast they can't believe it's over. My advice: don't give these people the satisfaction of chasing after them. They'll come to feel contempt for you, say bad things about you, and they certainly won't return to the relationship unless it is to pull the same stunt again. Besides, if you pursue them it just puffs them up even more and makes them more dangerous to their next 'victim.'"—Linda, 30

The Self-Involved Spouse

If self-absorbed types don't commit, how do some people manage to get them to the alter? Why didn't the narcissistic bride or bridegroom run away before the knot was tied? There are actually several reasons why a narcissist weds:

◆ The marriage might take place quickly—while both parties are still in the blissful merger stage of relating and before the narcissist has felt the urge to bolt.

◆ The narcissist feels that the marriage will lend him or her some prestige, and being associated with this particular spouse bolsters his or her status.

◆ An obvious one: the marriage might provide material advantages.

◆ The narcissist might wish to "prove" to himself and other people (relatives, friends, co-workers, business associates) that he is marriage material and therefore desirable and respectable.

◆ The narcissist might feel he or she has finally found someone who will devote their life to him or her and never criticize or expect from them things they do not wish to give.

But just because they marry doesn't necessarily mean they truly commit in the sense of making an inviolable pledge to be a partner come thick or thin. What if one's spouse is more invested in him- or herself than in maintaining the relationship?

Married, but Not a Couple

If you're married to a narcissist, you probably have the nagging feeling that although you are technically married, you are not actually a couple. Couples—in the true spirit of the word—are equal partners who share responsibilities, support one another, and understand when the other person is not functioning at their best. Everyone's needy sometimes, but in true partnerships, people take turns being the one who requires more tender loving care.

In relationships where one partner is primarily self-absorbed, the scales are always tipped in the same direction. The narcissistic spouse assumes they are the focal point of the marriage and the family. They hate it when their husband or wife is unavailable to them, even if they are drawn away by the needs of other family members or the demands of work.

The narcissistic spouse is more likely to ask, "Where's my dinner?" rather than "What should we have for dinner?" or, heaven forbid, "Can I help with dinner or make dinner?" They expect to be waited on—and not just in the kitchen. They assume they are entitled to full service in the bedroom as well, and that the sexual activities they prefer—when *they* are in the mood—are their prerogative.

The narcissistic spouse may expect their partner to take care of the bulk of the household chores, although they will make a great show of—and expect lots of kudos for—doing a few things at which they consider themselves proficient (for example, home decorating and backyard barbecuing). They assume that the household will run around their schedule and their preferences (they always get first dibs on that big screen TV, for example). They might spend a lot of time in activities that do not include the rest of the family if those are activities that win them public praise and recognition. Thus, the narcissistic spouse might be a workaholic, or a perennial "do-gooder" in the community, or a golf nut—relegating spousal and family needs to the backseat as they pursue other interests.

Speaking of praise, they will expect it to keep on coming. Fall behind on their daily dose of flattery and they will begin to resent you. Worse, it is entirely possible that they will look for adulation and affection elsewhere. Remember that the narcissist is fickle!

Getting Your Spouse to Notice You

Where are you in all of this? What happened to your dreams, your hopes, your needs? People wed to a narcissist can choose one of several paths. The first is to simply give in and assume that you will spend your life being the gardener, while your spouse gets to be the prized, much-tended flower. The second is to end the marriage, either by leaving or by refusing to feed your spouse's ego so that, in the end, they will be driven to find another partner.

But many people would prefer to keep the marriage intact but still attempt to address some of its imbalances. If that sounds like your situation, try giving your partner what they want to get at least some of what you want.

- **Convince your spouse that giving you what you want will reflect well on them.** Remember, narcissists are very concerned with outward appearances. They might well be happy to play the role of good spouse if they believe it will earn them the high opinion of others.

- **Always apply flattery before suggesting something your spouse can do for you.** When a narcissist's ego is full, they are apt to feel generous.

- **Use positive reinforcement.** When your spouse supports you in some way or does anything that is unselfish, reinforce that behavior with praise so that they will want to do it again.

- **When your spouse has a grievance, don't dismiss it.** Even if they are being petulant, engage in active listening. Remember to use echoing (paraphrase what they say to show you understand) and mirroring (let them know you are familiar with the feelings they are having).

- **Check in often.** Your spouse will be far more tolerant of you doing things on your own if you periodically touch base to remind them that you love them.

- **Flirt.** This is good advice in any marriage, as it's always a good idea to keep an element of fun and mystery alive. But narcissists actually crave this kind of sexual attention, and giving it to them will make them less likely to seek it elsewhere.

DP Disarmer

Praising your spouse in front of others will earn you extra goodwill. Narcissistic types enjoy being affirmed in public.

Above all, however, be sure not to lose yourself. Remember, you are doing these things to create a better balance in your relationship. Don't lose sight of that goal. In addition, under no circumstances should you drop your relationships with friends and other family members. They will help remind you that you are more than a mere extension of your spouse.

The Narcissistic Parent

Separating and individuating from our parents is part of the natural, healthy process of growing up. But try telling that to a narcissistic parent. They think of a child as either someone to serve their needs, a "mini-me" who will grow into an exact replica of them—or both.

The Merged Mother

In psychological literature, one reads mostly about narcissistic, "clingy" mothers. Perhaps it is only natural that this should be a more thoroughly examined dynamic than that of the child with a narcissistic father. After all, we all quite naturally start our lives in a state of oneness with our mothers.

As the renowned pediatrician and psychoanalyst D.W. Winnicott said, "There is no such thing as a baby." Mothers and infants are two interlocked beings that function as one system. They form a symbiotic team: bonding instinctively, and communicating intuitively. All mothers are in for something of a rude awakening when the baby starts to pull away and explore on its own. But narcissistic mothers are unwilling to do the right things, developmentally speaking, because they are unwilling to tolerate emotional discomfort and insecurity. So …

♦ Instead of urging her child to safely explore, she encourages dependence—often exaggerating the "risks" of leaving mother's side for a moment.

♦ Instead of helping her child to develop a realistic self-image, she pumps them up and gives them the sense that they are special—*just like she is*—so long as they continue to do as she wishes.

♦ Instead of disciplining them in an appropriate fashion, she overreacts with rage when they disobey her.

♦ Instead of offering empathy when they experience disappointments, she trains them to deny the fact that they are upset.

In short, the narcissistic mother does everything in her power *not* to raise an independent, self-reliant child. She wants, instead, a child who will put her needs first—not only when they are children but also when they are all grown up.

The Distant or Demanding Dad

Men, of course, can also be narcissist parents, and their effect can be just as destructive. Narcissistic fathers tend to fall into one of two subtypes:

♦ The Distant Dad is pretty much oblivious to the needs of his children and his wife because he is totally wrapped up in his own world and his own agenda. This type of dad can cause a child to try all kinds of extreme behaviors to get their father's attention. Another danger is that when dad is distant, mom is even more likely to rely on the child for her emotional needs. Thus, a triangle of narcissism develops.

♦ The Demanding Dad sees an opportunity to accrue glory through his children. He may pressure them to be top performers in academics or sports, counting their achievements as his own. This is the dad who can be found hollering instructions at the top of his lungs from the sidelines of his child's soccer game, much to the consternation of the child, the coach, and the crowd.

In short, the narcissistic father is either over-involved or under-involved in his children's lives as they grow. When they are grown, however, he will expect that they owe him extraordinary filial loyalty.

> **Manhole Ahead** _____
>
> If you recognize both your mother and your father as narcissistic types, you may
> wonder if you are doomed to remain overly attached to them or overly driven
> to please them. You may have been programmed to do so, but some children, for a
> variety of reasons, are very resistant and resilient. Nevertheless, it does not hurt to do
> a reality check—be honest with yourself about any over-dependencies in your relation-
> ship with your parents and try to temper them.

Grown Up, but Still Their "Baby"

Most grown children of narcissists manage to achieve some degree of separation from
their parents, or so it would appear. They move out of the house, pursue careers, get
married, and start families of their own. But if you are the adult child of narcissistic
parents, you already know that they still do not truly treat you as a fully independent
adult. Narcissistic parents are renowned for a number of difficult behaviors:

- **Giving unwanted advice.** These parents want you to live your life according
  to their script. They have no end of ideas about how your actions will reflect on
  them, whether it's why you should go to law school or why you should dump
  your current love interest.

- **Intruding and snooping.** They may barge in unannounced, or call every day
  and talk at great length. When they're in your home, they may feel free to peek
  into your drawers or browse through your outgoing mail. In their minds, they
  don't need permission—after all, they're your parents!

- **Tuning out or overreacting to "bad news."** Even a relatively minor setback
  for you can create a near-hysterical reaction in the narcissistic parent, who
  doesn't know how to process disappointment appropriately. Alternatively, they
  might not acknowledge that you could possibly have any problems.

- **Offering too much information.** There are things about our parents that we
  don't necessarily want to know—but narcissistic parents will discuss their most
  private matters anyway. Such moms and dads are also prone to blaming each
  other for their troubles and trying to get you to take sides.

- **Acting helpless.** Narcissists want attention at any cost. Although they do not
  enjoy feeling vulnerable, they are not above acting vulnerable if it gets them
  what they want. Sometimes parents believe that the best way to get their children's attention is to create situations where they appear to require an inordinate
  amount of assistance.

As parents age, such behaviors can become even more pronounced. Aging is tough on everyone, but narcissists take the process personally, rather than trying to take it in stride. As their youthful attractiveness and physical vigor diminish, they will often cling with greater and greater intensity to their children, who represent a chance for vicarious achievement and who are now tasked with taking care of them physically as well as emotionally.

Separating from the Narcissistic Parent

Separating from the narcissistic parent is a lifelong task. The only alternative is to estrange yourself from them completely, but most people prefer a less drastic route. After all, they're your parents. Still, unless you want your life to be your parent's life, you will have to take steps to preserve your identity and your integrity:

- ◆ **Echo and mirror your advice-giving parent.** Don't waste your breath telling them you don't want their input—they will give it anyway. Let them know you hear their concerns and opinions and that you will consider them. Then do what you decide to do.

- ◆ **Create a "border patrol."** Do not reward your parents for violating your boundaries. If they show up unannounced, be nice but let them know you are busy or on your way out. If they call too frequently, get caller I.D. and let them talk to your voice mail. Call them back when it's convenient.

 Manhole Ahead

Guilt is a big gun in the narcissistic parent's arsenal. If they fail to hear from you on their timetable, they may insist that they "thought something terrible happened" or they "thought you were dead." Remind yourself: *You didn't create the anxiety; they did.* You're not responsible for their feelings.

- ◆ **Give information on a "need to know" basis.** Your parents might give you too much information, but you don't have to. They don't need to know every detail of your life. The more they know, especially about things they don't approve of, the more they will express their anxiety and offer unwanted advice.

- ◆ **Consult third parties when your aging parents need assistance.** Many aging parents genuinely require assistance, the problem is that narcissistic parents might be all too willing to let their care consume your entire life. Before you do anything drastic, speak with knowledgeable experts: geriatric social workers, doctors, financial planners, attorneys, and in-home caregivers.

Finally, shield your own kids. It will probably come as no great shock that narcissistic parents are also narcissistic grandparents. No, you don't have to keep your kids and your parents apart. Just keep an eye on them when they're together. Try not to let your mother or father send your kids the wrong messages.

Tried and True Tactics

"When I was a child, my mother always tried to frighten me when I wanted to do something that would take me away from her, such as sleep over at a friend's house or go to camp. She made the world seem like a very scary place and I was an anxious kid as a result. When I had a son, I saw her trying to do the same thing to him. There is no use arguing with her. Instead, I limit the time my mom spends alone with her grandson and I'm always sure to remind him that Grandma is a nervous type and that she sometimes exaggerates."—Stacey, 27

The Self-Absorbed Sibling

In families where there are two or more children, one of the children is often selected by the parents to be the merged one, the one on whom high expectations are placed. Thus, you may have a sibling who is locked in a narcissistic dance with your parents while you are not. In a way that's good news for you, as you have been spared many difficulties.

But having a sibling who has borne the brunt of your parents' narcissism can be a challenge, too. She might be highly egotistical. He might intrude on your life in the ways that your parents intruded on his. If your sibling is self-centered, has boundary problems, and other traits we've discussed, you must—as you would with a narcissistic parent—try not to act out any script they try to force on you. Set limits on your involvement with them, don't share too much information, and live your life according to your standards.

One thing you cannot do, however, is imagine that you can change the relationship between your sibling and your parents. You know by now that the golden rule of coping with difficult people is that you cannot change anyone else. Now add to that: you cannot change the relationship that exists between other people. Your sibling and your parent will have to work out their issue their way—or not. The best you can do is manage the way you respond to them all.

The Needy, Greedy Friend

Lastly, we come to the self-centered friend. You might ask why on earth anyone would want a friend who is self-centered, but of course we find ourselves with all kinds of friends. Shared circumstances—such as growing up on the same street or being college roommates or being in the military together—create affiliations among all kinds of people. And let's not forget that narcissistic types can be very charming and entertaining! Maybe it's *fun* to be their friend—up to a point.

It's perfectly all right to be friends with someone whom you consider self-centered. The trick is to know *and accept* the limitations of the relationship. Enjoy the time you spend with them, and do the things you like to do together, but do not structure your entire social life around them. Make sure they're just one of a circle of friends, because they might be prone to canceling plans with you when they get a "better offer." Also, be sure that you are not your self-centered pal's only friend; you might become overwhelmed by their demands on your time. Moderation is the key to many things in life, and it certainly is the key when you have a friend who is narcissistic.

The Least You Need to Know

- ◆ Narcissists are prone to initiating brief, intense romantic relationships that they then end abruptly. Be wary and set limits with people whose sudden attentions and affections seem over the top.

- ◆ Some narcissists may marry, but they do not consider the marriage a true partnership. To get a narcissistic spouse to give you what you want, you'll have to supply heavy doses of flattery and positive reinforcement.

- ◆ Narcissistic mothers and fathers foster over-dependencies in their children and fail to view them as separate beings even when they reach adulthood. Reassert your own boundaries by keeping your private life private.

- ◆ In many families, one child receives the bulk of narcissistic "training" and becomes needy and self-centered. You can manage your response to your siblings but you cannot change the dynamic between them and your parents.

- ◆ It's all right to have a friend who is self-centered if you are getting some enjoyment out of the relationship—just don't expect too much from them, and don't make the friendship exclusive.

Chapter 7

What to Do About Public Narcissists

In This Chapter

- ◆ Picking your battles in the war on rudeness
- ◆ Dealing with rude and dangerous drivers
- ◆ Coping with cell phone abuse
- ◆ Handling narcissistic neighbors
- ◆ Managing narcissists in groups and committees

Public Agenda, a nonprofit organization that researches public opinion, says that 79 percent of Americans believe lack of respect and courtesy ought to be regarded as a serious national problem. Rudeness and road rage are rampant—and whom do we have to thank for it? In large part, needy, greedy narcissists.

In this chapter, we look at how the self-centered operate in public, and what you can do when their actions impact your environment, your safety, and your enjoyment of life.

Narcissists: A Public Pain

Narcissists may not have exactly cornered the market on inconsiderate behavior. A number of difficult types do their fair share. But when you consider the traits that narcissists possess, it's easy to see how they tie in to an attitude of selfishness and insensitivity with regard to fellow citizens:

- Their sense of entitlement leads them to think they don't have to play by written rules of behavior or unwritten rules of decorum.

- Their grandiosity leads them to believe that it's acceptable to inconvenience others, because their time is more valuable and their needs more important than anyone else's.

- Their denial of reality means that they never spend a moment thinking about the consequences of their public actions.

- Their lack of boundaries means they feel free to encroach not only on other people's physical space but also on their quiet moments.

Nearly everyone complains about the way self-centered people behave in public. But what can you do? How about confronting the offender every time you're the victim of impolite behavior? How about perfecting the art of the dirty look? How about writing a letter, starting a petition, or taking some other kind of civic stance? The answer is there is no single answer. You have to evaluate the elements of different situation.

Picking Your Battles

Directly confronting narcissists in public is the trickiest option. Sure, there can be a time and a place for making a comment to or request of a self-centered type, but you really need to pick your battles. You can't confront everyone.

For one thing, even if you quit your job, there aren't enough hours in the day to campaign against all the selfish, thoughtless folks on the planet. For another thing, you should take action only when it will most likely yield a positive result.

The Rules of Direct Confrontation

In each case, weigh your options. No one can make the call except you, but it helps to have some general guidelines. Say something only when …

♦ **You are in control of your emotions.** If you're really enraged, cool off before initiating any confrontation. Otherwise your behavior might end up being worse than the original offender's.

♦ **You can be heard without yelling.** Hollering over the roar of a crowd can stoke your anger, rev up bystanders who might want to weigh in (leading to who knows what kind of brawl), and embarrass the offender. Given how sensitive to criticism narcissists are, you won't get what you want by publicly embarrassing them.

♦ **You don't think the offender will get violent.** It's hard to know who is or isn't capable of punching you in the nose (or the gut), and sometimes you just have to trust your gut (or your nose). If someone is using a lot of profanity, that might be a sign of a short fuse. If they're showing off in front of friends, they might be inclined to pop you for effect. And exercise caution around anyone bigger and stronger than you. Why tempt fate?

♦ **Neither you nor they have been drinking alcohol.** Alcohol is a *disinhibitor*, and often adds fuel to any emotional fire.

♦ **You have thought about what you will say.** No smart cracks, please. And no name-calling. You always want your response to lead to a positive shift in behavior. Because narcissists are very concerned with image, try saying something that might convince them that changing will make them look better.

In each and every case, you'll have to weigh the benefits of saying something versus the benefits of saying nothing—or, in some cases, in doing something other than confronting a public pain directly. Ask yourself, "Am I the best person to take action?" As you'll see in this chapter, sometimes conferring with an authority who has more power in a particular situation is the best choice.

def•i•ni•tion

A **disinhibitor** refers to any stimulus—such as drugs or alcohol—that incites someone to relax their usual reservations and act inappropriately.

The Choice to Let Go

You might sometimes be tempted to instigate a direct confrontation even though your better judgment warns you against it. When this happens, you really need to check in with your ego. Are you tempted to confront because you would feel like a "wimp" if you didn't? If so, remember this: the active choice to do nothing *is* doing something.

There is nothing to be ashamed of if a thoughtful evaluation leads you to the conclusion that there is little point in taking action, or that taking action could be detrimental. On the contrary, your objectivity and levelheadedness is something you should be proud of.

Manhole Ahead _____

Don't let yourself be goaded into a confrontation you'd rather not have. If your companions think something should be done about an inconsiderate person, that doesn't mean *you* should be designated to do it. Don't allow yourself to be "guilted." Suggest ways your companions might deal with the problem if they don't feel equipped to do it themselves—perhaps by complaining to someone in authority.

Road Narcissists

Of all the offenses that the self-centered commit in public, the ones they make on the road are not only the most annoying, but they can also be the most dangerous. When narcissists get behind the wheel, they are the center of the universe, boundaries don't concern them, and the rules are for others. That makes for infuriating, and often risky, practices.

def•i•ni•tion _____

Road rage, also known as road violence, is the informal name for deliberately dangerous and/or violent behavior under the influence of heightened negative emotions—such as anger and frustration—involving an automobile in use.

Self-absorbed drivers routinely disregard other motorists, cut in front of you without signaling, and remain oblivious to what is happening around them. They use time in their vehicle to do everything from eat their breakfast to apply eye makeup to—of course—talk, talk, talk on their cell phones. Even if the offending drivers aren't in the accidents they instigate, they may leave a trail of them, or scary near misses, in their wake. They also often generate angry responses that fall under the collective term *road rage*.

Defensive Driving—Without Road Rage

Feeling enraged toward a driver who's inconsiderate, violates your space, or nearly causes you to smack into a guardrail or another car is perfectly understandable. We've all felt it. The problem is, when we're behind the wheel, that rage can all too easily turn into a provocative action on our own part.

Tragically, some motorists react in an over-the-top fashion. They follow the offending party in an attempt to extract the proverbial eye for an eye. They might blare their horn or shine their brights. They might tailgate or get directly ahead of their nemesis and then slow down. In some instances, motorists who've been automotively insulted by a narcissistic driver have actually gotten out of their own vehicles, pounded on the offender's windows, pulled the driver from their car and injured them, or even used a weapon. Sometimes they've used their own car as a weapon, ramming into the vehicle of the person who caused their intense anger.

Sound like good ideas? Obviously not, when you're thinking with a clear head. No matter how badly a self-absorbed driver behaves on the road, there is never any pay-off to reacting in kind. For one thing, there isn't a chance that you'll get the offender to rethink their behavior. For another thing, you'll stand a good chance of harming yourself or running afoul of the law. (Similar to your elementary school teachers, the highway patrol will not care one bit that "you didn't start it.")

So what can you do? The first and most important rule of the road under any circumstance is to drive defensively. And that is *especially* true when you've been affronted and you're feeling peeved. When that happens …

- Make safety your first priority. Maneuver to avoid a collision, not to retaliate.

- Use your horn sparingly. The purpose of your horn is to alert other drivers to your presence, not to stand in for yelling at the top of your lungs. Car horns are an extremely provocative sound—they'll likely only make an offending driver more offensive.

- Avoid making eye contact. In circumstances like these, eye contact can be perceived as a challenge by a narcissistic person. Keep your eyes on the road where they belong.

- Avoid hand gestures. Don't "flip the bird" or do anything like it. It might feel satisfying for a moment, but you'll only make matters worse.

- If the driver's actions were truly dangerous, note the make, model, and color of the other car, and the license number if possible.

- Put as much distance between yourself and the rude driver as possible. Although your urge may be to stand on the accelerator, let it up, and maybe even put on the brakes instead. Let the offender get far enough ahead that you are not likely to encounter him again.

- If you're really upset, pull over until you can collect yourself. A close call can leave you not only angry but also shaken and distracted. Take time for a few deep breaths so you don't endanger yourself or anyone else.

The road is no place for a showdown and no place to teach a lesson. Dealing sanely with a narcissistic driver is obviously one of those situations where "doing nothing" is actually a conscious, active choice.

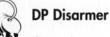

DP Disarmer

If you don't want to file a police report, but still want to vent, visit www.roadragers.com. Roadragers is not a law enforcement agency, but you can post a report that will remain online for anyone to access for research purposes.

After you arrive safely at your destination, pat yourself on the back. If the incident was really serious, and you believe the driver was being reckless and not just careless, you can call your local police station or the highway patrol and report it. The police consider aggressive, dangerous driving a serious public safety issue. Be sure to provide as much information as possible, including the time and place of your encounter, information on the car, and a clear description of what happened.

One Car, Two Parking Spaces

If you think narcissistic drivers are irritating to drive alongside, you've probably also noticed that they're no fun to park next to, either. Such drivers don't abandon their selfish ways just because they've stopped the car.

In classic "me first" style, they'll cut in front of you to get the space you've been patiently waiting for. Shake your fist, blow your horn—the odds that you'll make them apologize and retreat are roughly the same as the odds of their front fender being struck by a flaming meteorite while you watch with a satisfied grin.

Narcissistic drivers are also really good at "parking you in," parking so close to your vehicle that you practically have to pry it out with a shoehorn. And, of course, there's their favorite trick of all: parking their car across two parking spaces. (Especially annoying when spaces are in short supply and time is short, for example, at a commuter train station parking lot, or at your gym when you're trying to get to a popular workout class.) Self-centered drivers may feel entitled to more than one parking space because:

1. They drive a vehicle roughly the size of an ocean liner (although no formal studies have been done on the correlation between narcissism and the ownership of supersized vehicles, common sense says there is one).

2. Their car is "special" (new, expensive, customized, or all three) and they're afraid to risk it being damaged by the riff-raff.

3. Well, just because!

When you're denied a parking space because a car is splayed across multiple spaces, you might have a momentary fantasy about damaging it in some way. But "keying" someone's car or otherwise damaging it is obviously inappropriate. Sure, you can have the thought, but don't take the action.

How about a nasty note? It certainly is tempting to scribble a sarcastic diatribe for the offender to find when they return. And because you won't be around to confront the driver face-to-face, you might feel emboldened. But be careful. A note isn't a bad idea if you phrase it diplomatically: "Parking spaces are in short supply. Please be more considerate." But avoid foul language and insults: "Your car's a heap, you *%#@" because you never know when someone—perhaps a very large, muscular someone— will walk up just as you're writing the finishing touches.

Ask yourself, "Am I the best person to take action?" Consider who runs the establishment that the parking lot is affiliated with. Can you complain to management? You might be able to have them page the offender and ask them to move their car, or to post signage noting a "one car, one space" policy.

Tried and True Tactics

"Once, when I was really mad, I left a very insulting note on an SUV that had been parked across two parking spaces at my gym. I just grabbed the first piece of paper I could find, which happened to be the back of one of my business cards. Oops. I got quite a phone call later from the guy I'd called a "jerk" and a "moron." I steered clear of that gym for weeks! I think next time I'll talk to the club owner instead—or at least use a blank piece of paper."—Evan, 35

Messy Narcissists

Selfish, self-centered types seem to love making—and leaving—a mess wherever they go. At the prettiest parks, they'll leave a trail of empty bottles, food containers, tissues, and newspapers. At the beach, you'll find their flotsam in the water and their jetsam on the sand. In the movie theatre, they'll leave their gum under your seat and their popcorn … everywhere. In the restroom, you'll find their kids' disposable diapers.

Their penchant for littering is easy to understand if you try to think like a narcissist for a moment. *Why should I clean it up? That's someone else's job!*

Don't Go "Environ-mental"

The truth is, they're right about the second part—at least some of the time, someone else will clean up the mess. They might be paid workers, volunteers, or responsible Good Samaritans like you.

Is this fair? No. Can you stop it? Not usually—at least not on a one-to-one basis. Confronting a selfish litterbug in the act with a glare, a stare, or a pointed comment might work on occasion, but most likely you will be ignored, mocked, or socked if you go environ-mental. Besides, you can't spend your life policing public places. So try one of these two tacks, depending on your disposition:

- **Bag it up.** The truth is, the world consists of three kinds of people—those who mess things up, those who ignore the mess, and those who pitch in for the public good. No, it's not your job, but you'll feel better about the world and about yourself if you become one of the latter.

- **Help pass and enforce laws.** Many public places now post stiff fines for littering; this is especially true in state and national parks and beaches. Write to your legislators to encourage more and steeper fines. Report offenders to the appropriate authorities.

Whichever option you select, you won. You'll have the satisfaction of knowing that you're not part of the problem, you're part of the solution. That's a feeling a narcissist will never know. Well, maybe they will, but no one will agree with them!

Dealing with Inconsiderate Smokers

By now, nearly everyone understands the very real dangers of inhaling secondhand smoke. Not everyone who smokes is inconsiderate, but smokers who are narcissists present a special challenge. Remember, from their perspective rules don't apply, and boundaries are made to be crossed. No wonder their tendrils of toxic smoke are wafting into your airspace or across your dinner plate.

The good news is, even more than with littering, the law is soundly on your side. Workplaces, restaurants, even bars and other public venues are being designated smoke-free. If a policy exists, contact someone in authority. If such a policy does not exist, ask that it be put into effect.

Manhole Ahead _____

If you're traveling in other parts of the world, be aware that in many countries smoking is not the cultural taboo it is now in America. It might not have occurred to a smoker that they're bothering you. If they're just used to a different social contract, a little discreet coughing on your part might inspire them to at least turn the other way.

The Self-Centered Cell Phoners

Once upon a time, self-centered people's greatest noise-related offense had to do with the music they played and the volume at which they played it. Not surprisingly, narcissists assumed that everyone wanted to listen to their music—the louder the better! In recent years, the happy technological development of personal devices such as iPods have somewhat countered the effect of musical noise pollution.

But what technology hath given, it hath also taken away. Today, virtually every narcissist is armed with a cell phone and—apparently—a manual on how to use it to make everyone else's life miserable. They talk on their phones constantly, and at the top of their voice, even when they have nothing more to say except, "Honey, I'm on the train," and, five minutes later, "Honey, I'm still on the train." Sometimes they divulge personal information (about their love life, their medical conditions, their financial portfolio) that bystanders are forced to overhear.

And did someone say *ring, ring*? The phones of the obliviously self-centered go off anywhere and everywhere: at the movies, in the theatre (actors have stopped mid-scene in an indignant fury), in meetings, at dinner parties, in yoga class, even in church! It's not that narcissists have never heard of the "vibrate" setting. Why keep your calls to yourself when you can show everyone else how important you are? (Somewhat ironically, many of those songs you no longer hear via boom box are now loudly presented as cell phone ring tones.)

What to do? Reportedly, David Letterman tells his audience that if any cell phones go off during his taping he will crush them with a hammer. Jay Leno reputedly answered a woman's cell phone during one of his tapings, saying she couldn't talk and he'd have to take a message. If you have your own TV show, it's okay to try either one of these tactics. But for ordinary mortals, the following strategies can help:

◆ **Allow them to save face.** Let them know you're hearing what you shouldn't. If you say, "You're probably not aware of this but I can overhear your private conversation," you allow them the option of changing their behavior without getting too defensive.

◆ **Include "please" and "thank you" in requests.** There's no reason to be rude simply because someone else is. Influence by example.

◆ **When someone complies, stop talking.** There's no need to rehash what happened or to badger someone who has done what you asked. Forget the post-mortem rebukes and move on with your day.

Manhole Ahead _____

One way not to begin a request to a narcissist—or any other difficult person—is by saying, "I'm sorry." *You* are not the one who should be apologizing. As assertiveness trainers point out, this phrase disempowers you from the start.

Again, before you confront, think about whether you're the right person to do so. Does your location have a cell phone policy? Find out who is in charge of enforcing it. The manager might be the best person to intervene in a restaurant, a librarian in the library, and so on.

The Narcissistic Neighbor

Now we come to a special situation. Do you live next door or across the street from a narcissist—or a whole family of them? If you live in an apartment, do you live above or below them? If so, you have a unique problem. Even if you don't know them very well or pal around with them at all, you will have an ongoing relationship—until and unless one of you moves away.

Neighbors can instigate boundary violations in any number of ways. They can be noisy or messy. They can neglect to quiet or clean up after their pets. They can party 'til all hours—with their guest parked in your driveway. They can shine lights into your bedroom window. They can paint their house shocking pink, or midnight black. And, as is now a common problem in suburbia, they can keep making their house bigger and bigger and bigger until their McMansion dwarfs your more modest abode, crowding out its light and even diminishing its market value.

In some of these circumstances, help might be available from official sources. You may call the police to break up a loud late-night party, or ask the zoning board about a construction permit you suspect your neighbors never got.

But wait! You may be better off attempting to deal with the situation yourself. "Tattling" on your neighbors can lead to so much retaliation and counter-retaliation that your relationship will make the Middle East look like Woodstock.

Try to make nice with your narcissistic neighbors. I know you don't want to, but it's for your own good. Remember, you can ingratiate yourself to a narcissist by flattery. Find something about them or their dwelling or their pets to praise. Ask them about themselves and engage in active listening. After you've established a bond, you can leverage it to gently suggest modifications they might make to some of their practices—indicating that these are things they can do to benefit themselves. ("Gosh I love your adorable poodle. I hope she isn't allergic to all those chemicals we just put on the lawn.")

Being courteous and friendly toward a narcissistic neighbor isn't always easy, but it often pays. In the end, those late-night parties are more tolerable if you were at least invited.

The Narcissist in Group and Committee Settings

Finally, what do you do when you have an attention-seeking self-centered type taking up all the time of a volunteer committee, neighborhood board, or any task-oriented group—whether they are attending as a member or simply as a spectator? We've all run into them: the PTA mom who only wants to talk about her and her kids' issues, the co-op board member who only is concerned with the particulars of his apartment, the guy who attends all the town council meetings so he can expound on his theories of property tax reform, trash pickup procedures, and the hours of the local library. A group's agenda will obviously never get accomplished if such a person is allowed to monopolize the floor. But the more you try to deflect their soliloquies, the harder they dig in their heels.

Here's an instance where you need to invoke the inviolable authority of formal procedure. Make certain your group adopts a *written* policy of how meetings will proceed. Set up rules for making statements and asking questions. Make it clear exactly when in the meeting public comments will be heard. And outline which topics are and are not appropriate. (For example, a public Board of Education meeting is not the venue to discuss an issue between one child and one teacher.)

DP Disarmer

Many boards and committees use *Robert's Rules of Order* as their procedural bible. *Robert's Rules,* first published in 1876 by Army major Henry Martyn Robert after he'd presided over a church meeting and discovered that delegates from around the country did not agree about proper procedure, might be a bit formal for some groups—but it is still worth referring to for ideas on keeping meetings from being hijacked by difficult individuals.

The beauty of having written rules is that they apply to each and every person. Self-absorbed speakers—whether they like it or not—will be compelled to bow to the governing guidelines. They might protest that these rules, like others, should not apply to them, but if the group stands united, they will generally back down.

The Least You Need to Know

♦ Public rudeness at the hands of narcissists is rampant, but you can't fight every battle. Consider direct confrontation only if you can be heard without yelling, can control your emotions, and are not dealing with someone who might get violent.

♦ Selfish, self-absorbed drivers make the roads dangerous. Don't compound the problem with road rage; put as much distance as possible between your vehicle and theirs.

♦ The self-centered love their cell phones, and they want you to know it. Confront them politely, if you must, and consider whether you can enlist someone in authority to enforce a cell phone policy.

♦ Having a narcissistic neighbor can be a challenge, but you'll get much more consideration by befriending rather than complaining.

♦ To set limits of self-absorbed attention-seekers in committee and board settings, make certain your group adopts a written policy outlining how meetings will proceed and what types of statements and questions are appropriate.

Part  3

The Controllers

There's only one way to do something: their way. Meet "the controllers." In this part of the book, you'll learn about the tactics used by men and women with power agendas. You'll come to understand the many styles of controlling—some overt and some well hidden. In addition, you'll learn how to contend with controllers who pull out all the stops to get their way at work, at home, and in virtually every domain.

Chapter 8

All About Control Freaks

In This Chapter

♦ Discovering what turns people into controllers

♦ Learning what controllers fear most

♦ Understanding the four controlling styles

♦ Gearing up to deal with controllers

"He's so controlling. He never lets anyone else contribute."

"She's such a control freak. Everything has to go exactly her way."

Most of us have uttered these words about someone in our lives, whether it's someone in our family, someone at our place of work, or perhaps a teacher, coach, accountant, lawyer, doctor, committee chairman, or anyone with whom we have repeated run-ins related to issues of power.

Controllers can really get our hackles up, because they can make us feel like helpless children who are always being told what to do. Interestingly, childhood conflicts might be what caused those controllers to become the way they are.

What Creates Controllers?

As with narcissistic types, controlling types have personality traits whose roots run deep. Ask a person familiar with someone who always wants to run the show, and you'll probably hear, "Oh yes, they were always like that. Had to do things their way, or they just wouldn't do them at all!"

Controllers are very good at what they do, because they've been practicing for quite a while.

Early Power Struggles

Where does it all begin? Is there a hereditary factor that affects controlling behavior? Researchers have discovered a gene linked to certain obsessive and compulsive traits, which a controller may manifest. That may be just the tip of the genomic iceberg. But nature and nurture are a pair of slippery snakes, and genetic predispositions can play out differently in individuals depending on circumstances and environment. So, let's consider a circumstance that often results in the creation of a "little controller."

Each of us goes through a phase in early childhood when we harbor the exuberant belief that we can do whatever we wish. Newly mobile, we can walk or run wherever we want to go. Newly verbal, we can say—or scream—whatever we want in any setting or circumstance. If we don't want to do something—say, eat our peas, or go to bed—well, we just keep yelling and crying until we get our way.

Needless to say, most parents nip this worldview in the bud. For our own good, not to mention their peace of mind, they begin—generally in our second year—to set limits on our no-holds-barred approach to life. No, we can't run into traffic. No, we can't let go of their hand in the supermarket and career down the aisles yanking boxes of Froot Loops off the shelves. If we throw a tantrum, we get disciplined. If we can't share toys with our siblings, we get a "time out" from play.

Of course, it's all much easier said than done. Toddlers can be naturally stubborn, often dramatically so (hence the phrase "terrible twos"), and power struggles between parent and child can get thorny when children are especially recalcitrant or parents are too harsh, using physical force or emotional shaming to bend the child's will. If the struggles are especially intense and unresolved, the result can be that the child begins to develop strategies for exerting control in any area they can and in any way they can.

Freud used the term *anal-retentive* to describe people whose urge to control or "hold on to" things began in the toilet-training phase of life. But you don't have to be a Freudian (or be comfortable with his metaphor) to know when you are in the company of someone who won't "give it up." These behavior patterns may have begun as a way of expressing anger toward one's parents—of saying, in effect, *you're not the boss of me; I'm the boss of me*. But they have persisted well beyond childhood and now *you* are caught in the crossfire.

def•i•ni•tion

Anal-retentive is Freud's term for people whose obstinate and obsessive behaviors originated as a result of toilet-training struggles. Nowadays the phrase is such a part of our common vocabulary (comedian Phil Hartman played *Saturday Night Live* characters such as "Anal-Retentive Chef" and "Anal-Retentive Carpenter") that, without dwelling on its roots, we often use "anal" as a shorthand for implying that someone is obsessive or controlling.

Countering Chaos

Coming from a family where appropriate limits were *never* set could also lead to a controlling personality. Though we all resist limits to some extent, we do crave rules, routines, and order. Unless our mothers and fathers tell us what is wrong or danger-ous, we really don't know how to function or protect ourselves in the world, which then feels like a confusing and dangerous place.

Without limits, lovingly but firmly set, a child could develop a *reaction formation*. They will set their own rules and enforce their own constraints. These internal rules might be exceedingly rigid, but their stringency will allow the child to ward off the insecurity of not having a road map of rules to guide them.

def•i•ni•tion

A **reaction formation** is an unconscious psychological defense mechanism that switches unacceptable feelings into their opposites. Thus, if someone feels a sense of inner anxiety, they might devise a way to maintain outward calm.

What Controllers Really Fear

Regardless of what leads a controller to develop the way they do, all controllers fear the same thing: they subconsciously fear that relinquishing control in one area means relinquishing control in *all* areas. They have yet to accept the fact that only so much of life is within anyone's control.

Most of us acknowledge our limited personal power and the power of circumstance, but a diehard controller can't tolerate this aspect of reality. Instead they try to maintain the illusion that their actions can stave off the unpredictability of fate. Would-be human amulets, bent on warding off evil, they pretend no harm can befall them if they continue to orchestrate what goes on around them. They exert a great deal of effort to scanning their environment for potential threats to their autonomy so they can "head them off at the pass."

> **Tried and True Tactics** _____
>
> "The main thing I always thought about controllers was how anxious they made me feel. But when I learned that they can be among the most anxious people of all, I was a little less put out by them. Nothing changed except my perspective, but sometimes that alone can help."—Andrea, 36

Four Controlling Styles

Not all controllers exercise power and control in the same ways. Some are very forthright about their desire to dictate what happens, who does what, and when and how they do it. Others are much more subtle—even covert. Control can also be achieved through duplicity, even seeming passive.

The Volatile Controller

Volatile controllers get others to do what they want by holding a threat like a sword over their head. The threat is simple: if what they want to happen doesn't happen they will lose their temper.

You'll never hear such controlling types say this out loud, of course. It wouldn't do to warn: *Hey, if I don't get my way I'll pop my cork*. Instead, volatile controllers count on the fact that you've learned about their tendency to blow up either from direct experience or from their reputation. (The latter happens a lot in the workplace, where old employees warn new hires whom to watch out for.)

The "good" news, such as it is, about volatile controllers, is that although their blow-ups can be fierce and frightening, they are—like fast-moving thunderstorms—usually relatively short-lived. These people are not rage-aholics; that is, they're not addicted to the "rush" of anger—as people you'll learn more in this book's section on the truly toxic. In fact, controllers don't especially like losing their temper because doing so gives them a fleeting feeling of being *out* of control. They would rather intimidate by threatening what might happen, rather than actually losing their cool.

Along these lines, they are somewhat good at projecting all the signs that they're about to let loose some fireworks. They might:

♦ Stare and glare.

♦ Drum their fingers on a desk or table.

♦ Talk through gritted teeth.

♦ Start speaking … slowly … and … deliberately, enunciating every syllable.

Often, these signs are enough to inspire compliance. Imagine how our early ancestors felt when they were threatened by the close proximity to a simmering volcano. To appease its wrath, they'd sometimes offer a "sacrifice." We, too, often make sacrifices in the hopes of warding off an eruption. Sometimes that's okay, but we have to recognize when those sacrifices are too great.

Manhole Ahead

There are variants of volatile controllers who use tears instead of anger as their secret weapon. They send the message that if defied, they will unleash not fireworks but waterworks. (More about this in Chapter 10).

The "Smarter-Than-You" Controller

The smarter-than-you controller wants everyone to accept their authority because their knowledge, expertise, and logic are infallible. They've got an answer—yes, often a smart one—for every objection you could possibly make.

Are smarter-than-you controllers actually smarter than you? Maybe about some things some of the time, but certainly not about all things all the time. No human being is omniscient. And besides, there are different kinds of intelligence, including analytical, practical, creative, and—of course—emotional. The bottom line is that in refusing to be open to anyone else's ideas, the smarter-than-you controller proves they are, in fact, not the sharpest knife in the drawer. Truly smart people are open to new ideas.

To get a handle on smarter-than-you controllers in your life, remember this: *They draw their power not from their smarts but from your insecurities*. That's right. If you want to get this type of controller to accept *your* ideas, *you* have to believe in those ideas, and in yourself. Put your self-doubt on a shelf. Then you will be able to employ strategies that can gently and effectively get a smarter-than-you controller to redirect their attention from their idea to yours.

Tried and True Tactics

"I work with a guy who never misses an opportunity to mention that, years ago, he got a perfect score on his SAT. He's one of those know-it-all controlling types, and he uses this as a way of reinforcing the idea that we should do things his way because he was such a 'genius.' It took my own high school kids to remind me that the SAT is not a test of creativity, or flexibility, or people skills, or any other kinds of intelligence. Besides, as my son said, 'If he's such a genius, why hasn't he solved the mysteries of the universe?' I never ask that question aloud, but I sure keep it in mind, and it helps me stand up for my point of view."—Gene, 45

The Deceptive Controller

Deceptive controllers crave control so badly that, for them, the end justifies the means. They'll bad-mouth others, start and spread rumors, mislead, set one person against another, omit crucial facts, and sometimes lie outright. Sometimes, even when the stakes are relatively low, their approach is nothing less than *Machiavellian*.

def•i•ni•tion

Machiavellian is a term sometimes used to describe a person with a tendency to deceive and manipulate others for gain. It refers to the writings of sixteenth-century Italian political philosopher Niccolò Machiavelli, as set forth in his treatise *The Prince*.

Precisely because they are so good at what they do, it might take a while to realize how events are being orchestrated behind-the-scenes by deceptive controllers at work, in personal relationships, and elsewhere. Moreover, they're slippery when confronted, and they are very good at protesting—with some degree of believability—*"Who me?"*

If you can't always expose a deceptive controller's shady tactics, you can at least keep yourself from being a primary target by not painting a bull's-eye on your chest. Don't share secrets with deceptive controllers—they won't be secrets for long—and never discuss your self-doubts or fears with them. If you do, they'll just use them against you.

The Passive-Aggressive Controller

To say someone has a passive-aggressive style does not indicate, as you might think, that they vacillate between being compliant and being controlling. On the contrary: they're always angling for control, but they have learned to do so very indirectly. Their approach is often so slick or subtle that it takes a while to realize you're dealing with a passive-aggressive controller.

Perhaps you know someone who displays several of the seven signs of passive aggression. This type of person …

1. Repeatedly promises to do things and then "forgets."

2. Continually finds seemingly plausible excuses to delay taking action.

3. Says they wish they could do what you ask, but claims they are just not capable.

4. Withholds important information (or sometimes money or other resources) so that you are unable to take necessary actions when you need to.

5. Evades direct questions by offering vague or ambiguous responses.

6. Sometimes sulks and plays "poor me."

7. Expends extreme effort to maintain a friendly, cooperative persona.

If you know someone who fits the bill, wake up and smell the coffee! You are dealing with a person who controls by saying yes when they mean no, by stonewalling, or by playing the victim. If it makes you feel better, you are hardly alone in your frustrations. Passive aggression is a very common style.

DP Disarmer _____

In our culture we hear a lot about passive-aggressive males. But passive aggression is an equal opportunity style, and women can also be very skillful at sugar-coating their true agenda. If a woman or a man displays a passive-aggressive pattern of behavior, exercise caution. As they say: if it walks like a duck and it quacks like a duck, it's a duck.

Like any controlling style, passive aggression masks a great deal of anxiety. But the passive-aggressive person's anxiety is of a particular nature. This type of person, although determined to get what they want, dreads confrontation and conflict. If they *say* what they want, that would put them at risk of being questioned or challenged. Instead they devise diversionary tactics.

Confrontation is, to some degree, uncomfortable for lots of people, but that doesn't necessarily make them passive-aggressive. What distinguishes the passive-aggressive is more a fear of conflict than a dislike of it. This might well be due to a childhood dynamic where parents had zero tolerance for dissent. Coupled with the passive-aggressive person's fear, however, is a resolute, underlying determination to find a way somehow to circumvent the restrictions imposed on their self-expression. Under a compliant demeanor, they are stowing a pile of resentment.

Understanding the passive-aggressive's motivation doesn't make their behavior any more excusable or any less hurtful. But it does give you a clue as to why they so often leave you feeling baffled, insecure, and perhaps even guilty. They're exceptionally adept at *gaslighting*, making you feel as though you're the problem. If you buy their spin, you'll end up apologizing to them.

def•i•ni•tion

Gaslighting refers to the practice of getting someone else to doubt themselves, dismiss their own reactions, and perhaps even wonder if they're mentally unbalanced. The term comes from the movie *Gaslight*, in which Charles Boyer played a scheming husband bent on inheriting his wife's fortune.

Getting Ready to Cope with Controllers

With so many categories of people wanting to control things, it might seem like a wonder that you get to exercise any autonomy at all. How, you may wonder, can you deal with all these myriad string-pullers? As the next three chapters will show, you'll need a lot of different tools to deal with different kinds of controllers in different situations.

But as you get ready to cope with controllers, keep these basic guidelines in mind.

Consider Why You Comply

If you feel as though your strings are being pulled, think about who's pulling them and how they're doing it. Now look at any possible role you may be playing in perpetuating the situation:

◆ Maybe you're doing their bidding because you've gotten a bit lazy—too used to taking the path of least resistance.

- Maybe you were eager to let them be in charge because you really didn't want to take responsibility.

- Maybe you buried your head in the sand while a covert, controlling type repeatedly gave you clues about their agenda—perhaps because you don't like thinking critically about anyone, or you're afraid of seeming paranoid.

If you discover that you've been, to some extent, colluding with a controller, don't beat yourself up over it. Simply acknowledge your role. Doing so will help you unravel the situation.

Believe in Your Abilities

Controlling types are only too happy to help undermine your confidence. People who lack self-confidence rarely feel entitled to question the authority of those who claim it. You don't have to become a public braggart, but you do need to remind yourself of your accomplishments and your strengths:

- Remember the times your decisions have proved correct.

- Remember the times you beat the odds and triumphed over adversity.

- Think of the positive feedback you've gotten from others in the past and in the present.

If you feel you lack some skill that you consider crucial, don't throw up your hands. Make it your business to work on attaining it. That will give you not only new skills, but also a better self-image. The more you feel you *deserve* to be heard, the more you will find a way to make this happen.

Don't Be a Blabbermouth

Knowledge is power. Be careful what you tell controlling types about your desires and your plans. If what you want doesn't dovetail with what they want, they'll begin to make your life difficult.

Be especially careful what you reveal to covert controllers. And because we all reveal things both verbally and nonverbally, practice your poker face.

Manhole Ahead _____

Controllers are often quite close-mouthed about their plans, although quite skilled at extracting information from others. They love asking open-ended questions such as, "What do you think about such-and-such?" Ask them to be specific. Keep your answers brief and focused on one aspect of a topic. Never over-volunteer information.

Control Is an Illusion—Be an Illusionist

No one can control everything all the time. Even controlling types know this deep down. *They just don't want to be reminded of it.* They want to maintain the illusion of control. If you can help them to hang on to this illusion, you can often get things to go your way. The skill in doing this lies in convincing controllers that one of these things is true:

- They gave you the inspiration for your idea or plan, so it's really their "baby."

- The idea or plan was really theirs; you're just adding some finishing flourishes that they just hadn't thought of yet.

- Your plan, your idea will actually give them more power and control in the long run (at work, for example, by *you* handling the budget requests for your department, you can get your boss more funds).

Maybe you can convince them of all three! Be diplomatic when preserving an illusion. Use nonthreatening language to make your points. Say "we" instead of "I" whenever possible. And try phrasing your idea in question form, as in, "What do you think would happen if we tried …?"

Use Last Resorts Last

As mentioned in Chapter 3, sometimes you have to fight fire with fire. When all else fails, how do you out-control a controller?

One way, of course, is to go ahead and do what you want in spite of them. After all, unless someone is holding a gun to your head, they can't really force you to do anything, can they? But if defiance is what you choose, you must always ask yourself what the fallout will be and if you are willing to pay the price.

A second way is to appropriate their style. You can attempt to out-deceive a deceiver or be more passive-aggressive than a passive-aggressive type. But beware here, too, for these folks have had lots of practice. Since this is the only way they know how to do things, they're playing for keeps. A novice might have trouble beating them at their own game, and if you're not exceptionally skillful, you might just dig yourself into a deeper hole.

Sometimes a viable way to out-control a controller is to invoke the power of numbers. It is sometimes easier to stand up to a controller as part of a group, the members of which can unite and press for change. (The democratic process doesn't work in every situation, but when it does it's powerful stuff, as our country's founding fathers could attest.)

As always, use your psychological smarts where you can. Before you deploy fire, consider whether less drastic measures will serve you just as well, if not better. Get control of yourself, and you will be well along your way to preventing others from controlling you.

The Least You Need to Know

♦ Controllers generally begin in childhood, as an outgrowth of power struggles with parents or as a reaction to chaotic circumstances. The fact that they've been practicing these behaviors for so long makes them very adept at getting control.

♦ What controllers fear most is that if they relinquish control in one area, they will have to face the fact that much of life is beyond their control. They want to maintain the illusion that their actions can stave off the fickleness of fate.

♦ Controllers have four prevalent styles: the volatile controller threatens to erupt; the smarter-than-you controller preys on insecurities; the deceptive controller is underhanded; and the passive-aggressive controller controls by appearing to comply.

♦ Understand the role you play in a controller's dynamic. Reaffirm your own abilities, be cautious about divulging information, and help controllers maintain the illusion that they are in control while still moving your agenda forward.

Coping with Controllers at Work

In This Chapter

- ◆ Learning the four motivations of workplace controllers
- ◆ Handling tantrum-throwers at work
- ◆ Dealing with workplace know-it-alls
- ◆ Recognizing when "yes" means "no"
- ◆ Coping with controlling customers

Let's face it: it's not unusual for work to involve someone telling another what to do. You may not always want to do what you have to do in the way someone says you have to, but a certain amount of doing what's necessary is par for the course, whether you work in an office, a school, a store, a factory, or a farm. Sometimes you have to suck it up. That's why they call it *w-o-r-k*, and not *p-l-a-y*.

But what if your boss has crossed the line from rational delegating to demanding the unreasonable? What if the person being bossy is not your boss, but a bossy peer or even subordinate? What if there are people in your workplace who spend less time working than they do manipulating situations to get what they want—often at others' expense? This chapter addresses such scenarios, and will help you reassert control around controllers at work.

Controllers' Work Agendas

In Chapter 8, we looked at various styles of controlling. Workplace controllers can use any of those styles; they can be volatile; they can play "smarter than you"; they can be deceptive and duplicitous, or they can be passive-aggressive. Before you decide how to deal with a controller, scope out their mode of operation and their primary agenda. Knowing what they want can give you a leg up, because if they think you can help achieve their goal, they are apt to treat you better.

Most workplace controllers have one of four main motivations.

Material Gain

With some folks it's all about money. They will do whatever they have to—and demand you do whatever they want you to—if it means greater gain for them. Of course, what they crave isn't always merely cold hard cash. They also wouldn't mind a fancy company car, a prestigious corner office, and a sky's-the-limit expense account. If they're running a business, they want to see its profits soar.

The gain-driven controller is single-mindedly driven, and expects everyone they work with to be the same. They can be taskmasters and whip-crackers, expecting everyone to put in long hours and exert superhuman effort and dedication. They can also be cheapskates, expecting everyone to do their jobs on a shoestring budget with inadequate resources. Remember, they want to get—not to spend.

> ### Tried and True Tactics
>
> "My controlling boss was such a tightwad that he was actually harming the bottom line. He refused to invest in new computers for our graphic designers that could have saved all of us a tremendous amount of time, in turn raising productivity. One day I brought my teenager's state-of-the-art laptop into work with me, saying I planned to buy a new battery charger for it on my way home. I casually asked my boss if he'd like to try it out. I opened a program that we used all the time, but which operated about 10 times faster on the newer machine. Suddenly *he* had a brainstorm and we all had new computers."—Edward, 44

The good news is that material gain is a pretty straightforward goal. Controllers who seek it at least tend to be forthright in their tactics. They are often very volatile, but the bottom line is they value proven performance. Do things their way and they'll often reward you. On the other hand, if you want to do things your way, you'll have to help them discover that *they* will gain more by changing their tactics.

Risk Aversion

Some controllers are mainly concerned with fear of failure, and will do everything they can to ensure no mistakes are made. At work, they can be reluctant to delegate any responsibility for fear that anyone other than they will muck things up. If they do let others do any meaningful work, they'll insist on checking it not once, but twice or thrice—and of course they always find ways to "fix" it.

The risk-averse are creativity-crushers. They are loath to let anyone around them try anything different. Explain to them the potential upside of an innovation, and they will expound with great eloquence on the potential downside. Even if the risk is relatively small, they'll cite enough "evidence" to plow most objections under.

Risk-averse controllers often play the "smarter-than-you" game, and can be especially frustrating to innovators who feel they are wasting their breath trying to persuade them that in the workplace those who do not evolve become extinct.

The really innovative approach—albeit not always easy to execute—is to get a risk-averse controller to believe there is more risk in *not* changing than there is in changing. As always with controllers, it's best to help them come to such realizations "on their own."

Self-Preservation

Those obsessed with self-preservation want to appear invaluable and irreplaceable on the job, but they are not convinced of their own worth and ability. They're not big on working at work, but they are very big on playing politics: schmoozing and sucking up to some people; stabbing others in the back.

Self-preserving controllers generally use covert tactics. These are deceivers and passive-aggressives—proverbial wolves in sheep's

DP Disarmer

If a self-preserving controller clearly tries to get you to do their work, you have the absolute right to say "no." But it's best to decline diplomatically to avoid behind the scenes repercussions. Assure them you know this is their domain and they are the person best equipped to do this work.

clothing. They don't just want to look good, they want to look better than anyone else, so they find ways to make others look bad.

Meanwhile, who's doing the work? Maybe you are—especially if you are a diligent, competent but somewhat unassertive type. By arranging for others to do their jobs, self-preservers remain safe. If the work goes well, they win. If it goes wrong, sorry, *you* lose. After all, *they* didn't do it.

Personal Power

Some controllers simply want their own private kingdom. It might be a large kingdom, such as an entire business or corporation; it might be a tiny kingdom, such as a small department or business with just a few employees. Sometimes a controller is content to lord it over just one solitary person. So long as they have one subject over whom they can rule, they are happy. Just hope that subject isn't you.

Controllers interested in power may appropriate any and every controlling style. They are often versatile enough to alter their technique depending on who they're trying to get to dance to their tune. Those who are really power-hungry are also very good at identifying others' insecurities and going straight for the emotional jugular.

To defend yourself, it's best to know where you're weakest. Are you so insecure about your expertise you'll accept whatever they say? Are you so eager to please you'll do their work for them? Are you so scared of other people's anger that you'll sacrifice anything to stave it off? If so you may be unwittingly conspiring with the power-hungry to make yourself their serf.

But you're not alone. Often controllers do not seize power so much as they have it handed to them by people who don't know how to alter their usual response to controlling behavior. Read on to learn how to reverse this dynamic.

Watch Out, They're Gonna Blow

"He was the weekend manager of a restaurant. All us waiters used to literally tiptoe around him. We didn't want 'it' to happen to us."

"She was one of the partners at a law firm where I was an associate. I know all the associates feared 'it,' but I think the other partners dreaded it almost as much."

"He was the metropolitan editor at the newspaper where I was a reporter. When he called one of us into his office and shut the door, we quaked. 'It' might happen right then, right there."

The people being described above are volatile controllers in the workplace. The "it" is a grown-up tantrum: an angry, hostile outburst that leaves shock and awe in its wake.

Volatile controllers keep others in line by keeping them on edge. As unnerving as their actual explosions are, what's worse is wondering when those explosions will come. Some volatile types explode frequently, and others have predictable triggers for their wrath, but most behave erratically. A minor matter might sail right past them one day, but set them off the next.

Because it's impossible to read their minds and figure out when their own anxiety is about to reach a tipping point, it's impossible to know when a particular straw will break the camel's back. As a result, workers tiptoe around these types, being excessively careful to do what they think will please them. They are reluctant to question the controller's decisions or speak up in any way. They self-edit even their best ideas, because it's just not worth the risk that the controller will take what they suggest as a challenge to their authority.

 DP Disarmer

Want to tell off a volatile boss or co-worker? Go home, sit down, and write them a letter saying all the things you feel they deserve to hear. Then tear it up! You'll feel better. But whatever you do, don't write this letter as an e-mail. You might be too tempted to press Send—or do so in error.

Volatile controllers are often high on the workplace hierarchy, likely because their intense nature fueled their ride to the top. Once at the top, they are more apt "get away with" tantrums than people lower down the pecking order. However, sometimes a volatile controller who is not the boss will use the threat of a tantrum to lord it over others. Even high-powered executives, for example, have been known to quake at the thought of irritating the tantrum-throwing tyrant who runs the office copier center or mailroom with an iron fist. Unwittingly fill out a form incorrectly and their bewildering wrath could be unleashed.

How can you deal with a volatile controller at work? The trick is to realize that what you *don't* do is as important as what you do:

1. Don't respond in kind. If you've ever dealt with a toddler having a tantrum, you know that the most ineffective thing is to throw one right back. The same holds true for adult tantrum-throwers. You will only escalate the situation if you yell at them, insult them, or use sarcasm. Manage your response so that it is the inverse of theirs. If they grow more agitated, you must get calmer and quieter.

2. Don't confuse bark with bite. The good news about volatile controllers is that, other than pitching a fit, they usually don't take action at their targets. The volatile boss, for example, is unlikely to fire you in mid-rant. Remind yourself that they are only venting and it will be easier for you to keep from overreacting.

3. Acknowledge their level of concern. Although you should appear calm during a volatile controller's outburst, don't appear disinterested. Part of the reason these people are yelling is because they fear that no one is really listening to them. Show you take them seriously. Say, "I understand this is really important to you. I hear your concern."

4. Recognize your window of opportunity. After a blow-up, give volatile controllers time to calm down. After a breather, during which their adrenaline level will return to normal, see if you can arrange a private follow-up. At this juncture, you will probably find them in a rather mellow, accommodating mood. They're not especially proud of their erratic behavior and they will be open to your input. Indeed, you might find them surprisingly rational.

 Manhole Ahead

Don't empower volatile controllers by fueling their reputation as exploding grenades. This will only add fuel to the atmosphere of trepidation in your workplace, which isn't productive for anyone.

In addition to dealing with tantrum-throwers during and after outbursts, you can also practice some preventive techniques. One is to face and manage your own fear. Have you been yelled at before and survived? Then remind yourself the threat is not lethal. Another is to pose a direct question to the volatile person in your workplace. In the aftermath of a blow-up, you can ask them "What makes you angry? I'd like to avoid making you angry in the future."

Wise Guys

Just about every workplace seems to have its share of wise guys—men or women with predetermined ideas about exactly how things should and shouldn't be done. Outspoken, stubborn, and often quite articulate, they will tolerate no correction or contradiction. They know it all, or so they want you to believe.

Wise guys are driven by the belief that to be wrong is to be shamed. Rather than risk this feeling, they have perfected the art of making other people feel inadequate.

Do you have a new idea or a different approach to an old situation? Wise guys at work won't be grateful, and they certainly won't be encouraging. On the contrary, they are apt to question your motives. Are you trying to make them look bad? Are you a loose cannon? Don't reinforce their fears by attempting to publicly show them up. If you want even the slightest chance of getting your two cents in, practice these strategies:

1. Know your stuff inside out. These people speak with an air of absolute certainty and authority, giving the impression that only a fool would doubt them. They'll prevail unless you have, in your own mind, prepared a solid case for your point of view. Do your due diligence and double-check your research. You won't get anywhere unless you are grounded by hard facts.

2. Be humble. That's right. Even if you're sure you're right, don't get cocky. Make sure that "smarter-than-you" types feel that you respect their intelligence and expertise. Listen to their opinions and acknowledge their valid points. Mention that you are aware of good calls they have made in the past.

3. Create a bridge between your ideas and theirs. Don't come off as a rival expert. Find a connection between what they say and what you say. You are not trying to move away from their ideas, but are building on them. Use phrases such as, *"Expanding on what you said there ...."*

Manhole Ahead

Wise guys can be so infuriating that it's sometimes tempting to disagree with them reflexively, even if they are right. Beware this trap and pick your battles well. You'll only lose credibility if you argue just for the sake of argument.

4. Don't get your ego over-invested. Don't say "I, me, mine" in relation to your ideas. Remember, your goal is to get the idea across. Use phrases such as, "What if we were to try ...?"

If the person you are dealing with is likely to be in your work environment for the foreseeable future, you should also think about creating a long-term change in your relationship dynamic by using this person as a regular resource. If you get into the habit of consulting them whenever their expertise might be of value, you can build up a bank account of goodwill, so they won't feel so threatened if you occasionally have divergent ideas. Besides, as your mentor, they can take credit for having taught you well.

Sneaks and Snipers and Liars—Oh My!

If exploders and know-it-alls make the workplace less than Shangri-La, covert controllers turn it into a terrain booby-trapped with land mines. Of covert controllers at work, perhaps the most offensive are the unscrupulous, underhanded few who sneak, snipe, and lie on a routine basis.

Engaging in deception at work is an attempt to look good by doing harm. To this end, sneaks and snipers divide and conquer, sowing seeds of doubt and suspicion about the capabilities and dedication of others. Through innuendo (including everything from strategic eye-rolling to sarcastic remarks), rumor-mongering (*"Hey, did you hear that thing about Bob and that disastrous presentation?"*), and sometimes outright lying, they can turn employee against employee, department against department, and—their favorite—bosses against the other employees they see as their competitors.

Why does anyone believe sneaks, snipers, and liars? Because they spend a lot of time cultivating personal relationships. Friendly and "helpful" to anyone they think can help them, these opportunists build credibility by performing small favors (*"Latte anyone?"*) and establishing personal bonds (*"Say, how are the kids?"*).

If these people spent half as much time doing their jobs as they do maneuvering and manipulating, they'd be dynamos. But, alas, chances of reformation are slim. These people have engaged in patterns of deception for some time, often with some significant success. (They were probably the kind of kids that got away with blaming their errant behavior on a sibling, and who somehow got their elementary school teachers to believe someone else threw the spitball.)

Don't wait for these people to have an attack of conscience. Part of their problem is that they don't have a conscience. When you see a pattern of sneaking, sniping, and lying emerge …

1. Maintain polite but distant relations. To these folks, everyone is a potential pawn in their game. Don't accept favors from them or you may feel beholden to them. But don't deliberately antagonize them, either, because they are very vengeful.

2. Confront them *privately* if you catch them red-handed. Many sneaks and snipers are too clever to leave a trail of hard evidence. There's no point in accusing them of something you cannot prove, but if they commit something to paper, or leave an e-mail trail, or say something disparaging about you in front of witnesses who will back you, have a one-on-one chat with them. Make it clear that you know what has transpired, you don't appreciate it, and you expect that it will not happen again. A public confrontation will only raise the ante and provoke revenge down the line, because their dynamic is all about one-upmanship.

3. Remember that "loose lips sink ships." Mum's the word when it comes to sneaks, snipers, and liars. Every piece of personal information you give them, every opinion, every offhand observation, can be turned around and used against you. Most particularly, never complain to them—not about your workload, about a customer, or about anyone else you work with. If you do, you can rest assured your complaint will be passed on to the people you'd least like to hear it. Moreover, it will probably be embellished and exaggerated.

If you think of yourself as an outgoing, easygoing person, some of this counsel might be hard to swallow. You may protest that it's not in your nature to keep your guard up. Fair enough, but remember that dealing with difficult people successfully can mean changing your usual default responses. Tone down your natural, forthcoming nature around these folks, and you will make yourself less of an obvious target. With everyone else, you can still be as gregarious as ever.

The Yes-You-Along Game

Another favorite workplace pastime of covert controllers is the passive-aggressive sport known as the "yes you along" game. Yes-men (I'll use this as a generic term that includes yes-women) are the most agreeable folks you'll ever meet—on the outside. For them, no task is too difficult, no schedule too tight. They are 100 percent *can do*—until they don't.

When it comes to delivering—well, let's put it this way: if you asked them to deliver a pizza you'd starve to death. Of course, they'll never tell you that what you need isn't on its way. It's just … delayed for some reason. There's a funding problem, there's a resource problem, there's a technical problem. They don't have all the information. They weren't exactly sure of the deadline. But don't you worry, other than that, everything's coming right along!

Because they'll tell you all their excuses and continue to make promises in the nicest possible way—perhaps even throwing in some charming, self-deprecating humor—you'll find yourself in a quandary. Is it normal to feel mad at someone who is so gosh-darn affable?

Rest assured, your anger is a typical reaction to yes-men. Even though you recognize that these people are wielding control by managing to look good while doing nothing, it's not easy to know how to respond in a way that doesn't make you look testy and unreasonable.

Besides, as you might have noticed if you've ever lashed out at such a person, doing so doesn't get you what you want. Passive-aggressives dread direct conflict. Outwardly, they'll be hurt, and inwardly they'll be angry at you. This will translate to further delay and deferral.

Manhole Ahead

Tattling on a yes-man is generally not effective. Try to keep your negotiations between the two of you. These people simply seem so good-natured that few who have not been directly sandbagged by them can believe they have anything but the most sincere good intent. Consequently, yes-men are often "Teflon" employees—nothing sticks to them. They sail blithely on while *you* look like the difficult one.

It takes a while to recognize when someone who routinely says "yes" actually means "no." Anyone can have genuine obstacles thwart their good intentions once or twice. But if you ignore more than three instances when "yes" apparently means "no," you do so at your own peril. Instead, practice these strategies:

1. Make honesty a safe policy. Yes-men are quick to tell you what they think you *want* to hear. But what you *need* to hear is the truth: *What is the actual status of the project, and when will it be done?* Make them understand that you can deal with the truth, whatever it is, without blowing up at them.

2. Separate their actions from their character. If a yes-man hasn't delivered, discuss the ramifications of that behavior. Don't personalize your comments; stay objective. If you criticize their character, they'll completely shut down. Your opportunity to be heard will have been lost.

3. Don't accept unrealistic promises. Some yes-men don't just promise, they overpromise. *You need it Thursday? You'll have it Tuesday!* If you collude in this behavior, you'll only be doubly disappointed. Set expectations that are executable by a competent person, not a super-hero.

4. Clarify the commitment. After they agree to do something on a reasonable timetable, agree on interim deadlines when you can meet to discuss progress. Now put the commitment in writing.

5. Don't trust them with career-making or career-breaking matters. No matter what, you need to protect yourself. Don't entrust yes-men with any aspect of any work that is critical to your success. If you do, you'll find yourself out in the cold while they're still gainfully employed and yessing a new person along.

Of course, there's one more strategy that often seems very tempting. If a yes-man fails to deliver, should you jump in and just take on their commitment? After all, you know the old saying: "If you want something done right, do it yourself." Assuming you have not asked them to do something of a mission-critical nature (see Strategy #5), don't give in to this urge. If you do, you send the message that their behavior is acceptable and that you will bail them out. "Do it yourself" more than once, and you'll find yourself doing it forevermore.

Coping with the Controlling Customer

Anyone can be a controller in the workplace. Bosses may take most of the rap for such behavior, and are often the most blatant abusers. But in reality, peers and even subordinates can appropriate all kinds of styles to be just as controlling as those at the top.

However, this chapter would not be complete without mentioning that customers can also be controlling in inappropriate ways. Sure, customers are valuable. Of course you appreciate them and want to please them. But what happens if customers take advantage of your goodwill and dedication?

People in just about every line of work—from hairdressers to investment bankers—have run up against unreasonably demanding and controlling customers. They may rant and rave if things don't go their way. They might sully your reputation if they believe you're not paying enough attention to them. They might insist on being the expert even though they ostensibly have hired *you* to be the expert.

Your tendency might be to simply let them get away with these shenanigans. After all, their patronage pays the bills. But if you do that, you are setting yourself up to fail your other customers as you devote an excessive amount of time and energy jumping through the controller's hoops. And ultimately, you might have to sever your relationship with the controlling customer anyhow, because you've reached a breaking point.

Instead, change your reflexive response to your controlling customer and see what happens. Don't hesitate to try the strategies in this chapter on anyone—customers included—who is trying to exert inappropriate control.

The Least You Need to Know

◆ Volatile controllers create uncertainty about what will set them off and when they will throw a tantrum. But fear not, their bark is worse than their bite.

◆ "Smarter-than-you" wise guys equate being wrong with feeling humiliated. Don't show them up, show them a better way—one they can believe evolved from their own ideas.

◆ Sneaks, snipers, and liars turn the workplace into a minefield. When you recognize their *modus operandi*, maintain your distance, accept no favors, and approach only with great caution.

◆ Yes-men are eager to comply in word, not in deed, but because they dread conflict, you'll need to encourage them to be realistic.

◆ Anyone in the workplace, even a customer, can be a controller. You'll profit by using the same strategies with customers as you would with bosses, peers, and subordinates.

Chapter 10

Controlling Yourself with Relationship Controllers

In This Chapter

- Knowing the importance of undoing past patterns
- Cohabiting with demanding and passive-aggressive partners
- Handling know-it-all, martyr, and divisive parents
- Coping with controlling friends

Ah, how nice to get home from a hard day's work and be free from an environment where everyone's telling you what to do. Now you're your own boss, right?

Oh. Not so right? Of course all of us have obligations and responsibilities in our personal lives. To be in relationships is to share, to support, and, within reason, to accommodate one another's needs. But perhaps, like many, you have family members, or even friends, who expect you not to so much participate in shared decision-making as simply do what they want you to. If so, this chapter is for you.

Rewriting Control Scenarios

Relationship controllers use many methods to get their way. Some are blatant, some are subtle. Throughout this chapter, we look at strategies to address a number of specific scenarios. But keep one overall strategy uppermost in mind: controlling your impulses.

Having a controller in one's personal life is even more challenging than having one at work. At work, we're expected to behave as adults, and for the most part we do. Granted, we might sometimes *feel* like angry or abused children, but we still *act* professional. Indeed, our livelihood often depends on our ability to do so.

In our personal life, however, we are under no such constraints. Mistreat us and we take it straight to heart. We are more vulnerable and our deepest emotions are closer to the surface. Moreover, we are apt to quickly revert to our most immature psychological defense. If feeling controlled as kids made us want to scream, duck and cover, or simply submit to avoid a fight, those might be our typical first responses as adults. Whether we're faced with parents still trying to manipulate us or a spouse or a friend taking a controlling role, our initial urge might be to act how we did in the past.

Usually, that's not a wise path. You should have a much larger repertoire of responses at your command now than when you were a preschooler. The trick is to remember to access it. Yes, controlling spouses, friends, and parents can wear you down. But if you routinely holler at them, hide from them, or simply ask "How high?" every time they tell you to jump, you will only be perpetuating a negative pattern.

It's amazing how any people keep doing the same thing over and over and are surprised when they get the same result every time:

"No matter how many times I tell my controlling mom I'm all grown up now and she can't tell me what to do, she still tells me what to do!"

"No matter how often I nag my passive-aggressive husband for forgetting to arrange for a babysitter so we can go out, he still forgets to arrange for a babysitter so we can go out!"

Remember, you can only alter a relationship dynamic by changing your response. If you have been doing something for years that hasn't been working, it's time for something new.

DP Disarmer

Stuck in a rut with a controller? Try something different! Albert Einstein said, "We can't solve problems by using the same kind of thinking we used when we created them."

Contending with the Controlling Mate

Not so long ago, when two people joined hands in matrimony, someone promised to "obey" someone else. Now such an oath would be unthinkably politically incorrect. Nevertheless, many husbands—and wives—seem to think that their spouse should obey them anyway.

Sometimes wedding planning itself can offer the first glimpse of what's ahead, with brides-to-be (and occasionally grooms-to-be) micromanaging every aspect of the festivities with iron fists. Who sits next to whom? What color are the cummerbunds? They know precisely how it ought to be, and everyone else better fall into line.

Of course, controllers don't always show their hands so soon. Sometimes a honeymoon period—spanning a few months or so—passes before one partner starts acting as king (or queen) of the castle. Sooner or later, controlling types find ways to exert their will. Although some want to control every aspect of the relationship, others are chiefly preoccupied with controlling mainly one aspect—although they often do so with such tenacity that, for their spouse, this is more than enough.

 Manhole Ahead

A marriage license isn't a prerequisite for controlling behavior. Couples (including same-sex couples) who co-habitate are just as likely to get caught up in controlling dynamics as husbands and wives.

The Cheapskate Partner

One common control obsession in a long-term partnership is that of money. In any twosome, one person is often more concerned than the other with saving money, but controller cheapskates can be obsessed with stretching a dollar—and so stretch their partner's patience to the limit. Some insist on curtailing expenditures to the point where a partner feels continually deprived. Some insist on to-the-penny justifications for even routine expenditures.

Money-controllers are partly driven by genuine fear. They imagine that if they don't carefully control the purse strings, they and their family may be one step away from the poorhouse. Ironically, it really doesn't matter how much money they actually have. A money-controller can be a multi-millionaire or a middle-class Joe or Jane. The fear of being destitute is real for them, whether actual impoverishment is possible or not.

Aggressively challenge a money-controller and you will likely get a defensive tirade in return. *"You're lucky to have me taking care of this or we'd be broke! You have no idea of the value of a dollar!"* Unless you enjoy continual battles that go nowhere, direct challenge is not an effective strategy.

Nor does it work to react to a partner's strict money policy by secretly overspending as revenge. Sooner or later the secret always comes out, and you then have an out-raged partner *and* a pile of unpaid bills to contend with. Moreover, you'll only rein-force the controller's deepest fears: that unknown forces are conspiring—with *you*—to impoverish them.

Money controllers present a tough challenge. Their insecurities run deep, and money is a handy object onto which to project those insecurities. Follow these tactics if there's a money controller in your relationship:

- ◆ **Let them control *some* money.** The critical word is "some." Money control-lers really don't want to argue. They just want to feel safe. Many will respond well to a suggestion that you keep some discretionary funds that you will handle without interference. This is different than hiding financial transactions from the controller. The controller agrees ahead of time that they will write off a certain amount of money. *What the controller doesn't know doesn't scare them, so long as they agree not to know it.*

- ◆ **Ask them for advice.** Most money controllers have spent a lot of time thinking about financial matters such as long-term investments and short-term cost-cutting measures. You'd be surprised how insightful they might be if you'd stop being mad long enough to ask. When they feel you are listening, they feel safer and less alone in their concerns.

- ◆ **Use their concerns to convince them.** Remind them that it's risky to keep a partner in the dark about financial matters, or to deny them access to jointly held assets. *What if something happens to them?* Plan with them for worst-case scenarios and, somewhat ironically, they will feel better and trust you more.

DP Disarmer _____

Where controllers are concerned, reward any exceptions to the rule. If your fru-gal partner indulges in the occasional splurge, even if only an extra scoop of ice cream, don't needle them about their inconsistency. Instead, praise them. Always reward behavior you want to see continue.

The sooner in a relationship that you employ these strategies with a money controller, the better. In the beginning, you might be tempted to let a controlling partner handle all your joint finances because it is the path of least resistance, you don't want to fight, and maybe you never enjoyed dealing with money matters, anyhow. That's one less headache for you, right? But it usually doesn't take long for such acquiescence to turn into resentment. You'll find that the autonomy you so easily surrendered is harder to regain than it was to give up.

The Neat-Freak Partner

Another tough-to-live-with partner is one who insists on exceptional orderliness. In a day and age when many of us live a somewhat cluttered existence—coexisting with piles of unread magazines, stacks of unopened mail, and heaps of sporting equipment for whichever kid has an after-school practice—these controllers still believe in "a place for everything and everything in its place."

If neat-freak partners are not nagging everyone to straighten things up and put them away, they're doing it themselves. This second option might not seem so bad until you realize you can no longer find anything.

Like money-controllers, those consumed with neatness are mostly working at controlling their anxieties. On some level, they believe they can contain the chaotic nature of the world and their lives by, say, arranging books alphabetically on the living room shelves and moving the soccer balls from the dining room table (where the rest of the family might feel they rightly belong) to the back of the hall closet.

Neat freaks tend to take it personally when their partner is sloppy (or what they perceive as sloppy). They might scream, sulk, sigh, slam doors, or even storm out of the house if their high standards are not met. But probably they'll just race around tidying and reorganizing things until you feel so frustrated *you* scream, sulk, or do some door-slamming of your own. Either that or you just join in and make neatness a priority, even though you have other things you'd rather do.

Instead, try dealing with a neat controller with some of the strategies similar to those that can be effective with money controllers:

◆ **Agree on mess-free zones and messy zones.** They get to say which messes make them most anxious; you get to have some creative chaos.

◆ **Ask the neatniks about their system.** Do they really deal with all their mail and stacks of papers? If so, how?

♦ **Praise their slip-ups.** Many neat freaks keep a bit of mess "in the closet"—sometimes literally. If you spot a drawer or dresser or closet that is your partner's domain and whose contents are disorganized, don't say, "You missed a spot." Rather, say something positive about how this makes you proud of them.

Tried and True Tactics _____

"I got my husband to relax his neat standards by making messes sexy. When we both are feeling romantic, I take it off—all off—and leave it everywhere. He's not allowed to straighten anything up, or I get 'out of the mood.'"—Diane, 37

One important caveat bears mentioning when it comes to exceptionally orderly people. If you notice that their behaviors around preserving orderliness are so extreme and time-consuming that they significantly interfere with their normal routine, occupation, and social functioning, you might be witnessing symptoms of obsessive-compulsive disorder (OCD).

If your partner is distressed by his own behaviors and seems amenable to help, suggest a professional consultation. Treatment for OCD—sometimes a mix of behavioral therapy and medication—can be effective. Don't play doctor at home and insist that someone you suspect of having OCD "just stop" their compulsive behaviors. A sudden abandonment of their usual defenses can result in extreme reactions to the anxiety that arises.

The Drill-Sergeant Partner

The drill-sergeant partner usually has a "mission," and they carry it out as if your home were a boot camp and you were a buck private. This mission can be anything that they think is "good for you"—maybe it's a fitness mission, and they're determined to whip you into shape. Maybe they're on a diet mission, bent on getting you to trim down.

The drill sergeant could be on any kind of self-improvement tear and insist that you join in. They may not even sound like bad ideas on the surface: couples tend to thrive when they try new things together—and one person is often the motivating force. The trouble with drill sergeants is that they don't understand the word *moderation*. They're so zealous they can be scary. Whatever their latest mission is becomes a relentless cause.

Many partners will go along with a drill sergeant, sometimes kicking and screaming, until they simply can't take anymore and a blow-up ensues. Others will pretend to get with the program, but take revenge by secretly getting off the program whenever possible. For example, they'll join their mate on a low-calorie, low-fat diet, then sneak off for hot fudge sundaes. Some dig in their heels from day one and refuse to go along, only driving the drill sergeant to step up their attempts.

Instead of doing any of these things, try a strategy that often works surprising well. I call it "undoing by outdoing." Do them one better at their own game, becoming more zealous than they are about their mission of the moment. They want healthy eating? You'll go vegan, maybe macrobiotic. They want fitness? You'll sign the two of you up for a triathlon! (Never mind if they don't swim—it's time they learned!)

Resisting a drill sergeant only eggs them on, but joining in their enthusiasm, and then some, takes them by surprise and gives them pause. Did they really want things to go this far?

The Passive-Aggressive Partner

Finally, we come to a notorious kind of controlling partner. The passive-aggressive partner is so well known that sitcoms and comic strips abound with them. Advice on dealing with this dynamic has become its own industry. But it's really not all that complicated.

Passive-aggressives, as mentioned in earlier chapters, wield control by appearing to comply with your wishes—only to thwart those wishes in actual fact. In long-term relationships, passive-aggressives prefer the "yes, dear" mode. Ask your mate to make a dinner reservation, pick up their dirty laundry, or go online and pay the electric bill, and you will get a pleasant, affirmative response. The next thing you know, however, it's Saturday night and you are *sans* dinner plans, the laundry is still on the floor, and the power has been shut off—unless perhaps in the meanwhile …

1. You nagged, nagged, nagged until your passive-aggressive partner made a belated, half-hearted attempt to do what they agreed to, or

2. You did the jobs yourself.

The problem is that if you did either of these things, you are only perpetuating the cycle.

You have to remember why passive-aggressives are the way they are in the first place. They dread conflict. In understanding what they fear, you can help them to overcome the fear, and free them to act differently.

It's actually easier to deal with passive-aggressives in a committed relationship than any other setting. If the relationship is fundamentally loving and has a well of positive feelings to draw from, a partner has emotional leverage. Create a safe emotional environment in which it is all right for your mate to disagree with you and sometimes openly decline to do what you ask.

Take the dinner reservation dilemma. Why did your spouse say he'd take care of it and then not do it? Maybe he was being lazy and hoping you'd take care of it. But maybe he really didn't want to go out to dinner Saturday night. Did you ask? And if so, did you do it in such a way that he felt free to say, "You know, I'd rather stay home."?

The more reluctant your partner is to express her true feelings to you, and the more wary she is of an angry response, the more she'll default to the "yes, dear" approach. Create and perpetuate safe and open communication in your relationship. Make it okay for your partner to say "No," ask "Why?", or just say "Let me think about it for a while."

 Manhole Ahead _____

> Perception is reality. It may never have occurred to you that your partner is afraid of your anger. You don't think of yourself as a mean, scary person, and you're probably not. But it's all about point of view. Your partner may be transferring onto you all the anxiety they have about conflicts with their parents or other significant people in their history.

When you ask a "yes, dear" type to tell you what they really want, be prepared to hear their answers calmly. You don't have to agree with what they say, but you do have to listen to their feelings. If you don't, you'll be back to square one, with them merely pretending they'll do things your way. Wouldn't you rather have an honest response than continue to feel manipulated?

The Puppeteer Parent

Sometimes controlling partners really push our buttons because they remind us of our controlling parents. When our actual parents still try to run our lives, buttons flash red and sirens go off. We can't believe our mothers and fathers still expect us to do as they say. But, alas, many parents have never let go—much to their adult offsprings' chagrin.

Father (or Mother) Knows Best

Some parents control by using "smarter than you" tactics. These can be tough to deal with because, after all, you probably do recall a time when your mom and dad actually *did* know much more than you. In fact, there was probably a time—long, long ago— when you thought they knew everything!

Now you know quite a few things, especially about how you want to run your own life. Still, your dad insists on telling you everything from where to invest your retirement funds to what kind of weed killer to spray on your lawn. Your mother wants to tell you what to wear, how to cook, and—a big one—how to raise your own kids. They're in a rut, but that doesn't mean you should be.

If your usual reaction is to get angry and argue with them, you may have noticed that it doesn't stop them. Know-it-all parents are going to keep telling you what they think you should do whether you resist or not—and more so if you do. Instead …

- **Listen to intent rather than content.** Know-it-all parents can seem abrasive if you listen only to their detailed instructions. But try listening to their subtext. It probably amounts to: *I am so used to being responsible for you, it makes me anxious to think of you on your own.* Your parents telling you what to do doesn't mean they think you're stupid. It means they're worried and this is the way they express it. Yes, it's annoying, but it is less so if you realize they mean no offense.

- **Let them be right about something.** Your parents weren't always right before, and they're not always wrong now. (Remember: even a broken clock is right twice a day.) Take their advice once in a while, even on a minor matter (how long to cook the Thanksgiving turkey, when to rotate your tires). Let them know you've done as they advised, and say thanks.

- **Let them take credit for a big achievement: you.** It's all right to disagree with your parents, but better still to *respectfully* disagree. Remember that you got your smarts and your tenacity from them.

In the end, what advice you take or don't take from your parents is your call. And when you do reject advice, you don't always need to make them aware of it. They don't have a magic looking glass that enables them to see if you're following through with what they told you to do. As when dealing with all controllers, don't over-volunteer information. What they don't know won't hurt them.

What's the Martyr with You?

Martyr parents control through the passive-aggressive strategy of "sacrificing" for their offspring. They make a great show of putting their children's needs ahead of their own—although they claim to want no acknowledgement for doing so. (*I missed my bridge game to baby-sit my daughter's kids again. But that's all right. That's what I'm here for. I don't need to play bridge.*)

Martyrs pretend not to have personal needs, but they actually don't expect you to buy the pretense. As with all controlling parents, listen to the intent under their content. In reality, they are overzealous in taking care of their grown children to show those grown children how they would like to be taken care of themselves. If you don't make the kinds of "sacrifices" for them that they do for you, martyrs end up being resentful.

After a while those resentments build to a crescendo, and even though the martyr protests that they are still *fine, fine, fine*, anyone with the slightest bit of emotional savvy senses the awful truth: they are seconds away from turning on the waterworks. When they do, they will still protest that their tears and hurt feelings are "unimportant" and should be ignored.

 Manhole Ahead

Not sure if your parent fits into the martyr category? See if you can visualize them delivering—with a straight face—the punch line of this joke:

Q. *How many martyrs does it take to change a light bulb?*

A. *"None, I'll just sit here in the dark."*

Did someone say "guilt"? Yes, that's the secret weapon of the passive-aggressive martyr parent. They want you to feel guilty so you'll shower them with attention. Then they can insist they don't deserve it—thus setting the whole cycle in motion again. Obviously this is a no-win response, because the stakes will continually be raised.

It's perfectly all right to have a feeling and not act on it. Just because you feel guilty isn't a reason to rush to placate a martyr. Examine your guilt. Is it based in reality? If you have been taking advantage of your martyr parent, letting them do too much for you because it's become so easy, then use this guilt as a guidepost to stop doing so. The price is too high!

Likewise, if you've been neglecting your parent's legitimate needs for contact with you, use your reality-based guilt to fine-tune your priorities. Now, after you've used guilt to make appropriate adjustments, let it go. Don't use it as a stick to beat yourself with.

Divide and Conquer

Another type of parental covert control is a manipulative mode I'll call "divide and conquer." Divide and conquer involves a parent wielding control by creating subgroups within the family. For example, Mom, Dad, or both may complain to one of their grown children about how another is behaving, imploring the "good" child to intervene with the "wayward" one. In this way they get to give advice by proxy—avoiding any direct confrontation while still making their preferences known.

In another divide-and-conquer scenario, parents may offer financial rewards (okay, bribes) to the child who agrees to do things their way, or to give them more attention. *If you'll be living near us, we'll help with the down payment on your house.* Or: *If you'll come on vacation with us, we'll pay.*

> ### Tried and True Tactics
>
> "In our family, my parents planned to extend their divide-and-conquer control beyond the grave. They would continually tell my siblings and me they were rewriting their will to favor the child who did the things they wanted. Finally we all sat them down and explained that we had agreed that no matter what happened, we would divide any inheritance equally. That put an end to that."—Judith, 47

These divide-and-conquer techniques can often create a lot of ill will between family members, which is a shame because that's not really what parents want. They want influence and attention—not a family feud.

The best way to counter a divide-and-conquer parent is for you and your other family members to unite, not to divide. Never agree to convey a criticism to a sibling on your parents' behalf. Communicate openly with your siblings about any proposed parental financial favoritism. Now, talk to your siblings about what your parents' actual agenda is and what all of you can do to address their emotional needs.

Dealing with Controlling Friends

Why would any of us have controlling friends when we don't have to? After all, we're not bound to them by blood, or marriage, or any long-term partnership commitment.

But, as with other difficult types of friends, controllers can have their redeeming qualities. In fact, maybe it suited your needs at one time to have a friend who took charge. If you were a shy type or a late bloomer, their giving you a shove now and then could have been exactly what you needed. Maybe, every once in a while, it still is!

That said, controlling friends can be a nuisance if you let them interfere with your other relationships or commitments, or pressure you into doing things you really don't want to do (from drinking too much alcohol to spending your vacation camping when you'd rather be at a spa). But please note that the key words in the previous sentence are *if you let them interfere*, and *if you allow your friend to pressure you*.

Your friend might be in the habit of calling the shots. They have no incentive to break that habit, but if you are feeling manipulated, you do. So, when they pressure you to go along with them:

- Don't argue with them—decline politely to do anything you don't want to do.

- Don't offer excuses, or they will just try to talk you out of your objections—simply say, "Thanks, that's not for me."

- If possible, suggest other people who might be available to do the things your friend wants to do.

Ask yourself: what's the worst that can happen? Your friend might get mad. Can you deal with that? Okay. Your friend might find someone else to keep them company for a while? Can you handle it? Fine.

If your friend is a true friend, a sincere, loyal companion who just happens to have a controlling streak, your relationship can weather your changing its dynamic. If they find the change intolerable, then the reality is they wanted someone to order around more than they wanted a real pal.

The Least You Need to Know

♦ In long-term relationships, many control scenarios can be broken if we change our engrained responses and try something new. You can't get a different result by doing the same thing over and over.

♦ When controlling spouses try to dictate, consider what anxieties they are actually acting out, then choose a strategy that does not involve lashing out or being overly submissive but that acknowledges and addresses their deeper concerns.

♦ Controlling parents may be know-it-alls, martyrs, or family dividers, but if you hear the intent behind the content, you will find that they usually want certain kinds of attention more than they want literal compliance.

♦ Don't make excuses when controlling friends try to pressure you into doing things you don't want to. Just say, "No, thank you," and deal with the likelihood that they may find a substitute companion for that activity.

Chapter 11

Responding to Controllers-at-Large

In This Chapter

◆ Deciding what you want from controllers

◆ Approaching controlling teachers and school administrators

◆ Handling your kids' controller sports coach

◆ Dealing with bossy types on committees

◆ Coping with controlling professionals

Some people just have to be in charge, wherever they are—and, sadly, wherever *we* are. We run into controllers not only at work and at home, but at school, on the sports field, at the PTA and other community organizations, and in various professional settings. This chapter offers strategies for dealing with controllers-at-large.

The Self-Appointed and Self-Anointed

Controllers-at-large often seek out positions of power. No matter how small the realm, they want the top job: class Mom, coach of the Little League team, head of the Thanksgiving food drive, chairman of the recycling committee. If they can't obtain a power position, they simply attempt to turn whatever role they hold into a power base. And the more they act as though they are entitled to power, the more people fall into line.

But what about you? If you're reading this chapter, odds are you're pretty annoyed by the type of person who always has to be the big cheese. You're possibly a little tired of "going along to get along." So it's time to ask yourself: what do *you* want to do?

Let's start by looking at options. When we're irritated by a controlling type, one typical response is to try to seize their power for ourselves. Sick of being given orders, we decide it's time to step up and take charge. After all we can do it, right?

Well, yes. We can. But before you attempt to take over a position, always be sure to ask yourself this: *Do you really want this job?* Staging a challenge can be momentarily fulfilling. You've ousted a tyrant. You may feel avenged, and others may heartily thank you. But now *you* are the head coach, head fundraiser, head *this* or *that*. You've upped your commitment level, your visibility, and your vulnerability to anyone else who thinks *they* should be in charge.

If you're up for the job, that's great. But if you'd really rather get home early and watch TV, you've blown it.

 Manhole Ahead _____

There's no shame—and possibly some benefit—in not having to be in charge. Studies show that ambitious, hard-driving, controlling people (sometimes referred to as Type A personalities) are more susceptible than self-effacing laid-back types to heart attacks, stroke, and other stress-related illnesses. Ironically, it's more dangerous to your health to be a controller than it is to be subjected to one.

If you don't want to seize power from a controller, what else remains? One path is the path of defiance: you don't like this person and you're just not going to do what they say. Period!

Fair enough, but you always have to ask yourself what the cost of that defiance will be. You can refuse to bake oatmeal cookies for the bake sale like that annoying PTA president asked you to and the world won't come to a screeching halt. But if you refuse to bring your kid to soccer practice when their coach says they have to show up (right in the middle of dinner!) you might find them benched. You will have made your point, but the controller will have made a more poignant point in return.

Staging a power grab or being defiant are high-stakes maneuvers. Sometimes they *are* the right move, assuming you are clear about your motives and are willing to accept potential consequences. But these moves won't always result in getting you what, in many instances, you really crave from controllers: a little respect.

In lots of everyday situations, we are actually okay with controllers being in control. Most of us realize it would be foolhardy to try to take the lead in everything. No one is expert in all areas, and those who try to be can stretch themselves to the breaking point.

Besides, we're busy with many commitments. It's all right with us if we're not the one deciding what color to paint the mailboxes in our condominium complex or whether or what snacks will be served at the church social. It's *not* all right with us, however, if the person claiming dominion over such matters treats us derisively or dismissively:

- We don't want to be ordered about; we want to be requested to do things politely.

- We don't want to be treated as if we don't matter; we want to be given the message that our participation is important.

- We don't want to be patronized; we want to be spoken to as an equal.

It doesn't seem like a lot to ask. But that's the key—sometimes we do have to ask. As we'll see in the scenarios we're about to examine, if we do ask in the right way at the right moment, we might even get what we want.

School Daze

School is certainly an environment where control issues abound. Each school, indeed each classroom, is its own unique microcosm, with very specific set rules, standards, and expectations.

Being a student, or having a child who is a student, involves a certain level of acquiescence to those rules and standards. (It's hard to be a complete free spirit and contend with school at the same time.) But what can you do if you feel teachers or administrators are taking their power prerogatives too far?

Controlling Teachers

In the interest of full disclosure, I'll tell you that in addition to having been a student for many years and in many settings, I have also been a teacher. Having looked at this world from both sides, I know that to do their jobs, teachers do have to establish from the outset that they are "in charge" of their classroom. The buck stops with them. If they don't make this clear, the reality is that the students don't have a structured environment in which to learn—and that is not fair to anyone.

That said, being "in control" need not equate with being "controlling," wielding power in an unreasonably harsh or rigid way, or totally disregarding input from others.

But let's face it: most of us had to deal with teachers who were, in fact, controlling. They may have set rules and standards in their classroom that were far stricter than the guiding rules of the school at which they taught (say, loading students down with excessive amounts of work as compared to other instructors). They may be unreasonably punitive to students who commit minor infractions (grading a paper "F" because the typeface isn't the one they required). Or they might refuse to entertain any point of view, no matter how legitimate, that does not agree with their own.

Although a student can't very well mutiny against a teacher and take over the classroom, students (or their parents) have certainly gone over teachers' heads to deal with such situations. You don't need an advanced degree to know that this is not going to gain you or your child the teacher's eternal goodwill. Of course, sometimes there's the option of trying to switch to another class—but because there will likely be another difficult teacher lurking in one's future, it's really a better idea to try to deal with the one you've got and see what you can accomplish.

If it seems to you that a teacher is acting in an unreasonably controlling way:

- **Construct a thorough, intelligent presentation.** Frame a calm explanation of your grievance and include a proposed solution to what you see as the problem. Teachers respond well to research and organization. They'll be more receptive if you're obviously prepared.

- **Talk with the teacher one-on-one.** Never, ever challenge a teacher's authority in front of students. It makes it harder for them to do their job.

- **Make it clear you're starting with them.** Teachers would far rather resolve problems without third parties and red tape. Let them know you feel the same.

Manhole Ahead _____

Never "show off" for other students by poking fun at a difficult teacher. For an example of how this dynamic ends up, rent the movie *Fast Times at Ridgemont High* and see what happens to Sean Penn's character on prom night at the hands of a disrespected history teacher.

If your goal is to elevate your teacher's level of fairness and respect, remember the golden rule of doing unto others as you would have them do unto you. You can count on the fact that *virtually every teacher has had their share of difficult students.* If you want to achieve your goal, don't be one of them.

Principal Principles

I've heard it argued that people who become school administrators—principals, deans, and so on—have a bent toward being petty dictators. They gravitate toward such professions, some say, because they can carve out fiefdoms of personal power. That's a generalization, of course, and there are many laudable reasons for going into academic administration that have nothing to do with a petty quest for power. On the other hand, whether they deliberately seek it out or not, a personal kingdom is what an academic administrator winds up with. Some rule more wisely than others.

School administrators set disciplinary policies—from dress codes to honor codes—and enforce those policies. They are also instrumental in determining what students learn and when they learn it. If you believe these polices are in some way unreasonable and you want them altered, first you'll need to consider: *Do you want an exception to the policy or do you want the policy changed?*

As always, knowing what you want should determine how you proceed:

- **Requests for exceptions are best dealt with one-to-one.** Even the most seemingly dictatorial administrators could be more inclined than you think to consider exceptions to stringent rules *if you can make a sound argument.* If you confine your argument to the case at hand, you will not be perceived as challenging the administrator's overall power stance, and you allow them to "save face."

- **Requests for policy changes are best dealt with by a force of numbers.** If you believe a policy is not working or is unfair, shop around (discreetly) for allies who feel the same way. Collect signatures on a petition and request that the administrator meet with a small, representative group to hear your concerns. You represent a "customer base" that will be harder for an administrator to ignore than a lone individual.

DP Disarmer

If you're canvassing for like-minded individuals to join you, be *sure* they're willing to back you up in public. People who blow off steam privately but are unwilling to take a public position will only complicate matters by stoking your indignation. You'll be alone in the hot seat trying to manage an overload of anger.

Keep in mind that even the most seemingly controlling administrator does not rule solo. They are always beholden to a school board, a board of trustees, or some other overseeing body. Approaching this body represents a logical next step if an administrator is unresponsive. But, as when dealing with teachers, be sure to save this strategy until you are certain you need it. Administrators with a controlling bent can become extremely defensive if you try to make an end run around them.

Controlling Coaches

If you've ever been a member of a sports team, you're no doubt familiar with another power position: the coach. Coaches are the closest thing to earthbound deities as far as players are concerned. They get to say what you should eat, when you should sleep, what you should abstain from. Most of all, of course, they get to say who gets to play, in what position, and in what games.

When you're devoted to a team and committed to a sport, it's not uncommon to do whatever the coach says—even though you might grumble about it after you're out of earshot. After all, if you don't fall into line, you might be deprived of the one thing you want most: getting in the game.

But what if the player is your child? Given our enthusiasm for and preoccupation with children's sports these days, it is the rare parent who hasn't cringed when their would-be budding athlete is harshly criticized, yelled at, or—perhaps worst of all—unceremoniously benched by an officious baseball, soccer, lacrosse, basketball, football, or hockey coach. To complicate matters, this coach is often *one of the other parents*.

The apoplectic amateur coach who treats even a five-year-olds' T-ball match like the seventh game of the World Series has become a cultural stereotype—for the simple reason that there truly are so many of them. And yes, these over-the-top weekend warriors probably are taking out frustrations from other parts of their lives on the field. Perhaps they're disappointed to have ended up as computer programmers or mortgage brokers rather than as first basemen for the Yankees or tight ends for the

Green Bay Packers. But even though you're tempted to say all this when they mistreat your kid—don't.

Dealing with a controller on your own behalf is one thing. If you misjudge your approach only you will suffer the consequences. But when your child is involved, you are an advocate. You have to remember to see things through their eyes.

No, your kid might not enjoy being publicly chastised or being relegated to the side-lines for a missed play. But odds are that they will enjoy you making a scene or getting physically aggressive with their coach even less. Besides, you need to consider whether you are being too much of a *helicopter parent*. Perhaps your child needs to learn to handle situations like this on their own. (We all have to learn to deal with difficult people sometime.)

def•i•ni•tion

Helicopter parent is a popular term for parents who hover too closely over their children and who rush in to help with every situation—whether their help is actually needed or not.

That said, if you genuinely feel your child is being unfairly singled out or bullied by a coach, and your child is still too young to start speaking up for himself ...

♦ Approach the coach one-on-one.

♦ Speak with him when he's *not* feeling immediate pressure (for example, never complain during a game).

♦ Be prepared to step up and pitch in.

This last point is crucial. These coaches may be supremely annoying but, to be fair, they are usually doing quite a bit of work and giving up quite a bit of their free time. If you have a better idea about how things should be done, you should be prepared to shoulder some responsibilities. Some coaches might suggest this, but you might have to suggest it yourself. Either way, be prepared to stick around and model for the controller how things can be done in a less provocative way. Being a positive force your kid can be proud of is the best way to counter the negative effects of an overly controlling coach.

Controllers in Committee

Just as most of us have ended up participating in some school or community group with a self-centered type who only wants to focus on their personal issues, most of us have also ended up in such situations with people who want to do good for all—so long as all agree that their vision is best.

Controllers in committee may be PTA moms determined to raise money for various projects. They could be co-op or condo honchos gung ho for property improvement, from one-color-fits-all paint jobs to water-conserving shower systems. They could be charitable volunteers determined to save a species, cure a disease, or fund the garden club's reference library on flowering vines. Their cause might be frivolous or meritorious, but either way they will go at it as if it is the most significant mission in human history since the race to the moon.

And you? You'll be given an assignment. Maybe several. And if you decline you will be made to feel—you guessed it—guilty. Yes, guilt again. Remember, this can be a powerful weapon in the controller's arsenal. How can you possibly refuse a controller's request if his request is clearly being made on behalf of the greater good?

But what if you don't believe in their agenda? What if you disagree with their methods? What if you think you have some interesting ideas of your own?

Of course, your initial strategy should simply be to speak up. There may well be others on the committee who feel as you do, and based on the force of that "critical mass," the process of change can begin. However, some committee controllers work hard at keeping discourse to a minimum. If this happens:

- **Know—and use—the committee rules.** Formal organizations have sets of by-laws. Look them up and use them to your advantage. They may offer guidelines for meeting protocol, and—if the going gets rough—for changing leadership.

- **Take the initiative.** In a volunteer organization, there's nothing stopping you from doing *more*, is there? If you don't like your assignment, dispatch it quickly and then do the thing you really think will make a difference. If you're right, your actions will speak for themselves—and serve as their own reward.

- **Examine your goals.** Ask yourself why you're on this committee. Is it because you really believe in the cause? Or is it because of habit or what you perceive as social pressure? Consider that there are plenty of other ways to make yourself useful.

DP Disarmer _____

Ad hoc committees, those that are set up solely to respond to a particular problem or situation, may have no governing rules *per se*. In such cases, get your voice heard by suggesting a "round-robin brainstorm," in which all participants take turns offering their ideas for a certain amount of time—perhaps three to five minutes.

When you volunteer to participate on a committee or board bent on helping others or improving circumstances, your altruistic efforts ought to serve as an antidote to stress. Studies show that helping others can be calming and life-affirming. If, however, your efforts become a source of stress because of a controlling person, maybe you can help in another capacity.

Professionals as Controllers

Sometimes the professionals we engage can be highly controlling. We all depend on the expertise and experience of doctors, lawyers, accountants, and the like, we also sense when the fine line between guidance and totalitarianism has been crossed.

In some situations, the latter might be a good thing. Some of us need a despotic doctor to read us the riot act every now and then. If we have been willfully doing things that are bad for our health (refusing to schedule important check-ups and screenings, eating an all-bacon-and-cupcake diet), then choosing and sticking with a controlling doctor—say, one who threatens to expel us from their practice if we persist in our self-destructive ways—could be a lifesaving strategy in itself. Who cares if they're abrasive if they're all that stands between us and an early grave?

Likewise with attorneys and accountants. Perhaps a lawyer's advice—no matter how irritating—has saved us from a lawsuit. Perhaps our fuss-budget tax accountant has helped us survive an IRS audit and come out smelling like a rose. (There's something to be said for an anal-retentive accountant!)

But what if their dictates seem excessive in light of our particular needs? Controlling doctors have been known to irritate their patients by berating them for so much as a gained pound, or refusing to even discuss alternative treatments. Controlling lawyers frustrate their clients by being so hyper-cautious that those clients feel hamstrung in their day-to-day affairs. And hyper-controlling accountants have been known to hit the roof if their clients exceed their usual expenses by a few dollars.

At such points, we have to wonder: is it our body or our doctor's? Is it our money or our accountant's? Is it our life or our lawyer's? If we don't like the answers, it might be time to shop around for another professional.

Naturally, you have every right to disagree with someone whose services you retain. But you'll have to assess whether you're actually being heard. If your concerns are not being addressed thoroughly and thoughtfully, or if you are spending an inordinate amount of your time (and your money) arguing, it won't do any harm to find out who else is out there.

Remember, it doesn't matter who you are dealing with or in what capacity: when you pay the bills, you are the boss. Be a wise consumer and search for professionals who are knowledgeable and who will share that knowledge in a way that is palatable to you.

Tried and True Tactics

"I experienced a very trying situation with my children's pediatrician. In my opin-ion, she would prescribe antibiotics too aggressively—sometimes for conditions that may have been viral, such as ear infections. I preferred a less invasive approach and began to explore herbal remedies and homeopathy. When I mentioned what I'd learned, the doctor said my kids would no longer be welcome in her practice if I so much as mentioned this again. I stopped talking about it, but asked around until I found an M.D. who used herbs and homeopathy when possible. Then I transferred my children to the new doctor's care."—Patricia, 35

The Least You Need to Know

+ Think about what you want from a controller before you take action. Do you really want to challenge them and end up in charge, or do you simply want to be treated with respect?

+ For teachers and administrators, a certain amount of control comes with the territory—but if you seek a change, do your homework before you make your case, and find a way to help them "save face."

+ Think before you challenge your child's controlling coach in an inappropriate way. You are your kid's advocate, but consider whether your child will appreciate being embarrassed by you.

+ Committee controllers want to do good their way. If you have a better idea, find a way to float it to the group, and take the initiative in carrying it out.

+ Professionals such as doctors, lawyers, and accountants can be overbearing—you'll have to carefully weigh the good they do versus the emotional toll they take. If the latter outweighs the former, shop around. You are the customer!

Part 4

The Obstructionists

They're always in the way: raining on your parade, micromanaging, second-guessing, taking their own sweet time, or doing everything they can to evade responsibility. In this part, you'll get acquainted with a spectrum of difficult people whose frustrating gambits always end up impeding your forward motion. There are ways to get around obstructionists wherever you encounter them. This part of the book will show you how.

Chapter 12

All About Obstructionists

In This Chapter

- Why pessimists won't be positive
- How perfectionists torture you—and themselves
- Why some people just won't decide
- Why tortoise types take their time
- How whiners feel they win
- How to gear up to cope with obstructionists

You've got places to go, people to see, and things to do. You've got little time—and even less patience—for people who say no, who don't know, or who go slow. You're tired of nitpickers and whiners. But, alas, such types are ubiquitous. You can't mow them down, so you need to help them get out of the way or learn how to go around them. But, first, of course, you have to understand them.

As with other sorts of difficult people, knowing what makes obstructionists of all kinds tick can help you select the most effective strategy for dealing with them. This chapter gives you an overview of various obstructionists and helps you understand how they think and what motivates them to behave in the ways they do.

The Pessimist

"If it rained soup, we'd all have forks."

So predicts the pessimist. Their stock in trade is gloom and doom. Nothing, they believe, could possibly turn out right—or, if it did, it would merely be a momentary distraction from the devastating event that was lurking just around the corner.

We've all encountered pessimists, and it's hard not to be affected by their negativity. Most of us readily acknowledge that bad things happen sometimes, but we don't automatically jump to the worst-case scenario. But pessimists are so skilled and so relentless at prognosticating potential pitfalls that sometimes their perspective brings down even the sunniest personalities. And negative types not only demoralize us, but stifle our creativity and prevent us from pursuing opportunity. As the saying goes, "When opportunity knocks, pessimists complain about the noise."

Just how did pessimists get so good at being so negative? Chances are they came from a long line of pessimists. Negativity can be emotionally contagious, and if one's family embraces a glass-half-empty philosophy, that will profoundly affect one's viewpoint. Some pessimists hail from families or cultural backgrounds where it's believed that saying positive, optimistic things is just tempting fate to pull the rug out from under them. Such people might also go out of their way to find a negative thing to say about even the most apparently positive situation ("Sure, I won the lottery, but wait until I get my tax bill!") because they believe such protestations will keep envious people from afflicting them with the "evil eye" (thus inviting sure misfortune).

Either way, it's hard to tolerate perennial pessimism in people around us. Our initial temptation might be to argue with them, and to try to spread some sunshine into their cloud-covered firmament. But as anyone who's ever seen *Star Wars* knows, it's not always so easy for light to vanquish darkness. If you're going to counter a pessimist's viewpoint, don't insist that life's a bowl of cherries. They'll just remind you about the pits. Instead, address their concerns as *valid* ones, while trying to help put them in perspective. For example:

- Because pessimists view negative events as permanent, try to reframe them as temporary. ("I know this quarter's sales results were a setback, but they just reflect all the bad weather we had.")

- Because they see negative events as having a universal impact, reframe them as limited in scope. ("Just because one person stopped dating you doesn't mean you'll never get married.")

◆ Because pessimists feel powerless, remind them about the areas in which they have some control. ("I know your boss hasn't promoted you, but you have an impressive resumé and you can look into changing jobs.")

By agreeing with a pessimist that there is indeed a problem, you make it easier for them to agree with you that there might—just might—be at least a partial solution. But let's be clear: this won't work with all pessimists.

As with most difficult behaviors, pessimism comprises a spectrum. There are run-of-the mill negative types and then there are super-pessimists who seem to take almost a perverse pleasure in trying to bring as many people down to their level as possible. The former type might be convinced that "things may be going wrong, but we can do better"; the latter will always insist "things are going wrong, and there is nothing we can do to keep them from getting worse."

If your efforts to help a pessimist reframe their concerns are continually shot down, you need to switch to a self-protective mode. Don't internalize their message. When you are around them, be sure to remind *yourself*—no matter what they say—that all things pass, that one bad circumstance need not taint every other situation in your life, and that you do have the power to effect some level of change, even if that change involves only your attitude (which, of course, can have a profound impact).

DP Disarmer

Negativity can be contagious, but so can a positive outlook. If you must routinely be in the company of a pessimist, seek out the company of optimists to counterbalance the impact. You'll feel better emotionally, and physically, too. Studies show that optimists avoid the toxic biochemical reactions that stress caused by pessimism can trigger. For example, optimistic moods lower levels of cortisol, a stress-related hormone that depresses immune function.

The Perfectionist

The perfectionist obstructs by needing to get things right—exactly right—before moving forward. They often spend countless hours fussing over minutiae—from the exact wording of a report to the exact shaping of the garden hedges to the precise arrangement of a vase full of peonies.

Although there's nothing wrong with having high standards, the perfectionist's standards are so high as to be unattainable. Perfection is not only elusive, but to some extent objective. Who can really say when a report, a flower arrangement, or anything else is "just right"? Couldn't it always be better? "Of course it could," says the perfectionist.

Many think of perfectionists as controlling types, but what distinguishes the true perfectionist from the demanding controller is that perfectionists are just as hard on themselves—or harder—as they are on everybody else. Nevertheless, the perfectionist's insistence on personal flawlessness often serves as a drag and makes other people's lives difficult.

When a project of any kind passes into a perfectionist's purview, it stalls. The perfectionist wants to leave their mark on it—a perfect mark, of course. They need to get it right and avoid mistakes. That requires lots of time. Moreover, while they are scrutinizing one aspect of a project, product, or process for tiny flaws that they can correct, larger problems may go unaddressed. For instance, what good is a report worthy of a Pulitzer Prize if its facts are outdated by the time the perfectionist gets done with it?

Perfectionists are not likely to relinquish their behavior, however, no matter how much you point out its imperfect consequences. Such logic is usually lost on them. Perfectionists often had mothers or fathers (or both) with unrealistically high expectations. Their relentless efforts toward precision can reflect the internalization and repetition of their parents' constant demands. That's not a syndrome one can snap out of overnight.

One thing you can try is to prevent a perfectionist from delaying a critical task or project where time is of the essence. Get them to focus their attention on an alternative task instead. Even the most meticulous perfectionist can perfect only one thing at a time. Find a task they can sink their teeth into ("Can you proofread this?" "Can you figure out how to keep my soufflé from falling?") and tell them how much it requires their impeccable touch. While they're busy with one thing, they'll let you tend to other matters. This is a variation on a behavior modification technique known as *incompatible behavior*.

def•i•ni•tion

The **incompatible behavior** technique is based on the simple idea that it is impossible to do two things at once. Instead of teaching someone to stop what they are doing, give them something else to do.

The Chronically Undecided

If you want to picture the epitome of a chronically undecided person, think of Shakespeare's Hamlet. The Prince of Denmark questioned his every perception and was torn about each and every decision—including whether to kill his uncle or himself ("To be or not to be: that is the question").

Happily, most of the indecisive people we know don't go quite this far! However, the chronically undecided do sometimes make us imagine how much easier life would be if they weren't a part of it.

When faced with making a decision, most of us are prepared to do so based on available information. Sometimes there is less information than we might prefer, and we have to "go with our gut." Indeed, some of life's biggest decisions (whether to make a bid on a particular piece of real estate, whether to accept an intriguing job offer) have to be made quickly on a proverbial wing and prayer.

We know that not every decision we make will turn out exactly the way we hoped, but—as they say—that's life. We're prepared to take our knocks if we have to. But people who always say "maybe" or "I don't know" instead of "yes" or "no" don't think in those terms. They'd rather linger indefinitely at a fork in the road than risk choosing the wrong path. Needless to say, the result is that they won't get anywhere. And if you are waiting on their decision to proceed, neither will you.

It's easy to get irritated with an indecisive person. Their wishy-washiness can stymie our progress. We might even have to sit by and watch while others seize opportunities we have missed because a chronically undecided spouse or boss or co-worker's stalling has impacted our ability to act.

Sometimes we're in a position to do an end run around an indecisive type, either by making the decision ourselves and being willing to take responsibility, or by consulting another decision-maker whose "yea" or "nay" can override an "I don't know." Ideally, though, if you have an ongoing relationship with an indecisive person, it would be helpful to explore ways of helping them feel more comfortable with taking a stand.

It could very well be that such people never *had* to make a decision. Perhaps their families never empowered them to make choices, preferring to take an authoritarian "do as I say" approach. As a corollary, it's very likely that the chronically undecided never were taught any decision-making skills. They are probably insecure and apprehensive when someone asks them to make up their mind, because they don't know their own mind. If you get irritated and become impatient with them, they only become more frightened and more reluctant to take action.

If your relationship bond is strong enough, you might be able to model for them how decisions can be made:

◆ You can construct a list of pros and cons together about a particular course of action.

◆ You can weigh the inevitable unknowns that factor in to any such process.

◆ You can float worst-case scenarios to assess the downside of any decision. (It might sound scary, but such bugaboos are less menacing when put into words than when they are vague fears floating around in an indecisive person's head.)

Tried and True Tactics

"My boyfriend got better at making decisions because of our discussions after he had missed out on a couple of really good career opportunities. I think I helped him realize that making *no* decision was, in fact, a decision. It was deciding 'no' by deciding nothing at all. My boyfriend finally realized that, even if he was going to say 'no', he might as well take ownership of that choice. He has, and he now says he feels much more in control of his life."—Erin, 27

If you're encouraging someone to go ahead and make a decision, it's also crucial that you let them know that you will accept whatever decision they make. *That doesn't mean only accepting it if you agree with it.*

They'll also need to believe that you will not hold it over their head if it doesn't work out. Remember, you want to impress on them that some decisions turn out to have been wiser than others in retrospect. When that happens, we make the best of things and move on. No Monday-morning quarterbacking!

The Terminally Tortoiselike

Some people are fast thinkers, fast talkers, and fast walkers. Some go at average speed most of the time, but quicken their pace when deadlines are tight or the stakes are high. But some people, regardless of what's going on, are simply, and maddeningly, s … l … o … w. While they saunter, others will be left simmering. *What's wrong with these slowpokes? Are they just lazy?*

In some cases, perhaps they *are* lazy. Some people just can't be bothered to rush, and they hope that if they take long enough to do something they won't have to do it, or won't be asked again. But other slow-going types might just think of themselves as careful, thorough, and deliberate. They identify with the eponymous reptile in Aesop's fable "The Tortoise and the Hare"—slow and steady, but ultimately coming out ahead.

Ironically, finding out what sort of slowpoke you're dealing with may take some time itself. If you have an ongoing relationship with a tortoise in your personal life or at work, you'll need to observe what their end results typically are. Are they slackers or sticklers?

If they seem to be continually delaying and delaying until someone else picks up their ball and runs with it, you'll have to resist the temptation to rush in and take on their task as your own. If you do that, you'll only reinforce their lazy behavior. (Because this behavior can indicate a passive-aggressive pattern, you'll also want to refer to the appropriate sections in Chapters 8, 9, and 10.)

On the other hand, if this tortoise tends to eventually get where they're going and do a good job of it, you can probably help them speed up, at least to some degree, by rewarding what behavioral psychologists call *approximations*—for example, by rewarding incremental steps on the road to a new behavior.

- Try breaking the tortoise's tasks down into small, manageable bits.

- Then, instead of focusing on how slow the tortoise is going, praise them for each bit of progress they achieve.

- Next, agree on a timed goal for the next bit that they agree is realistic, and praise them when they meet that.

You will probably notice that as their confidence grows, they will agree to shorter and shorter timed goals going forward. And, even more importantly, they will meet those goals.

DP Disarmer

Some slowpokes are herd animals. Sometimes they'll move more quickly when they are moving with a crowd. If possible, put them in situations where they are working alongside others who are involved in doing similar things. Watch and see if this speeds them along. If so, continue to use this strategy.

The "Woe Is Me" Whiner

Woe and worries, worries and woe: so goes the cycle of a perpetual whiner. We all have our problems, but the whiner's problems seem to impact everyone else. Somehow their issues seem so all-consuming that they get in the way of the day-to-day functioning of entire families, workplace teams, or other groups.

Some whiners whine about nothing much. They don't have extraordinary problems, they just don't know what to do except complain *ad infinitum*. On the other hand, many whiners do seem to be living under a rain cloud. When they say, "Everything happens to me," they're not really exaggerating that much.

It's probably not that they were born under a bad sign or cursed by a malevolent wizard in their youth. More likely, their lack of proactive behavior over time has tended to make what problems they have grow larger (neglect to pay your bills one month, and next month your bigger bills have late fees attached; neglect to repair your car and you get stranded at inopportune moments). Moreover, their firm conviction that only bad things will happen to them makes their unconscious minds virtual bad-luck magnets. They can only see problems, so in some subtle way they're drawn to problematic situations.

Where does all this leave you? Often stuck in a morass of real or imagined difficulties right along with them. How can you accomplish anything when you have to stop every five minutes to respond to the latest bulletin on what's gone wrong now? How can you move forward when you continually feel compelled to stop and rescue a lover, friend, family member, or co-worker in the throes of yet another crisis? They need a loan, they need a ride, they need extra time off from work, they need a shoulder to cry on ....

Reacting in a constructive way to "woe is me" types—particularly those with serious troubles—is especially hard for those of us who think of ourselves as kind, compassionate folks. Our initial reflex will be to drop whatever we're doing (and let them off the hook for whatever they *should* have been doing) and commiserate with them. After all, how can we think about our own needs when these people are so beset with trials and tribulations?

But before you evaluate if such a response would actually be compassionate, think for a moment about what might be driving such people. Many whiners believe deep down that the only way they can get someone to show love and interest in them is by offering up their misfortunes. Indeed, this might have been true with some of the people in their past, which is what generated their tilt toward *masochism*. The trouble is that they are carrying this baggage into the present, and if you play along with their script, they have no reason to alter it.

def•i•ni•tion

Although **masochism** initially referred to sexual gratification achieved via humiliation and physical pain, it has also taken on a more general psychological meaning as the tendency to enjoy misery of various kinds, especially to be pitied by others. The word comes from the name of the nineteenth century novelist Leopold von Sacher-Masoch, whose writings centered on self-abusive predilections.

Unlike the universal pessimist, the "woe is me" whiner does not believe that things will go badly for everyone. In fact, they think that everyone else has a wonderful life and an abundance of luck compared with them. So when dealing with a "woe is me" whiner ...

♦ Don't try to argue them out of their sad-sack persona—it's an argument you can't win.

♦ On the other hand, don't agree that they have an inordinate share of trouble— this actually just eggs them on.

♦ Don't tell them you admire their fortitude—that spurs them on as well.

♦ Don't try to help them solve their problems—they'll just come up with new problems.

What should you do? Try what's known as the "least reinforcing response." Another behavioral technique, the least reinforcing response is based on the idea that any response, positive or negative, can fuel a behavior from someone whose primary aim is to get attention. If an attention-seeking behavior provokes no response whatsoever, it will typically fade away.

When animal trainers use the least reinforcing technique with, say, chimps or dolphins, their goal is to literally give no response whatsoever if the animal acts in a mischievous way. They offer no rebuke; they don't even make eye contact. They simply turn away and do something else. Of course, in human affairs, offering no response whatsoever can sometimes be a socially awkward choice. But try to give a socially appropriate response that is least reinforcing. If you can't say nothing, say something polite but noncommittal such as, "I'm so sorry to hear that"; then go about your business, adding a "please excuse me" if needed.

Coping with Obstructionists

As you can see, obstructionists come in many flavors. You'll need to observe their motives and methods before trying to resolve the particular obstacle they represent.

In the next three chapters, we'll look at specific ways to deal with obstructionists in various circumstances, including some scenarios where you may decide that going around them is a more viable and efficient choice than trying to get them to budge.

But however you deal with obstructionists, try to keep any anger in check. Many obstructionists don't actually mean to slow you down. Although that is a result of their behavior, that might not be its goal. The purpose of their behavior often has far more to do with them and their internal issues than with you and your schedule.

Besides, showing anger and impatience toward an obstructionist might satisfy you for a moment, but your show of irritation can actually have the opposite effect of what you would wish. If you blow off steam at an obstructionist and demand they speed up, cheer up, make a decision, stop nitpicking, or stop complaining, your own behavior can inadvertently fuel theirs by provoking their anxiety. When people are anxious, they default to old behaviors; they don't magically develop new, constructive ones.

Finally, remember that although we live in a continually accelerating world, in a culture with increasing demands at a breakneck pace, many things worth doing—and worth doing well—do require some time and thought. Before you lash out at someone who is slowing you down, take a moment to ask yourself if it might not be a good idea to slow *yourself* down every once in a while. Take a breath or two, or ten. Center yourself. Then, and only them, figure out if this is a moment when you really need to go as quickly as you think you do. If so, put your strategies for dealing with obstructionists into play; if not, try to relax for at least a little while.

The Least You Need to Know

◆ Pessimists usually come from a long line of doomsayers—in some cases you can reframe and slightly modify their unilaterally gloomy view, but in other cases you have to buffer yourself with positive thoughts and positive people.

◆ Perfectionists are hard on others, but hardest of all on themselves—their dynamics are hard to undo, but you can often keep them from impeding your general progress by encouraging them to focus on a specific task that calls for fastidiousness.

♦ Chronically undecided types can use a prod when they're stuck at a crossroad—if your relationship with them is strong, capitalize on it by modeling your decision-making process, and let them know you won't second-guess them.

♦ Slowpoke tortoise-types might be trying to slack off, but they might just be a bit too methodical—it helps them if you break goals down into shorter increments and praise them each time they make timely progress.

♦ "Woe is me" whiners, unlike universal pessimists, think everyone's life is rosy except theirs—agreeing or disagreeing with them doesn't help, and helping them with their problems doesn't help; just give a minimal response to avoid reinforcing their behavior.

♦ In general, try not to display anger and impatience toward an obstructionist—that would be counterproductive, as such behavior will only serve to fuel theirs.

Chapter 13

Getting Past Obstructionists at Work

In This Chapter

- Getting past perennial naysayers
- Dealing with nitpickers and micromanagers
- Handling those who say "maybe"
- Coping with slow-motion co-workers
- Contending with whiners at work

At the end of a long day's work, it's often satisfying to think back over the things we've accomplished: Did we create something we're proud of? Did we educate or inspire anyone? Did we resolve any nagging problems? Did we—literally or figuratively—build any bridges or put out any fires? Did we satisfy any customers? Did we make any money? If we can honestly answer yes, we're proud of ourselves. It might have been hard work, but it was worth it.

Some days go better than others, of course. We're all used to those times when no aspect of our work seems to be moving toward closure. It's frustrating no matter what the reason. But when the reason is that someone else is continually holding us up and thwarting our best efforts, it's downright infuriating.

How can we circumvent these pessimists and perfectionists and other relentless roadblocks? That's the subject this chapter addresses.

Naysayers and Idea Slayers

You probably know what it feels like to come up with an inspired idea at work. You've figured out something that will motivate people, improve a product or service, or save time and resources—or perhaps even do all these things at once. As a result, you feel energized and excited. You can't wait to bounce your revelation off others whom you hope will be just as jazzed as you are. And then it happens. You run smack up against a "no" person.

That Won't Work!

Just as every workplace seems to come with its allotment of can-do, positive types whose attitudes tend to be "let's go for it!" so does every work environment have its allotment of negative types who are about as happy to encounter a new idea as picnickers are to encounter a swarm of bees.

Workplace pessimists appear to have a personal mission to shoo away virtually any new idea. It doesn't matter how strong the rationale behind it, nor how many others agree that this inspiration would represent a sound course of action. And heaven forbid anybody thinks the new idea would be fun! That will really get the pessimist to shoot it down.

 Manhole Ahead

Naysayers don't always say "no" in a direct way. Watch out for phrases such as, "Let me play devil's advocate ..." and "With all due respect ...." These can represent early warning signs that your idea is about to be pummeled.

Pessimists love to expose the downside of any "what if" scenario you raise. They'll tell you why what you propose is too impractical, too risky, too costly, too similar to what your competitors are doing, or too unlike what your competitors are doing. All the while they'll shake their heads, roll their eyes, or cluck their tongues, as if to imply that you are being a naïve, impulsive simpleton who has not thought any of these things through.

You might think you have the situation beat if you show up with thoroughly crunched numbers showing just how successful your idea can be. But even this strategy can backfire, as many diehard pessimists are wont to point out that certain ideas can be "too successful."

"What happens if we just can't keep up with customer demand?" they want to know. "What happens if our competitors start to imitate us?"

Sure, you might have good answers to such questions, but you have to remember that to pessimists determined to squelch an idea, no answer you can give will be good enough to overcome their reluctance.

Getting Past the Big "No"

Sometimes you might have to just go around a pessimist at work. If the pessimist is a member of a team that operates by consensus, you may need to build support for your ideas with the rest of the team so that the power of numbers will prevail. If the pessimist is your boss, you might have to find a way to get the idea in front of their boss (subtly, perhaps casually floated as a hypothetical, so you will not appear to be deliberately overstepping). But before you go either of these routes, try these approaches:

- ◆ **Take the onus on yourself.** If you believe the pessimist in question is in part motivated by fear of being the fall guy, assure them that you will take full ownership of and responsibility for the plan.

- ◆ **Suggest a small, limited trial.** Dissuade the pessimist from predicting dire universal consequences. Find a way to test your idea for a short time or with a limited group. Keep the financial investment at a minimum. If things go well, propose expanding your plan a little at a time. (Less severe pessimists may be able to tolerate risk in incremental doses.)

- ◆ **Raise their objections before they do.** Be prepared for all the worst-case scenarios you think the pessimist will offer up. If you bring them up first, they may warm up to you, which can only help your cause.

- ◆ **Agree they might be right.** Finally, agree that your whole idea could end up in unmitigated disaster. Some pessimists are so extreme in the negativism that this could actually hold some appeal. After all, if your idea fails, they get validation.

One word of caution: even pessimists who are being negative out of reflexive habit might, on occasion, be justified in having certain reservations about moving forward in a particular fashion. Just because someone is a pessimist doesn't mean they aren't sometimes also being realistic. It always helps to listen to what someone is actually saying and what their concerns are before you start attempting to change their minds.

Picky, Picky—Very Tricky

Have you ever been eager to move a project along only to have it hijacked by someone who wants to make it "perfect"? There's nothing wrong with wanting to do the best job possible, but perfection *per se* is a tricky concept. Who's to say when something is so good it could not possibly be improved upon? The workplace perfectionist—that's who! (Or so they'd like to think.)

Self-appointed arbiters of flawlessness can stop any endeavor cold in their quest for the ideal. You say you detailed that car? You missed a spot. You say your brochure is ready to send to the printer? Try another font.

If the perfectionist works *with* you or *for* you, you can generally extricate yourself from falling into this time-consuming rabbit hole by citing a pressing deadline set by a supervisor or customer. But if you work *for* the perfectionist, woe is you. Perfectionist bosses are well known for sapping morale as they sweat the small stuff at their subordinates' expense. Remember how you felt when your English teacher gave you back your school composition marked "DO OVER" with a red pencil? That's about how good you'll feel when your micromanager sends back the report you painstakingly researched because he doesn't like your margin size.

If you don't do something, you might spend your life word-processing instead of making any sort of genuine progress. But what can you do? Try these strategies:

- **Ask for your boss's "big picture" opinion.** Remind your boss how much you value her insights and instincts. When you hand her something, pay her a compliment that reinforces her authority, and give her an "assignment" that will encourage her to tap her valuable experience and expertise. The more confident she feels about this macromanagement aspect of her job, the less she might desire to nitpick.

- **Limit "do-over time" by avoiding careless errors.** If you know what your perfectionist boss's hot buttons are, do yourself a favor and brush up on the skills you need to avoid his ire. If he's fussy about grammar, for example, familiarize yourself with the proper use of the semicolon and steer clear of misplaced modifiers. Why deliberately invite nitpicking?

♦ **Distract him with a less critical project.** If your boss is the type who just likes to obsess on *something*, make sure it's not *your* project that's got his attention. He can only nitpick one thing at a time. Steer him toward something that won't suffer from a slow, thorough going-over. While he's laboring over that, he's apt to wave your other project through.

Perfectionist micromanagers don't generally mean any harm to those who work for them, even though it may feel that way. Chances are that if you could peer inside their minds you would find they are more critical of themselves than they are of anyone else.

Knowing how perfectionists think won't cure them. But sometimes just being less defensive around perfectionists will relax them a little bit, which can only help you both.

Wishy-Washy Every-Which-Wayers

In the world of work, clarity can count for a lot. Studies show that working with direct, decisive people—even if they err on the side of downright bluntness at times—is generally less stressful than working for those who seem not to be able to make up their minds.

In the workplace, most of us like to know where we stand. We also appreciate confidence in others. On the other hand, we feel insecure when we don't know which way the wind will blow—or if indeed it will blow at all.

Studies also show that decisive, direct types make the most effective organizational leaders. So how, you may well wonder, do so many wishy-washy indecisive types seem to wend their way up the ranks—if not to the top, then at least high enough where they can torment lots of other people? The answer is probably that wishy-washy types are unlikely to offend anyone above them in the workplace hierarchy. In some organizational cultures, that alone can be enough of a plus to carry an every-which-way type along.

But none of that helps you when your pet project is brought to a standstill by someone who can't commit to a simple yes or no. Whether with regard to small decisions (should we use staples or paper clips?) or more important ones (should we lower our prices to undercut the competition?), "maybe" just doesn't cut it. If you're at the mercy of someone who won't cough up a clear "yea" or "nay," you're trapped in a quagmire.

The obvious temptation is to go ahead and make the decision yourself (apologizing later, if need be) or to seek a "thumbs up" from someone higher on the ladder.

Depending on the exact circumstances, such strategies could work—but be advised that they could potentially create problems. Usurping a decision-maker's power (yes, even a decision-maker who makes no decisions) can put you in the hot seat. If in 20/20 hindsight you turn out to be wrong, you may well be portrayed as rash and impulsive. Worse, even if you turn out to be right, you could be perceived as a maverick who might not be so lucky next time. If your workplace culture does not tend to reward individualism, you could lose even by winning.

Before you do anything drastic, consider if you can nudge an indecisive type toward a decision. Try not to let them know how impatient you are, as this will only feed into their reticence. Instead …

♦ **Keep the options simple.** Don't put five versions of something in front of a wishy-washy type, or give them elaborate options from which to choose. Do as much pre-editing of choices as possible before you present something to them, so they will not have to make more than one basic decision.

♦ **Explain the time constraints.** State clearly what the time frame for action needs to be, and be sure to say *why* these time constraints apply. If you explain the timing rationale objectively, an indecisive type is less apt to feel that you are pressuring them needlessly.

♦ **Be clear about the "no action" consequences.** Continuing to remain objective, explain what the effects of taking *no* action will be. Remember to be very clear: no decision is a *de facto* decision.

DP Disarmer

Don't ask a wishy-washy type to decide anything while they're online. They'll Google the subject until they drop. Where wishy-washy types are concerned, there is definitely such a thing as too much information.

Finally, keep in mind that some wishy-washy types are actually happy to get off the hook when it comes to saying yes or no. However, they do very much want to be kept in the loop. Rather than actively avoiding them, you can try presenting a decision as all but a *fait accompli* that merely requires a rubber-stamp approval. Try running something by them with a quick "This is good with you, right?" They might be all too glad to say, "Er, sure. Go ahead."

Stuck in Slow Motion

Another type who can roadblock you at work is the tortoiselike slowpoke. In today's high-speed business climate, this plodding type can be especially annoying. They truly are anachronisms, throwbacks to an era when most people were at least a little more methodical in their approach to their jobs.

No matter what you do, sluggish types are not apt to speed up to a degree that will please the frenetically fast-paced. But you might be able to spur them on a little if you keep your cool and try these tactics:

- **Team them with high-energy types.** Energy has a way of rubbing off on people. Pair low-energy types with their opposites and the slowpokes may pick up the go-go "vibe."

- **Reward baby steps.** Even a little improvement in terms of pace should be noted and commented on in a positive way. You don't have to be effusive, but do offer an "attaboy" wherever and whenever you can.

- **Don't give slowpokes ASAP projects.** If you're in a position to assign work, do all you can to mete out assignments that demand speed to those who are best able to cope with that demand. Slowpokes will do a fine, thorough job on matters that are not quite so time-sensitive.

Keep in mind that while some slowpokes might be trying to slack off, others are probably just endowed with less "oomph" from the start. Pediatricians will tell you that even infants can be categorized as active or less active types, and that this aspect of newborn temperament is genetically based.

A slowpoke who's driving you crazy might be trying to get out of doing work, *or* they might just be doing their best. One way to distinguish between the two is to remain observant and notice whether the workplace slowpoke seems to race out the door when work is done with apparently lots of energy for *non*-work-related activities. If so, that's a tip-off that you have a slacking passive-aggressive type on your hands. (If so, re-read the appropriate sections of this book.)

Tried and True Tactics

"If you want to know if someone is just acting slow at work or is really slow by nature, try pulling out of the parking lot behind them. See how long it takes them to pull into traffic and how fast they go—or how slow they go—after they get there.

"I once did this with a slow worker and realized he was not trying to goad me personally by being slow on the job. This was just the way he approached everything."—Dan, 40

It's My Crisis and I'll Cry If I Want To

Perhaps nothing can bring a workplace to a grinding halt faster than someone who is very vocally enmeshed in a personal "crisis." Of course, nearly everyone has legitimate troubles at some point, and there are certainly times when work must take a backseat to critical life issues. The problem lies with those who react very dramatically and who attempt—often very successfully—to get lots of others involved in their dilemmas.

You also may have noticed that I put the word "crisis" in quotes, because what constitutes a crisis can be very subjective. Some people consider it a crisis if their big screen TV is out of order, if they've discovered their first gray hair, or if their cat spent the night coughing up hairballs. Others only react histrionically if they've got genuine troubles—perhaps serious financial or health issues affecting themselves or family members.

Either way, those who seek to draw co-workers, supervisors, or subordinates into their unfolding dramas (especially when those dramas seem to unfold one after another) can be a real drain on productivity. Ironically, this is because most people are so nice, so considerate, and so compassionate, that they really feel compelled to offer assistance in whatever ways they can—from providing a shoulder to cry on to covering the afflicted person's workload, to offering personal aid—even emergency babysitting or giving a personal loan.

Be careful here! It's easy to get sucked into someone else's crisis because you feel bad for them. But if someone is the type who makes molehills into mountains, you won't help them by agreeing that a minor glitch deserves the same level of concern as a major problem. In a similar vein, if someone seems to perennially attract major problems, you won't help them by contributing to an ongoing high drama level and immersing them in pity. This dynamic creates even more high-stakes problems, as certain types of people seem to court trouble (albeit on a less than fully conscious level) so they can garner attention.

If you're faced with someone who whines over every little thing, or seems to always be in the grips of disaster, do yourself and them a few favors:

- **Don't ask for details.** The more you ask, the more they'll tell you—in the hopes that you will keep on asking.

- **Don't get personally over-involved.** No matter how sorrowful their story, it is not your job to bail them out. If you find yourself volunteering extra time outside of work to help them, or tapping your own wallet, you've gone too far.

- ◆ **Don't ask them what's wrong if they look upset.** Some people don't begin a litany of complaints with words, but rather by sporting a sad-sack expression and a demoralized posture. They are probably waiting for an invitation to wax eloquent on the woes that plague them. Your casual caring comment of "Is something wrong?" or "You look down in the dumps" will give them *carte blanche* to spill their guts.

- ◆ **Give them space and privacy.** If it is within your power to do so, try to provide whining or crisis-prone types with a workspace a bit off the beaten path (a corner beats a centrally located cubicle). This will keep them from being too great a distraction. Besides, after you remove their audience, they will have less incentive to over-dramatize.

- ◆ **Don't do their work for them.** You can't possibly do two jobs well, so both will suffer. Besides, you won't help them by thinking your attempts will "cover up" for them and make them less vulnerable. If they truly can't manage their work, some sort of temporary substitute may be in order.

What about offering someone a little time off during a crisis? Good idea or bad? The answer is: it depends. If it's within your purview to grant this, and if it appears that taking some time off could actually help someone resolve a pressing issue, you can offer it. But make sure you do so with the stipulation that when they return they will have their minds on their work.

Of course some people will abuse this privilege, and you will have to monitor such situations judiciously. On the other hand, you might find that those who prefer complaining rather than actually fixing the problem might refuse your offer. They might not really want time off as much as they want public sympathy.

If you work for a mid-sized to large organization and are genuinely concerned that someone with whom you work is distracted by a serious life problem, check with your company's human resources department about the availability of services that might be offered via an Employee Assistance Program (EAP).

EAPs used to be thought of as the place one referred employees with substance abuse problems, but they have changed and greatly expanded since that first "Occupational Alcohol Program" of the 1940s.

Modern EAPs offer employees and their families confidential help from professional counselors in areas that include marriage and family counseling, financial and legal difficulties, child-care and elder-care-related matters, and more. The number of companies offering EAPs has also increased significantly, as companies have come to the enlightened conclusion that life stressors can substantially affect on-the-job performance and morale.

Credentialed CEAPs (Certified Employee Assistance Professionals) are more qualified than you to provide the appropriate level of care to an employee with a pressing life problem. They will meet the challenge with the necessary level of expertise and objectivity.

The Least You Need to Know

- Workplace pessimists love to tell you why something won't work—by agreeing with them you might get them to give you a go-ahead in the hopes that they'll be proven right and the onus will be on you.

- Nitpicking bosses are actually hardest on themselves—one way you can defuse their micromanaging is by boosting their confidence and asking for their "big picture" guidance.

- Indecisive types want to be kept in the loop even if they don't like making decisions—instead of avoiding such people, try to present their choices so that they are as clear and simple as possible.

- Slowpokes at work may be passive-aggressive types, or they might just be inherently low on energy. The latter won't improve vastly but they can be goosed by praise and by pairing them with high-energy types on the job.

- Workplace whiners may complain about serious or trivial woes—either way, don't do their work for them or spend your off-the-job time helping out; it won't help them (or you) even if you think that's the compassionate thing to do.

14

Handling Relationship Obstructionists

In This Chapter

- ◆ Living with a negative spouse
- ◆ Coping with crisis-prone parents and siblings
- ◆ Dealing with nonparticipatory family members
- ◆ Handling friends who bring you down

You don't pick your family; you do pick your friends. But either group of folks can lift you up or bring you down.

Husbands, wives, mothers, fathers, sisters, brothers, and pals can provide tremendous forward motion in our lives, offering inspiration, ideas, energy, and a healthy dose of cheerleading. But when their support is absent, or when they're actually a drag on our momentum, we experience the impact profoundly on both a practical and an emotional level.

It's not always easy to counter the effect of family members and friends who, wittingly or unwittingly, have become obstacles in our path. This chapter offers some guidance.

The Negative Partner

The great majority of us marry filled with optimism. Whatever our personal goals, we can only imagine that our spouse will be a helpmate as we pursue them. And of course we have joint goals as well—things that we envision achieving as a couple based on our synergies and our all-for-one and one-for-all attitude.

Sometimes things work out this way, but sometimes they don't. Sometimes a spouse who is pessimistic, perennially problem-prone, or habitually slow and indecisive can distract us and sidetrack us from the goals we once held so dear. We may still love our partner, but that doesn't keep us from being somewhat resentful of them.

As when dealing with difficult spouses of any type, we need to look at an obstructionist mate not merely as an individual but as our partner. The way two partners respond to one another can perpetuate a negative dynamic, but when one partner changes the pattern, positive movement can take place.

The Grass-Is-Greener Outlook

Have you ever had the experience of receiving what you thought was good news—a promotion at work, a "thumbs up" medical check-up, a win in your stock market portfolio—only to have your spouse immediately point out the "downside"? ("That promotion means more late nights"; "Your doctor didn't do all the tests he should have"; "The market is ready for a correction.")

Have you ever just felt upbeat for no particular reason only to have your spouse question whether you've gotten into the cooking sherry? (What other explanation could there be for an "irrational" good mood?)

If so, you know what it's like to live with a pessimist. Living with a partner who always sees the negative side can be particularly soul dampening. In the safety of our home, in the company of our trusted mate, we want the freedom to feel all our feelings—including the good ones! Sometimes we want to talk about "blue sky" ideas that may or may not come to pass, imagining the best-case scenarios. Sometimes we want to be assured that everything will be okay, even if deep down we know it might not be. We don't necessarily want to inhabit a fairy-tale dreamland with our spouse, but neither do we appreciate coming home to a house of horrors!

The pessimistic partner is good at telling us what's wrong with our outlook, what can go wrong with our ideas, and why our neighbor's grass is—and always will be—greener. They are *not* so good at letting us convince them that their negativity is unwarranted; in fact, you've probably noticed that the more you try to argue a pessimistic partner out of their viewpoint, the more entrenched they get.

Stop arguing! Try these ideas instead:

- **Curb your enthusiasm.** When pessimists are given news prefaced by breathless exclamations such as, "Guess what wonderful news I have!" they immediately shift into contrary mode. Offer what you consider positive news objectively, with minimal editorial comment. Your spouse may not respond in the usual reflexively negative way.

- **Pose a hypothetical.** Along the same lines, try presenting good news as a hypothetical before you present it as a fact. ("What would you think if I were offered that promotion?") It will give your partner time to digest an event before it occurs.

- **Give voice to their anxieties and concerns.** Anticipate and articulate your spouse's objections to good news before they do. ("I know you'll be concerned about this promotion's impact on our free time, and we should discuss this.") Your mate will feel understood and validated.

- **Don't exclude them.** Think about whether you present good news only as it pertains to "me" and not "we." Make sure your partner knows that you are including them in any future scenario that you foresee.

- **Don't exaggerate.** Hyperbole on your part ("We're going to be zillionaires!") will only incite exaggerated naysaying ("We're going to end up homeless!").

Manhole Ahead

Agreeing with a pessimistic spouse does have its limits. Never compare your spouse negatively to someone in your social circle, even if they insist that so-and-so is more successful, or better looking, or what have you. Deflating their ego in this way will only make them gloomier.

Finally, take a realistic look at where you fall on the optimism/pessimism spectrum. The way couples dynamics work, it is possible that you and your partner have become polarized over the years. You might have moved to the far optimistic end of the spectrum and your spouse to the extreme pessimistic end. All in all you've balanced out, but is this kind of balance the healthiest arrangement?

Ask yourself: could it be that you have become glued to your rose-colored glasses in part out of spite? Do you refuse to even consider possible negative consequences because you don't want to give your spouse the satisfaction? Or are you perhaps afraid of feeling even a little bit doubtful or worried and therefore content to let your partner express your unwanted feelings?

It's never a good idea to embrace a point of view simply because it's 180 degrees off someone else's. You might find your spouse is less attached to his or her position if you're willing to be more flexible in yours.

The Stick-in-the-Mud Spouse

When you and your mate were courting, chances are you engaged in lots of activities and did a fair amount of socializing. Now you may find your mate has evolved from the life of the party into a world-class couch jockey or *mouse potato*. The idea of getting up, getting dressed up (even slightly, such as putting on shoes), and going out to visit friends or do the town may hold about as much appeal for them as a root canal.

def•i•ni•tion

Mouse potato is the colloquial term for someone who is more or less permanently affixed to their computer screen, in the way a couch potato is affixed to a television screen.

As we saw in Chapter 10, some partners adapt a passive-aggressive approach as they strive to maintain their loaf-about-the-house status. They *say* they want to go out, but they always seem to "forget" to make plans, or contrive some reason why they just can't do it. But others are forthright about their stay-at-home preference and downright proud of being a stick-in-the-mud.

"Who me? Go where? Why?" they want to know.

Good question! Have you remembered lately to tell your spouse how much you actually enjoy their company and like spending time with them? If not, you should. That beats accusing them of having their behind glued to a Barca Lounger—even if the latter would appear to be the case.

If you want to get your spouse unstuck, try the following:

♦ **Build a social activity around their favorite passive pastime.** If they like watching football, get tickets to an actual football game. They won't mind swapping the couch for seats at the stadium—and maybe on the way home they'll be amenable to stopping for dinner.

♦ **Invite others over to share in their potato-hood.** If they're hooked on home shopping, have a home shopping party. If they're stuck on the History Channel, have a history party (maybe in costume). After you've gotten other people to come over, the conversation should branch out and before long your spouse might be able to tear their eyes away from the tube and truly socialize.

♦ **Plan a "something for everyone" vacation.** Even a stick-in-the-mud can be talked into a vacation if that vacation includes lots of loafing—say, on a cruise ship deck or on a beach. While they're in their ultra-relaxed "vacation head," they are often more amenable to trying new activities. Many are reassured by the fact that no one they know will see them and so allow themselves to be a little looser.

Tried and True Tactics

"My husband, who never went out of doors unless he had to, discovered golf at a resort vacation I planned. It wasn't exactly what I had in mind in terms of getting him inspired to do some activities with me, but it turned out okay. Even though I don't golf with him, I appreciate the change that has come over him. He is more active, in a better mood, and has more friends. Because of all this, he is also open to doing many more things together as a couple and with other couples."—Cindy, 47

Perhaps the most important thing to know about dealing with a stick-in-the-mud spouse is that it is all too easy to use them as an excuse for turning into a stick-in-the-mud yourself. Then you get to sit around the house feeling bad about yourself *and* resenting them. If you can't budge your stick-in-the-mud, you can at least budge yourself.

It's perfectly all right to socialize without your spouse if your spouse really would rather not socialize. You'll feel better about yourself for having spent time with friends, gone to the gym, taken an adult education class, or pursued a hobby. And when your spouse does—eventually, even occasionally—turn off the TV, you will have something interesting to share with them.

The "Poor Me" Partner

Perhaps no type of obstructionist spouse is as difficult to deal with as one who is constantly in a state of real or perceived crisis. Of all the people in the world, apart from our children, our partner is the one whom we feel we should "drop everything" to help. We are right to feel that way, of course. (The vow said, "In sickness and in health," right?) But is dropping everything to help a perennially crisis-ridden spouse always the best way to truly help them?

Before you abandon or at least back-burner all your other pursuits to help a spouse in crisis, try to remain calm and consider what you can realistically provide. If your spouse needs home health care, for example, are you really the best person, or would bringing in a professional—even part-time—actually be better for the patient and your relationship? If your partner needs help taking care of one or two aging parents, should *you* rush in where, say, their siblings have failed to do so?

Look carefully at the situation to see if you can discern any recurring patterns. Are you always moving to a new city so your spouse can take a new job after being fired from the last one? Perhaps your spouse would benefit more from some occupational counseling than from your tacit agreement to uproot the family over and over again.

Now what of the partner who has a penchant for turning every bump in the road into an opportunity for melodrama? What of the spouse who reacts to a leaky faucet as though the roof were caving in? What of the *hypochondriac* who treats every minor tension headache as the harbinger of a brain tumor?

def•i•ni•tion

A **hypochondriac** is a person excessively preoccupied with their health who constantly searches for reasons to believe they're seriously ill. Such a person usually spends an inordinate amount of time detailing their real or imagined symptoms to others.

Clearly, it doesn't help you or a partner who is prone to this type of hyperbole if you let yourself get caught up in their intensely exaggerated reactions. Most likely, what they really want is attention. And although it's alright to give them attention, you will only perpetuate their "poor me" dynamic if you do so by sympathizing their self-inflicted suffering.

When responding to a noncrisis crisis, say as little as possible, and use language that is as neutral as possible. Don't agree that the situation is dire, but don't try to disprove their feelings, either. (You can't disprove a feeling, and you'll only start a fight by trying.)

Your lack of engagement in their woes might result in an initial escalation of their complaints, but only briefly. After a while, when they see this behavior is not going to be rewarded, they will ease off. That's when you should give your spouse some positive attention. Flatter them, hug them, be sweet to them when they are calm, and they may not feel so strong a need to dramatize in the future.

Problem-Prone Parents and Siblings

Bad enough that we feel guilty if we don't "do enough" for crisis-prone partners, but we often feel the same way with regard to problem-prone parents and siblings. If we're not careful, dealing with the problem-prone could become our full-time job.

But the truth is that some of us are more apt to be cast as family problem solvers than others. This dynamic may have been preset for decades. That's because families are typically organized by mutually agreed-upon roles. Though rarely articulated, these roles profoundly affect issues such as distribution of power, guidelines for intimacy, patterns of communication, and allocation of work within the family.

Some common roles include:

- **The parentified child:** This is the offspring designated as mature, levelheaded, and organized. They are often made to feel responsible for the well-being of others in the family, including that of their own mothers and fathers. (This parentified child is often, though not always, the firstborn.)

- **The identified patient:** This person is considered the one with emotional problems—for example, some form of instability that may include depression, anxiety, anger management issues, or substance abuse. If the family were ever to enter counseling, they would identify this member as the one who really needed the help.

- **The black sheep:** This person is always in trouble—or perceived to be. Some children may be so firmly entrenched in the black sheep role that even when they have successes, neither they, nor their siblings, nor their parents recognize them as such.

- **The pacifier:** Often, though not always, the middle child is the pacifier—an emotional hub who can speak to any and all family members and stay cool. The pacifier tries to calm everyone down and keep everyone happy. When other family members are arguing, the pacifier becomes the liaison and peacemaker.

- **The clown:** A family clown can also be a pacifier, albeit one with a different style. The clown tries to keep everyone from arguing or complaining by distracting them with humor. (The clown often successfully deflects criticism away from themselves, because "everyone loves a clown.")

- **The lost child:** The lost child is the "one that got away"—the one that is considered beyond help. In some cases, the so-called lost child might be doing just fine, but because they have become estranged from the family, others may be discouraged from reaching out to them or even mentioning them.

If you are a parentified child, you are doubtless a "go-to" person when a crisis situation—big or small—impacts another family member. Your "job" would be to offer pragmatic assistance.

If you are the pacifier, you may also be called to duty in crisis, although your job will more likely be to bridge any differences that have arisen between family members who disagree as to what course of action should be taken. (In other words, everyone will hope you can "talk some sense" into everyone else.) Can you refuse this duty? Sure, but if you do you had better be prepared for resentment, as you will upset the family balance. A dynamic that has been decades in the making can't be "fixed" overnight.

def•i•ni•tion

Gravitas is a serious or solemn attitude. When it is said that one speaks with gravitas, the implication is that one's words carry weight.

Rather than upset your family's equilibrium, it's a good idea to acknowledge your role and use it to your advantage. If you are the parentified child or the pacifier, you are probably used to trying to wade in and "solve things." Instead, use the *gravitas* of those roles to help order and calm prevail.

As someone who can command the attention and respect of other family members, you have the power to help them help themselves. Encourage them to refrain from acting impulsively, and to consult bona fide experts (doctors, lawyers, financial planners) about wise courses of action where appropriate. Most of all, encourage them to keep each so-called crisis in perspective. Every family, no matter what their dynamics, has been through good times and bad. Remind them of the times they've come through adversity, perhaps all the stronger for it.

No-Show Relations

As much as some family members bog down your life by being omnipresent, others have a way of putting a crimp in things by being perennially absent.

Have you ever tried to plan a wedding, bar mitzvah, or simple summer barbeque only to be to put off again and again by relatives who aren't sure when they can make it or are notorious for backing out at the last minute? If so, you know how these "no show" relations can drive you to distraction.

What's their excuse? You name it. Or rather, they'll name it for you:

- They're just so busy with work.
- Their kids have a baseball/soccer/basketball/football/lacrosse game.
- They're overcommitted to the PTA/Boy Scouts/Junior League/bowling league.
- They can't get a pet sitter.
- They have to wash their car/hair/golden retriever.

It might seem as though you're low on their priority list, and indeed you might be. On the other hand, these could be the kind of people who really don't commit to anything, except perhaps at the last minute (the kind of people who, proverbially, would miss their own funerals). Regardless, your strategy should be the same: don't wait for them.

If experience tells you that these relations will never give you a clear-cut answer, stop asking. Simply tell them what will be going on and say you hope they can make it. Your no-show relations may raise a fuss at first when you change the way you deal with making plans. But, overall, you will be lessening your stress and you will not be lessening your chances of getting together with them. In fact, when you don't give them an opportunity to hem and haw, you probably will see them more often.

DP Disarmer _____

If no-shows continue not to show, take the tack of spontaneity. Some people who cannot firmly commit to social dates are actually very amenable to a last-minute drop-by. (Plus they just won't have time to come up with excuses.) You'll never know until you try!

When Friends Drag You Down

Finally we come to the matter of obstructionist friends. Do you have friends in your life who …

- Are perennially pessimistic when you tell them about any new venture in your life?

- Try to talk you out of making any changes?

- Are "wet blankets" who can never make up their minds about whether they want to do something until it is too late?

- Seem to want to talk only about the latest in a long series of troubles in their own lives?

You've read enough about obstructionist types by now to know what some of their motives probably are. But a more immediate question for you is, *What is your motive for letting these people become roadblocks in your life?*

We sometimes cling to friendships out of habit more than any pleasure, comfort, or stimulation these relationships provide. If you have a friend who continually drags you down and is really a source of discomfort for you, it might just be that your relationship has run its course—at least in terms of being a primary, intimate bond.

There may be no need to sever ties completely, let alone abruptly or unkindly, but you can scale back your relationship. Indeed, this might be happening more or less on its own. For example, if you have moved forward and your friend has not, you may feel disinclined to tell them about changes in your life, and find yourself calling or scheduling time with them less and less.

Of course you can still keep old friends in your e-mail address book or drop them a holiday card. There's something reassuring about keeping a tether between ourselves and people who were meaningful at a stage of our lives. But you do not need to feel obligated to keep friends who have become obstructionists.

If, on the other hand, you are reluctant to redefine a friendship with a person you consider a drag, you will need to ask yourself why. What's in it for you to keep a pessimist around? Are you using them to scare yourself and prevent yourself from taking any risks? Are you anxious about broadening your experiences or social circle and therefore hanging around with someone who eschews new people, places, and things?

Be honest with yourself. Your feelings won't hurt you, but your denial of them might. For example, denial may cause you to scapegoat a friend rather than face your own fears.

The Least You Need to Know

- The pessimistic spouse can become more negative depending on how you present good news—try not to boast or exaggerate, and don't cause them to feel excluded.

- The stick-in-the-mud spouse can often be coaxed off the couch by planning a favorite activity outing or inviting people over—but if nothing helps, be sure not to let them turn you into a stick-in-the-mud as well.

- The spouse who reacts to mild bumps in the road of life as major crises probably just wants your attention—but don't reward them for their hysterics; give them positive attention only when they are calm.

- What you are asked to do in a family crisis may depend on the role you play in your family of origin—if you are the one parents and siblings turn to, use your influence to help them help themselves.

- Don't let family members obstruct your plans by being noncommittal—keep moving forward, and you may be surprised how often they happen to find themselves free to join you.

- If you're letting your friends obstruct your life, consider that you might be friends simply out of habit, or that you might be using them as an excuse to obstruct yourself; either way, it could be time to re-evaluate your relationships.

Chapter 15

Surviving Social Obstructionists

In This Chapter

- ◆ Facing up to fear-mongers
- ◆ Coping with fairness fanatics
- ◆ Handling bureaucrats
- ◆ Getting around lazy pedestrians

Obstructionists are ubiquitous in our society. Most of us can probably think of daily examples of people in the public sphere whose purpose seems to be to discourage us from doing anything, or to throw endless obstacles in our path if we try to go ahead in spite of them. In some cases they are even doing these things because they believe it is their job.

It's no simple matter to get where you're going in a world of relentless road blockers, both professional and amateur. This chapter offers some useful detours.

Social Scarers: "Watch Out, Don't Do That"

"Watch out, don't do that!" was a common phrase all of us heard from our mothers and fathers when we were growing up. Good thing, too. As children we sometimes needed to be protected from some of our own daring (and sometimes reckless) impulses. Thanks to our parents' warnings we learned not to cross the street without looking both ways, not to run with scissors, not to ride a bicycle without putting on a helmet.

But now we're all grown up and everyone is still telling us what to watch out for. Dire warnings and grim prognostications are on every newscast and every piece of product packaging. If we took them all to heart, we might find ourselves unable to do anything for fear of the risk involved.

We appreciate sensible, prudent warnings. An "ounce of prevention" at airport check-in lines is a sound practice. Yes, we move along more slowly, but we are safer. Warnings can also make us rethink personal behaviors that might need rethinking. Who can quibble with warnings on cigarette packs, for example?

But there is a general sense that things have gone too far. We all need to come up with a personal strategy for filtering the messages of fearmongers, so that risk aversion doesn't turn into life aversion.

Paranoid Pundits

If you want reasons never to leave the house or get on with your life, all you have to do is turn on TV news. There is usually a barrage of scary feature stories: "Is Sun Tanning Addictive?"; "Can Your Golf Cart Go Out of Control?"; "Is Your Supermarket a Safety Hazard?" Even if you decide to stay home, it would appear you have a problem ("How Much Bacteria Is in Your Kitchen?"). In fact, you're in danger even if you decide to stay in bed ("Could Your Mattress Be Full of Mites?").

We all know that many of the most cataclysmic predictions of recent years—killer bees and Y2K computer Armageddon—have failed to materialize. Yet we are so immersed in the *culture of fear* that even if we shrug off such stories on the outside, most of us can't help but entertain a kernel of anxiety when our channel surfing yields a potpourri of paranoia.

If we tune in to late-night or Sunday morning televised news pundits, our fear level can be even more severely elevated. Many social critics seem bent on increasing ratings by offering shock-value estimations of the state and fate of the union and the world.

def•i•ni•tion

The **culture of fear** is a term that refers to the feelings of dread and anxiety that predominate in contemporary public discourse, changing how people conduct their lives and relate to one another.

Turning off the TV is obviously one way to stem the tide of fear-inducing messages that discourage us from doing pretty much anything. But getting a quick TV news fix is, for many, an ingrained and tough-to-break habit. If you're not about to relinquish it entirely but want to feel less stymied by fear, consider putting yourself on a TV news diet. Stick with one source of news you consider reliable and relatively nonsensational.

In addition, watch with a critical eye. Be aware of scaremongering techniques:

- Deliberate inclusion and omission of facts (some relevant facts are shown and some are not).

- Distortion of statistics or numbers (an infinitesimal statistical probability is exaggerated, sometimes by comparing it to an even more insignificant risk factor).

- Portrait of a single, isolated event as a social epidemic.

- Use of fear-inducing terms and hyperbole.

- Oversimplification of complex and multifaceted situations.

Of course, TV news is not the only culprit. Hollywood has become quite adept at spreading paranoia and exploiting primal fears (snakes on a plane, anyone?). Newspapers, magazines, radio, and blogs often do their share. It's necessary to be a wise consumer of information on every front.

We all have our fears, rational or irrational. And we all know that bad, scary things do happen in this world. The trick to not being paralyzed by those who peddle fear is to not to let realistic, reasonable concerns be blown out of proportion or to let imaginary fears take on a life of their own.

Legal Eagles

Another source of fear-based social paralysis comes to us via the legal profession. But there is no need to blame, let alone bash, lawyers *per se*. After all, we all know by now we live in a society where people are prone to suing companies or organizations for what can only be considered petty matters. Lawyers are doing what has come to be their jobs when they try to keep their clients in business by advising them to post warnings (Hot Coffee!) on their products.

But taking each and every warning to heart would immobilize us. Consider these warnings, all real and all winners chosen from among hundreds of entries in the annual "Wacky Warning Label" contest, conducted by Michigan Lawsuit Abuse Watch:

♦ A heat gun/paint remover that produces temperatures of 1,000 degrees warns users, "Do not use this tool as a hair dryer."

♦ A folding baby stroller warns, "Remove child before folding."

♦ A kitchen knife label warns, "Never try to catch a falling knife."

♦ A label on a baking pan advises, "Ovenware will get hot when used in oven."

♦ A cocktail napkin with a map of the waterways around Hilton Head, South Carolina, printed on it adds the caveat, "Caution: Not to be used for navigation."

♦ A 5-inch brass fishing lure with a three-pronged hook on the end warns, "Harmful if swallowed."

DP Disarmer

To remind yourself how extreme and how silly some of our warnings have become—and to give yourself a good laugh—visit common sense-promoting web-sites such as www.m-law.org (Michigan Lawsuit Abuse Watch), www.cgood.org (Common Good), and www.overlawyered.com. If you've got good examples, they'd all be happy to hear from you as well.

The problem is not, of course, that any of us are likely to stop using ovenware or baby strollers because of such inane warnings. Rather, it's how many of us have become reluctant to start a business, offer a product or service, or even volunteer in our community for fear that we will be the victims of a frivolous lawsuit. After all, if big manufacturers are obviously concerned about such matters, why shouldn't we be?

Until and unless judges begin to dismiss all frivolous lawsuits out of hand, or until our legal system is changed so as to discourage such suits (for example, by making the plaintiff in a frivolous case pay all related costs), the reality is that a certain amount of prudence is a wise course of action. But if we ever hope to become enterprising in any meaningful way, there comes a point where careful becomes too careful.

Let common sense and common decency be your guides. If you're offering a product or service, or are working on a volunteer basis, of course you want to operate with people's best interests in mind. Sure, warn them if there's some evident risk, but try not to scare the heck out of them, or yourself. (And check out the advice for dealing with litigious types in Chapter 19.)

Fairness Fanatics: Idealistic or Impractical?

Another group that tends to throw up roadblocks in the public arena is fairness fanatics. We all agree fairness is a noble thing, a democratic value. We want to try to create a fair society where all have access to opportunity. That is our ideal, and it's a good one. But in real life, idealism often butts up against pragmatism and progress.

The truth is that not everything in life can possibly be 100 percent fair. And to some degree whether something is fair often boils down to a matter of opinion.

Even our highest court is often divided over what is or isn't fair to whom, but ultimately a decision is rendered. Nevertheless, anyone who has ever sat in a meeting about, say, whether children who are not especially good at soccer should be excluded from school soccer teams has seen how hard it is to bring such an issue to closure.

Those who cry "fairness foul" are very likely to get our attention. After all, we want to be reasonable and considerate. We'll grind any process to a halt to examine it for fairness chinks and cracks. If we find any, we'll try to plug them.

But some fairness diehards are never satisfied. They still want to know if whatever decision has been arrived at would be fair in every conceivable case, even in extremely unlikely scenarios.

How do you deal with a fairness fanatic? Check out these suggestions:

- **Agree with them.** As with many people, fairness fanatics will often back down when you affirm their feelings. Tell them you agree that a given policy might not be completely just in every possible case. Lament that such is often the case as we search for what's workable.

- **Set a future date when the policy can be reviewed.** If it's necessary to move forward now, suggest a date to revisit the proposed solution. At that time it can be amended if necessary.

- **Remind them of the integrity and empathy of the individuals involved in the process under discussion.** Not all fairness boils down to policy. Remind fairness fanatics that the people who will be administering the policy are reasonable and caring human beings.

Fairness in any cooperative enterprise requires balancing of different interests. Often it's enough to set basic principles and count on the human element to do the rest. If you can get a fairness fanatic to appreciate this, you will have achieved a great step forward. If you can't, you can always fall back on majority rule. If it's good enough for the Supreme Court, it should be good enough for them.

> ### Tried and True Tactics
>
> "What are the criteria for whether a test is fair? As a professor I've had students tell me that my tests were not fair to those who had not studied. At that point all I could do was agree. Yes, the test was unfair to nonstudiers.
>
> "It is futile to try to have a logical argument when you're presented with an illogical premise. Just because someone invokes the word "unfair," don't feel you have to over-sympathize with them, let alone pander to them."—Adam, 35

Dealing with Bureaucrats

Some people's jobs involve the somewhat ironic practice of getting their tasks accomplished by doing what appears to be placing obstacles in other people's paths. We call these people bureaucrats. (Though on a bad day we have many other names we might resort to calling them.)

The term "bureaucrats" was originally offered to administrative or government officials, but the word has evolved to mean anyone who applies rules rigidly. If you've ever encountered one—and who hasn't?—you have had your patience sorely tested. But maybe it's time to change your approach.

How to Charm a Bureaucrat

Sooner or later, we all have to deal with a bureaucracy. Perhaps we need to renew our passport, or register a new car at the Department of Motor Vehicles. Perhaps we need to resolve a misunderstanding with the Internal Revenue Service, or wrangle a green card from the Immigration and Naturalization Service.

We know we're going to have to deal with a lot of red tape, and so we're probably prepared to have some degree of patience. Even so, we often run into sticklers who refuse to accept certain documents and question the validity of others. They insist that forms we thought were properly filled out have to be redone. They refer us through a Kafkaesque maze of fellow bureaucrats instead of helping to resolve an issue at their level. Moreover, they seem to take a peculiar sort of joy in prolonging our discomfort and taking up our time.

Suddenly, the patience we promised ourselves we would exhibit runs out. We are at the end of our proverbial rope. But on whom do we take out our frustration? On the very person who has all the power in the situation and who can only make our lives more difficult.

Of course, this makes no sense in terms of getting what we want. Whether a tough bureaucrat is actually being sadistic or is simply doing their job as they see it, losing your temper will only make them more inventive in finding ways to halt your progress. If you want to move on, don't lose your cool. Instead …

- **Take a deep breath—literally.** Instead of letting something adversarial come out of your mouth, calm down by taking in some air. Make sure you push it way down to the abdomen. Hold it a moment and release slowly. This only takes a few seconds, and you don't have to make a big show of it.

- **Smile.** You won't feel like smiling, but simply doing so will make you feel better. Besides, moving the edges of your lips upward will remind you that what you are about to say should match your facial expression. (Note: a small smile will do, not a maniacal grin.)

- **Call the person by name.** If they are wearing a name badge or if their desk or booth has a name plaque, this will be easy. If you see both a first name and a surname displayed, use the surname prefaced by "Ms." or "Mr." If you don't see a name, simply ask. Inquire in a friendly manner so they don't get the impression you are going to use the information to complain about them.

- **Acknowledge that you understand their role.** Affirm that you know what their job is and that they are doing it well. ("Driver licenses are important documents. I know it's your job to make sure the information on them is accurate.")

- **Explain your question or concern and ask their advice.** Never say they are wrong, although you can suggest that their organization's communication has confused you. ("I understand you can't accept this piece of I.D., but I thought the information on your website meant this was okay. I'd hate to have to lose another morning's work to come back. Is there anything you think we can do?")

- **Float solutions to expedite matters—if you have them.** ("Could I possibly run out to my car and bring back an insurance card with my address?")

♦ **Whatever happens, end with "thank you."** Even if you don't get what you
want, be sure to end your conversation politely. The next time you come back,
you might run up against exactly the very same person. Don't give them incentive to impede you any further.

Like it or not—and I know you don't—bureaucracy is a fact of life. It's also getting
more convoluted. Security-related identity checks are more thorough as security concerns continue to heighten. New privacy-protection laws such as HIPAA (the Health
Insurance Portability and Accountability Act) necessitate increased red tape to control information access. The more regulations we have, the more people are paid to
enforce them. Learning to be nice to bureaucrats is a skill everyone needs to cultivate.

Getting Service from Customer Service

Another fact of modern life is the increased need to deal with employees at customer
call centers to obtain services such as phone or cable installation or repair, to check
on an insurance claim or credit card statement, or to track a product order. We've all
run into situations where those whose job it is to *provide* service seem bent on actually
depriving us of service. They ask too many redundant questions, don't understand the
urgency of our problem, and fail to provide a timely solution.

If you've ever found yourself losing your temper in such situations, you're not alone.
But if your anger has prompted you to yell at the person on the other end of the line,
you have surely noticed that this never gets your problem solved any sooner. In most
cases it slows things down, and in some cases it results in the representative hanging
up on you. Then you have to start all over again!

The next time you're frustrated in such a situation, keep these tips in mind:

♦ **Stay attentive during voice mail prompts.** It's easy to becoming impatient
as soon as we have to start wending our way through the automated voice mail
menu. "Press 1 for this and 2 for that …" *Can't we just talk to a person already?*
But, sadly, if we want to talk to a human we have to follow the script. Don't start
off on the wrong foot with a human because you're mad at a machine.

♦ **Answer the representative's questions cooperatively.** Yes, they will often ask
you to verbally repeat a 16-digit account number that you've just punched into
your touch-tone phone pad. Arguing with them won't alter this rule. (Remember
their supervisor might be listening in.) Like you, they probably wish the system
wasn't set up this way, but it is.

DP Disarmer

Pressing zero, as you may have noticed, usually does not allow you to shortcut a voice mail system and get to a human any sooner. However, if you think you will be calling again, make a note of the series of prompts that get you to your destination. In the future, you can speed things along by punching them in before the automated system finishes asking for them.

♦ **When they say their name, greet them.** In most cases, the customer service rep will volunteer their first name near the start of the conversation. It's a good idea to repeat it back in a friendly greeting (for example, "Hi, Tiffany, I'm Mike. Let me tell you why I'm calling …"). If you can spare half a minute, ask them where they are (call centers can be anywhere on the planet these days), and how the weather is.

♦ **Have all relevant information handy.** You will slow yourself down if you have to stop the conversation to start rummaging through checkbooks or billing statements. Try to anticipate what they might need to know and have it at the ready before you make the call.

♦ **Explain what's been done already, if anything, and why the matter is urgent, if it is.** Be thorough, but don't share your life history. It's enough to say, "My office phones still don't work and I'm losing business." You don't need to detail an hour-by-hour chronicle of the saga.

♦ **Sympathize with how the system hamstrings them—then ask for a supervisor.** If the call representative is unable to help you, agree that it would be difficult for them given the constraints of the system (in other words, don't assign blame to them). Politely request that your call be transferred to a supervisor who perhaps might have a little more leeway.

When you get a supervisor on the line, follow the rules as above, but now add some flattery. Let them know you feel confident that someone of their stature can resolve the problem. If they can't resolve it immediately, ask for a method by which you can get back to them directly because they have already been so helpful.

Sidewalk Slackers

Other people who slow us down in public settings are people who simply move slowly, whether on foot, on a bike (though, annoyingly, not in the bike lanes), or on those electric-powered scooters that some have dubbed "sidewalk SUVs." (Originally designed for the handicapped, stores can hardly keep these scooter gizmos in stock as they sell out to the admittedly "just lazy.")

We can attempt to barrel by these sidewalk slackers, of course, and why not? After all, we've got places to go and things to do.

Nevertheless, it's wise not to be reckless under any circumstances. The temptation to get around a slow-moving sidewalk slacker can be so overwhelming that we neglect to think about what might be on the other side of them.

No matter how angry we get, it's just not worth endangering anyone's safety—not your own, not an innocent bystander's, and—no—not even the slacker's. A simple "pardon me" can go a long way toward getting cooperation. (And somehow it always sounds more gracious than "excuse me.")

If that doesn't work, move to a more declarative statement, such as "On your left." This doesn't "ask," it "tells": *I'm passing on your left—I'd do something if I were you.*

This declarative phrase also works especially well in situations where you want to bypass someone who plans to stay still on a moving escalator or a pedestrian ramp of the sort found at airport terminals—as opposed to walking briskly along as the conveyance moves. Unwritten social codes dictate that those who stand still in such situations should stand to the right. But slackers often plop right in the middle of foot traffic—oblivious. They may appear to be in a daze, but your little warning will shake them out of their reverie.

 Manhole Ahead _____

It's hard to say "excuse me" to someone wearing an iPod. Oh, you can say it all right, but they won't hear, and that makes for an unsafe situation. If you need to bypass an iPod wearer, don't bother yelling. Try a very gentle tap on the shoulder. Or do what a friend of mine does—carry a small placard in your purse or briefcase that says "Pardon me." If all else fails, cross the street.

The Least You Need to Know

♦ In our contemporary culture, fearmongering has become something of a national pastime—keep your perspective and your sense of humor, and don't be too careful to live your life.

♦ Those who persistently cry "no fair" can slow down any process as they insist on an ideal rather than a workable solution. Agree with them that life's not fair, but remind them that most people operate out of integrity and empathy.

♦ Bureaucrats and customer center call reps are people, too, even though their jobs mandate that they follow time-consuming, obstructionist procedures. Be cooperative and polite and you will get through the system a lot faster.

♦ When trying to navigate past a sidewalk slacker, keep safety in mind. Alert them of your intentions as politely as possible.

Part 5

The Truly Toxic

This part of the book discusses coping with people who are beyond garden-variety difficult types. It offers measures for those who want to stop being victimized in their professional or personal lives by the abusive, the emotionally cruel, or the double-dealing. It also offers advice for spotting dangerous strangers and how to protect yourself from them.

Chapter 16

Crossing the Line

In This Chapter

- How to tell if someone is toxic
- What underlies toxicity
- Why you shouldn't make excuses for the toxic
- What to do when someone is toxic only to you
- How to deal with toxic individuals

Up until now, this book has mainly focused on types of people whom we find difficult because their behaviors irritate, frustrate, and sometimes confound us. But there is a more extreme type of difficult person—a type whose actions and attitudes can be deeply disturbing, abusive, menacing, and ultimately destructive. We call these people toxic, because we have the sense that they are capable of causing serious harm in the way that a poison can.

Obviously, none of us wishes to be poisoned. Ideally, we'd like to forego exposure to all toxic people. Indeed, sometimes we can spot early warning signs and manage to steer clear, but in certain situations this won't be possible. When we are exposed to a poison, we need an antidote. When we are exposed to a toxic person, we need antidotal strategies to counter their dangerous effects. But first, in the name of self-protection, we need to know more about toxic people and what makes them tick.

Signs of Toxicity

Have you ever had to use a toxic household substance—a weed killer or a paint remover, perhaps? You'll notice that detailed warning labels alert you to its possible effects. *Caution, harmful if swallowed. If necessary, contact a poison control center.* If only toxic people came with such clear markings.

They don't, of course. Yet somehow, most of us have a gut instinct, a sixth sense that alerts us when we are in the presence of someone who has the potential to cause us harm. This early warning system is really just our eyes, our ears, and our emotional intelligence working quickly in unison.

Here are some things you may notice about a potentially toxic person:

- They often say things that are highly inappropriate in a social situation.

- They seem incapable of the niceties of communication, such as making small talk.

- They sometimes reveal way too much personal information.

- They sometimes use foul or hostile language.

- Their emotional reactions are either noticeably strong or radically different than what you would expect.

- They react severely or irrationally to minor annoyances.

- They might look smug or laugh when you would expect them to look sad or sympathetic.

- They do not appear to maintain a supportive social network.

- They may be loners, or appear able to maintain intimate relationships for only short amounts of time.

- The relationships they do maintain seem troubled and tumultuous.

- They are either oblivious to the unsettling effect they have on other people, or are aware and take pleasure in it.

We may notice such things even from a safe distance. Observing a toxic person from afar, we get a sense we might want to limit our interactions with this person. But if we do or must interact with them, their dangerous nature only becomes more obvious because of how they make us feel.

Harmful Reactions to Poisonous People

When we interact with a toxic person, we react throughout our *mind-body system*. A toxin can affect any part of us, including intangibles such as moods—which in turn can impact our overall health. In some cases we sense this looming threat ahead of time and approach gingerly, with our guard up. Nevertheless, it's a good idea to monitor reactions closely when around anyone you think might be toxic.

def•i•ni•tion

The **mind-body system** is a conceptual understanding of our interrelated psychic and physical self. In practical terms, this concept informs contemporary medical and psychological thinking with regard to such matters as stress-related illness.

Psychological Symptoms

If a typical run-in with a difficult person can be compared to having to cope with a mosquito, a run-in with a toxic person feels more like defending oneself against a snake. Annoyance does not begin to sum up what we feel.

We might feel frightened, or at least unaccountably nervous. We might also feel confused about how to proceed, and doubtful of our own ability to deal with the situation effectively. Of course we might feel angry and want to lash out, but something tells us this is not a sound strategy. Who, after all, wants to anger a snake?

If we get close enough to experience the fangs of a toxic person (even just as much as a cutting remark), we can experience a whole range of reactions. We may feel defeated, humiliated, enraged, demoralized, anxious, confused, dazed, or even panicked.

Sometimes our intense emotion is focused directly at the toxic person; however, it can also be aimed at us. That's because some toxic people have a way of filling us with self-doubt and making us feel inadequate. Not knowing what to do with these feelings, we might be prone to acting out inappropriately.

If we fall into a pattern of allowing toxic people to harm or dominate us over a period of time, we may start engaging in self-destructive acts such as overeating, abusing drugs or alcohol, becoming passive and lethargic, acting out at work or in relationships, and generally sabotaging what is good in our lives. We mistreat ourselves in part because we don't know how to deal with our intense emotional negativity toward another person, and because we don't like ourselves when we feel sad, mad, or afraid.

Physical Symptoms

Going hand in hand with our emotional symptoms could be a host of physiological symptoms. During or after an unsettling encounter with a toxic person, we might experience:

- Headaches
- Muscle tension
- Queasy stomachs
- Shortness of breath
- Backaches
- Stiff necks
- Facial tics
- Flushing and even itches and rashes, as if our skin is "crawling"

In some cases we might experience temperature extremes: feeling warm and even sweating profusely, or feeling as though chills are shooting up our spine.

One very common symptom is tightness in the throat. Because physical symptoms sometimes can reflect emotional conflict, one might suspect this is because we are attempting to restrain ourselves from saying something profoundly negative.

 Manhole Ahead

Do not ignore your body's messages about toxic people. Over time, passing physical symptoms can add up. Prolonged stress due to toxic relationships may result in a psychosomatic illness—an illness generated at least in part by psychological causes—such as ulcers, irritable bowel syndrome, and even heart disease.

Don't Ignore Your Instincts

Tragically, despite the intense emotional and physical reactions we have to toxic people, and the powerful sixth sense that something is "off," many of us spend quite a bit of time and energy *denying* what we know to be true: that someone is toxic. In spite of the evidence, we make excuses for them. *They can't really be like that*, we think. *They can't really mean me any harm. I'll give them another chance.*

Why do we ignore our gut instincts in this way? Maybe because we find the reality of a clear and present danger posed by another human being just too scary. Maybe we think of ourselves as "not nice" for even imagining that others could have unsavory motives. Maybe we've been abused by someone for so long that we no longer realize that what's happening is not right. Maybe because after exposure to a toxic person we begin to act like them, meeting hostility with hostility, and so think we are the "bad" ones.

Tried and True Tactics

"I went for a long time tolerating an abusive boss because I felt so much hostility around him I thought I must have some 'issues' of my own. It took me years to realize that I felt aggressive and hostile *only around him* because I was taking on his feelings. I learned that when I am acting in a way that is totally foreign to me, I might be in the presence of a person whose toxic emotions are contagious."—Ed, 46

In many cases, we make excuses because we are trapped in a pattern and simply have no idea whatsoever how we can extricate ourselves from it. Sadly, the longer we deny the reality that someone is toxic, the more we become invested in that denial. After all, to change our viewpoint *now* would be tantamount to admitting that we have been duped and deceived for years. Everything we believed to be true about our world could be turned upside down. But as devastating as this may be, it is not as devastating as remaining shut off to reality.

If you truly believe someone is toxic to you, they are. You can attempt to talk yourself out of it, but if you keep ending up in the same place, you have to pay attention to the writing on the wall. If your mind and body are sending you danger signs, do not ignore them. They will only grow louder and more disturbing, and your discomfort will only increase. No matter what changes you might have to make, it is better to recognize toxicity for what it is than to pretend all is well.

What Makes Toxic People Toxic?

How do toxic people become the way they are? Why are people mean, nasty, and sneaky? Why are there human beings who seem to take joy in belittling, degrading, hurting, or tricking others? The truth is there are no definitive answers to such questions, only theories.

Some people will tell you that toxic people are just plain evil—that they are "bad seeds" born without conscience. Some will say that they have chemical imbalances that affect their thinking and behavior. Some will point out that they have often been victims themselves at some point in their lives. Any of these things—or indeed any combination of them—could be true. And any of them could be part of a "chicken and egg" effect where causes become cyclical and problems become self-perpetuating.

In the end, you might not have any idea what drives a toxic person to act as they do. It is useful, however, to understand that no matter what the precipitating cause, most toxic people do share certain underlying dynamics. Understanding these can offer a glimpse into how their minds work, and can help you devise self-protective strategies.

The Self-Esteem Drought

Although many toxic people appear to be completely confident—even righteous—such posturing is often a defense against deep feelings of low self-worth. And even though they seem to have very thick skins, they may in fact be hypersensitive to criticism.

The egos of toxic people are often so frail that they bolster those egos by trying to tear other people down. They embody a kind of defensive aggressiveness. Only by inflicting suffering on others can they distract themselves from their own distress.

Envious Rage

Not surprisingly, the thing that most distresses toxic people with a low self-image is when someone else is doing well. They hate it when anyone else earns praise, gains stature, or accrues material gain. They hate it when others seem happy in love or content at work. They don't even like it when someone is simply having a nice day, which explains why they often seem so bent on ruining it.

Sometimes a toxic person can be specifically jealous of something that belongs to another person. They might crave for themselves, for example, the corner office that was given to a co-worker or an award that was bestowed upon a rival. Often it's just a general attitude of pathological envy.

Pathological envy is the tendency to evaluate one's status and well-being solely by assessing how well one is doing in comparison with others. The result of such envy is, as Aristotle said, "Pain at the good fortune of others."

Even if the achievements of other people do not objectively detract from the toxic person's own standing, a toxic individual is apt to be threatened when anyone to whom they compare themselves displays any sign of worth. The more "deserving" the envied person actually is, the more the envier becomes incensed. And the more incensed the toxic person is, the more determined they are to destroy the other's good fortune.

DP Disarmer _____

A toxic person might well try to "throw you off the scent" by praising your accomplishments. If you sense some insincerity (they could be stingy with praise or obsequiously over the top), remain gracious and, above all, humble. Never flaunt your achievements in front of a toxic person—you're just asking for trouble.

Is There Any Excuse?

You might be kindhearted enough that you feel badly for toxic individuals. You might be able to imagine how painful it must be to live inside their heads. And you might lament the fact that *perhaps* their path to toxicity could have been avoided had they been born with a different genetic blueprint or into different environmental or family circumstances.

If so, your compassionate nature is to be commended. But do not let it determine whether you will choose to defend yourself from toxic people. The fact is that when it comes to defending your body, mind, and spirit—not to mention your career, your reputation, your healthy relationships, and your material possessions—from threats posed by toxic people, *it does not matter if they have an excuse.*

When you need a strategy for dealing with a toxic person, find one as quickly and dispassionately as possible. You are not judge or jury here, you are a potential victim. As such, you need to be primarily concerned with your right to live your life unfettered by a poisonous individual.

Someday, on Earth or—based on your belief system—perhaps in heaven, a toxic person might have to face up to what they have done. They might be brought to justice in one way or another. They might see the error of their ways. Who knows? They may even, ultimately, feel remorse. But none of this can be your concern, or your responsibility, if you are in jeopardy right now. If you have faith that an earthly or sublime system will make things right in the end, hold on to that faith. But first and foremost, take care of yourself.

One Man's Pal, Another Man's Poison?

One more thing worth mentioning is that it is possible for someone to be toxic to you but not necessarily to everyone else. Toxicity can be very specific. Think of it this way: there are times when a number of people are exposed to a certain virus or bacteria— some get sick, some don't. It depends on where each person's particular immunities or vulnerabilities lie.

Some toxic people are selectively hostile. They may be reasonably well behaved around people whom they do not envy, for example, but vicious toward those who have personality traits, relationships, or material things they covet. If you are one of the unlucky ones they do envy, look out.

Some toxic people are primarily dangerous to people with whom they share a certain type of relationship that pushes their hot buttons. For example, someone might be a toxic boss, but a perfectly adequate parent. Conversely, they might be quite well behaved at work, but emotionally abusive toward their spouse or kids. Some mothers might torment their daughters, but behave tolerably well toward their sons.

In addition, you may view someone as especially toxic because you have a particular sensitivity. For example, if you had an abusive parent, you might be especially reactive to anyone who acts similar to that parent. Although someone else might view their behavior as unpleasant or even crazy, they might not be as personally affected by it because they don't have your unique emotional history.

Whatever the reason, if you experience someone as toxic *to you*, you must protect yourself regardless of how others perceive them. You cannot expect everyone to agree with you, nor should you expend your energy trying to convince someone who's impervious to an individual's toxicity.

 Manhole Ahead _____

Just as someone who is toxic to you might not be toxic to another, someone who is toxic to another might not be toxic to you. File away any warnings as potentially useful information, and keep your eyes and ears open. But in the end you will have to make up your own mind and behave accordingly.

Getting Ready to Protect Yourself from the Toxic

The next several chapters will outline strategies for dealing with toxic people in the workplace, in personal relationships, and in public. But some general rules always apply whenever you encounter someone who sends danger signs:

♦ **Give toxic people a wide berth.** If you were walking through the woods and noticed a poison mushroom, chances are your instinct would not be to pick it, handle it, and sniff it. Instead, your gut would tell you to leave it be. The same should hold true for toxic people. Don't seek out their company if you don't need to, and don't interact with them any more than you have to.

♦ **Don't intentionally provoke them.** As tempting as it might be to lash out at toxic people verbally or physically, this will only increase the likelihood of putting yourself in danger. In addition, because toxic people are so envious, don't flaunt your achievements or your happiness before them. Play your cards close to the vest.

♦ **Don't give them a taste of their own medicine.** It can also be tempting to be as nasty to toxic people as they are to you. But try not to sink to their level. This only gives them a perverse kind of satisfaction, and it makes you feel bad about yourself.

♦ **Avoid getting sucked in by temporary niceness.** If a toxic person suspects you are on to them and suspects you might break off contact or stop playing by their script, they might temporarily act sweet and sensitive. They might even apologize for past transgressions. Don't buy it. They are doing this because they need to keep their victims victimized, no matter what it takes.

♦ **Seek support and learn your rights.** There are many ways to protect yourself from a toxic person. If you are being harassed or abused at work, investigate company policies and consider contacting human resources. If you are being abused at home, consider reaching out to organizations that can offer emotional and even legal support.

There have always been people in the world that we would now call toxic. Reading the oldest myths and stories confirms that there have always been villains, just as there have always been heroes. This is not going to change.

It is important to remember, however, that we do not have to be at the mercy of toxic people. With determination, support, and the right set of strategies, it is possible to break free of their influence and be heroic in your own life.

The Least You Need to Know

♦ Toxic people don't come with warning labels. Listen to your intuition and pay attention to your emotional and physical responses.

♦ There are many theories about what causes toxic people to be as they are, but all toxic people share low self-esteem and a pathological degree of envy.

♦ Don't make excuses for the toxic. No matter how great your compassion, you still need to protect yourself.

♦ Toxicity can be specific—someone can be toxic to you but not to someone else, and vice versa.

♦ To guard against dangerously toxic people: keep your distance, don't be provocative, resist acting like them, resist being seduced, and learn to seek support.

Chapter 17

Responding to the Ruthless at Work

In This Chapter

- ◆ Why some people are abusive at work
- ◆ How to handle toxic, troublemaking co-workers
- ◆ What to do when your boss is toxic
- ◆ How to defend against toxic subordinates
- ◆ What to do if you must quit

Work is tough, and difficult people can make it tougher. But toxic people can make it almost unbearable. Most of us spend more waking hours at work than we do with our families or pursuing any other activity. These days, most of us spend less than eight hours a day sleeping and more than eight hours a day working. Imagine how hard it is to be exposed to toxicity for that length of time, day after day.

But if you are reading this chapter, perhaps you don't have to imagine. If you have a toxic person in your work environment, read on for some effective strategies.

Abusers at Work

Sadly, people who behave abusively at work are not uncommon. In some cases, these people are generally toxic types, a bane to all they meet. But in many cases, people who behave shamefully at work may behave perfectly acceptably in other environments. It is only in the workplace that their demons are unleashed.

Work, especially in times of fierce global competition and economic uncertainty, can be hyper-competitive. Some see it as dog-eat-dog, and they want to be the canine that *has* the meal—not the one that *is* the meal. They mistakenly think that anything goes at work so long as they get ahead or feel powerful.

Some people also view work as a place to dump all the toxicity accrued from other troubling areas of their life. If they have an inadequate love life, home life, or social life, work is where they can get even, even though their co-workers or employees have nothing to do with their outside-of-work circumstances.

These days, abusers at work don't literally crack whips similar to *Simon Legree* of yore. But they find many ways to torment those under them or around them. Sometimes they even manage to torture those who are above them in the workplace hierarchy.

def•i•ni•tion

Simon Legree was a character—a vicious plantation owner—in Harriet Beecher Stowe's famous American novel *Uncle Tom's Cabin*. The name has come to be associated with someone who is overtly cruel to those who work for them.

Invalidators and Troublemakers

Sometimes the people who work alongside us—who are supposed to be cooperating with us and aiming to achieve the same goals—torment us the most. The methods of toxic co-workers vary, and they are sometimes as subtle as they are sinister. Nevertheless, they are insidious.

The Constant Critic

One common form of a toxic co-worker is the constant critic. Such a person will typically contribute nothing of value, but rather spend all their time invalidating what others do. Invalidators take pleasure in belittling the efforts of others. They go beyond being nitpickers. They mock and devalue, even if—and sometimes *especially* if—a colleague's work deserves praise.

The constant critic has a way of knowing exactly what your insecurities are and preying on them. If you're apprehensive about making a presentation, they will be sure to sit in the front row rolling their eyes, yawning, and nudging the person beside them as if to say, "Look at this clown." If you're uncomfortable executing a task or planning an event, they will go out of their way to point out to you and everyone else the one detail you overlooked—regardless of the fact that what you accomplished was overwhelmingly successful.

Invalidators are fond of sneak attacks. They might build you up only to tear you down later. They may pay you a left-handed compliment such as, "Wow, great job. That's a much better job than you usually do. Did you have some outside help?"

Of course, critics won't always criticize you to your face. They will store up nasty things to say about you to others, especially things that cast doubt on your value to the organization. They will bad-mouth you to those who have power over you, or who are supposed to assist you. They will cast doubt on your competency, and blame you for anything that goes wrong.

If you directly confront a constant critic about something they said directly to you, they will probably say you misinterpreted their remarks. If you confront them about something they said behind your back, they will deny it—or claim they were misunderstood by a third party. Even though you know in your heart they are lying, there will not be much you can do about it. In fact, directly accusing a constant critic of belittling or bad-mouthing you only gives them a peculiar kind of satisfaction. It's far better to at least pretend to ignore them.

Think back to the dynamics of the schoolyard when you were a child. Remember the mean kids who taunted other kids? (Yes, they might have been toxic adults in the making.) If you recall such scenarios, you probably also recall that the kids who got picked on the most were the ones who reacted. The more dramatically they reacted, whether with tears or recriminations, the more they got abused. It was the kids who feigned imperviousness ("sticks and stones will break my bones") who eventually were spared.

The game is the same in the workplace. Pretend to ignore your critic, but do what you must to make certain their words won't sully your reputation.

 ◆ **Be absolutely sure to document everything so you can defend your record should anyone's criticisms be taken seriously.** Keep thorough notes on your accomplishments and when and how you accomplished them.

- ◆ **Don't retaliate by labeling.** If you hear someone has bad-mouthed you, even in a very untruthful and vicious way, don't respond by calling them a pathological liar or a psychopath. If you voice a complaint, focus on the behavior: what they *did* or *said*, versus what you think they *are*.

- ◆ **Build and nurture positive, productive relationships.** The best way to make sure people think well of you, despite a critic's constant negative spin, is to be the sort of person people know they can trust and rely on. If people know you as consistently dependable, friendly (though not obsequious), and resourceful, a toxic person's attacks will have little practical impact on you. Indeed, it could backfire.

In addition, don't assign guilt by association. If a critic bad-mouths you to someone else, don't assume that other person takes them seriously or thinks ill of you as a result. The other person might be well aware of the critic's agenda. Your best move is to spend some time with the third party yourself—because you are your own best goodwill ambassador.

DP Disarmer _____

Many people don't keep good notes at work because they don't like to write or don't have the time. It's worth taking a time-management course and perhaps a writing skills course to address such matters. Making this essential task easier will make you more likely to continue to follow through.

The Instigator

The toxic instigator will try to provoke a conflict between others. They hope that while they stand on the sidelines and gloat, people they have manipulated into disliking one another will get into a nasty confrontation.

The instigator is not above telling an outright lie to Person A about what Person B allegedly said about them or did behind their back. But sometimes they spread their poison indirectly, by starting a rumor they claim to have heard through the grapevine. Sometimes they take a germ of truth and then twist or exaggerate it until it takes on a life of its own.

It would be convenient if we could tell with certainty when someone is actually lying or stretching the truth, but we can't hook a co-worker up to a polygraph. There are, however, often little giveaways that alert us to the fact that someone is being untruthful:

- Not making eye contact.

- Touching one's nose while speaking (perhaps expecting it to grow, as Pinocchio's did).

- Licking one's lips while speaking.

- Turning one's body away while speaking.

- Placing objects (such as a coffee cup or newspaper) between oneself and the listener.

- Displaying stiff and limited facial expressions.

- Displaying facial expressions that are incongruous with spoken words (such as smiling slightly while sharing bad news).

- Making hand gestures that are slightly delayed from the words they should accompany.

- Stuttering or clearing one's throat while talking.

- Using fewer contractions (such as "I did not" instead of "No, I didn't").

DP Disarmer

If you think someone's lying, change the subject of the conversation quickly, and see whether the liar becomes noticeably more relaxed. If their demeanor really changes, be alert.

Some toxic people are extremely adept at lying. If someone tends to lie across all areas of their lives, they might be so well rehearsed that they can hide most tip-off signals. Some toxic liars even come to believe their own lies over time and don't reveal any signs of inner conflict or anxiety. Nevertheless, common sense will tell you that if they've lied in the past, they are capable of lying again. Your gut can lead you in the right direction, so heed it well.

The Opportunist

The opportunistic type of toxic co-worker will hit you when you're down. When you're busy, distracted, or absent from the workplace, they'll seize that moment to undermine you, cast doubt on your dedication, or question the quality of work you've yet to finish. They'll try to take control of your projects, customers, or initiatives.

Because you won't be around to defend yourself, they'll feel free to spin their point of view. By the time you can devote your attention to the situation, it could be too late. You might have been deposed or at least deemed less than critical to the task at hand. To whom does everyone turn for guidance now? To the opportunist, of course.

The best way to defend yourself against an opportunist would be to clone yourself and be in all places at all times so that you can defend your interests. But because that's not possible …

- **Never divulge your schedule or whereabouts to an opportunist unless you must.** If they know ahead of time that you'll be absent, they'll be able to plan their attack.

- **Know whom you can trust to update you on what's going on.** Having loyal colleagues who will tell you what's up is the next best thing to having proverbial eyes in the back of your head.

- **Check in as often as possible.** Even if only for a minute, poke your head into a meeting you cannot attend. Give a quick call to colleagues on your cell phone, or send a quick e-mail from your Blackberry. A little contact goes a long way in reminding people you are still concerned and connected.

DP Disarmer

Distinguish between private and public aspects of your personality and your life. You should rarely, if ever, air your private thoughts, attitudes, hopes, dreams, fears, or plans at the workplace—especially if that workplace contains toxic opportunists. Edit your public self so that no one can capitalize on your perceived weaknesses.

As always, one of the best overall strategies you can use to counter a scheming toxic opportunist is to develop a reputation for consistency and reliability. People will be less likely to switch allegiances midstream when they feel sure that you will resume your capable role as soon as you can.

Toxic at the Top

As difficult as it is to work with toxic people, working *for* them is tougher because of the obvious power differential. Your boss can influence events, decisions, and outcomes in a way most co-workers cannot.

To prevent toxic bosses from being destructive to our careers, we are often willing to put up with a great deal from them that we might not tolerate from others. At the same time, a toxic boss can counteract any joy or satisfaction we might otherwise get from work. Precisely because they are in charge, their lack of integrity and disrespect for us can be profoundly demoralizing.

Big Bully Bosses

Toxic bully bosses are often exploitative. They are infamous for crossing the line when it comes to what is and isn't appropriate to ask from an employee. To flaunt their power, they might ask you to do chores that are of a clearly personal nature (*"fill out my kid's college application"*; *"pick up my dry cleaning and my drugstore prescription"*). They might call you at all hours with trivial requests that could obviously have waited until later.

When it comes to actual work-related tasks, bullying bosses may dole them out at an unreasonable rate or with sparse or incomprehensible instructions—as if setting you up to fail. When you do inevitably fail, or dare to request additional guidance, they will berate you. They may question your competence, even laugh at you or call you names (sometimes four-letter ones). Worst of all, they often prefer to do such things in front of an audience—or at least loudly enough so that people cannot help but overhear.

Sadly, workplace hierarchies are famous for bringing out the bully in people, especially those who need to "prove" their power—perhaps because they don't feel powerful or respected in other areas of their lives!

Sexual Power Players

In some cases, toxic bosses use their power to sexually intimidate those who work for them. *Sexual harassment* does not always come from a supervisor. As any number of people with war stories can attest, it can come from co-workers as well. However, when the boss is making suggestive remarks or directly or indirectly asking for sexual favors, the victim feels immense pressure and so resists drawing the line. After all, the boss could retaliate.

def•i•ni•tion

Sexual harassment, as defined by the U.S. Equal Employment Opportunity Commission, can consist of unwelcome sexual advances, requests for sexual favors, and other verbal or physical conduct of a sexual nature when submission to or rejection of this conduct explicitly or implicitly affects an individual's employment, unreasonably interferes with an individual's work performance, or creates an intimidating, hostile, or offensive work environment.

Although we might reflexively think of sexual harassment as something men do to women, this also need not be the case. The victim as well as the harasser may be a woman or a man. The victim does not have to be of the opposite sex. In fact, the victim does not have to be the person harassed but could be anyone affected by the offensive conduct. What sexual harassment really is about is less sex than power. Some toxic bosses use sexual harassment as one of many tools in their arsenal of abuse.

Sexual harassment is a form of sex discrimination that violates Title VII of the Civil Rights Act of 1964. If you need to take formal action, remember that for acts to qualify as sexual harassment, they have to be unwelcome. Do not make the mistake of "playing along" with your boss if you are offended by their behavior. In the long run, it will take away your legal leverage.

Do-It-Yourself Protection from Toxic Bosses

If you work for a medium-size or large organization, you probably have a formal avenue for making a complaint about a toxic boss. But before you go that route, consider dealing with your boss directly. If—but only if—you think you can handle this without giving in to anger, tears, or fears, try the following:

- **Arrange for a conversation in private.** A bully won't back down in front of an audience. An exception to this is if you feel physically or sexually threatened by your boss, in which case you must remain in view—if not in earshot—of others.

- **Specify the behavior that's unworkable and ask them to stop.** Be clear about what your boss is doing that bothers you. Explain how it negatively impacts your performance. Do not discuss your private emotions.

- **Help your boss come up with alternative behaviors.** If possible, come up with an example of acceptable behavior from his own repertoire. If your boss treats others better than he treats you, request that sort of treatment.

♦ **Don't play amateur psychologist.** Restrict your discussion to specific behaviors, not theories of what motivates the behaviors. Do not label or diagnose your boss.

♦ **Consider recruiting allies.** If your boss's abusive behavior extends to others, consider requesting a meeting with the boss as a group. It's less likely that a toxic boss can pull an "I don't know what you're talking about" routine if more than one person can verify events.

It is always difficult to confront, and confronting a superior is especially anxiety provoking. But many toxic people dislike direct confrontation as much as you do. You might find they back off and look for other targets if you become "too much trouble" to manipulate.

Enlisting Help

If you work in a situation where a human resources department is available, you should seriously consider using whatever formal grievance process is in place. These processes are meant to protect employees from retribution and to encourage them to come forward and report unacceptable behavior.

Good organizations know that bad bosses are bad not just for morale but for the entire organization. Bad bosses create a climate of fear, which is hardly a climate where innovation will thrive. They put people in a defensive rather than a productive mode. Moreover, they create stress, which can lead to illness (hence medical expenses and absenteeism).

Formal complaint processes vary, but they are generally detailed in employee handbooks or posted online at an employee portal. Read and understand the procedures carefully before you take action. Weigh the seriousness of what you are doing and proceed judiciously. Be prepared to offer as much documentation as possible to validate your claims. Stick to the facts and be as objective as you can. Understand that even if you are dealing with a truly toxic terror, there is still a chance they will survive the scrutiny you bring to bear and continue to be your boss when all is said and done.

Manhole Ahead _____

You might or might not be afforded confidentiality if you complain about your boss. If you fear retribution, consider complaining anonymously. Some companies have anonymous hotlines which employees are encouraged to call if they witness abusive or illegal behavior.

Toxic Subordinates

People who work for you have the potential to be just as toxic as those you work for. You might think this would not be as much of a problem, because you supposedly hold the power cards. But, in fact, one can easily be undermined by a toxic employee.

A toxic employee can harm you by failing to keep confidential matters confidential inside or outside of the workplace, by failing to display loyalty and appropriate workplace decorum. In addition, they might interact negatively with other employees. You may find they lack modesty, refuse to accept accountability, or refuse to act with any level of predictability. They may be quick to become defensive and aggressive when questioned.

Can't you just fire them? That's easier said than done in most cases. Toxic subordinates are often willing to portray themselves as the victims of abuse or discrimination if their tenure is threatened, making you look like the bad guy. To defend yourself …

- ◆ Keep careful records of their transgressions, including dates, times, and details.

- ◆ Put any and all reprimands and warnings in writing.

- ◆ Detail their shortcomings when it comes time for formal performance reviews. (They will have to sign off on these, and though this does not constitute a "confession" on their part, it is at least an acknowledgment that they are aware you see a problem.)

The best way to protect yourself against a toxic employee is, of course, not to hire them in the first place. If you are in a position to hire, be sure to verify all data on resumés and verify all references by contacting them personally.

Thanks to the Internet and e-mail, background checks are easier now than they've ever been. *You* are the one who is at fault if it turns out you hired someone who padded a resumé or who lied outright about prior experience or academic degrees. Don't be so snowed by an impressive interview with a charismatic personality that you take a potential hire at their word. Many toxic people have a winning way about them—until they are in the door.

Remember, it is always harder to fire someone than it is to hire them!

Toxic Organizations

Defending yourself against toxic co-workers, bosses, and subordinates is easier in some organizations than in others. If the *organizational culture* itself is toxic, you have a difficult path ahead.

def•i•ni•tion

Organizational culture is the values and norms shared by people and groups in an organization, the ways employees interact with each other and with stakeholders outside the organization. They guide standards of behavior and ideas about what is and is not acceptable.

Sadly, some organizations are themselves devoid of conscience. Even though some individuals may display exemplary ethics, the culture as a whole is skewed to reward only success—at any cost. In such organizations, there is tacit agreement to look the other way when wrongdoers misbehave so long as they are contributing to profits or to the overall celebrity of the institution. In such places, a bullying boss can easily be confused with someone who has "great leadership skills," and opportunistic employees and self-serving newcomers can be hailed as "go-getters."

Mere survival can be difficult in such a situation. But if there are financial or career-driven reasons why you must stay, know that you probably cannot swim against the tide. The best you can do is to adhere to your own standards within the greater context, and engage in self-care that will keep your stress level manageable.

To the latter end, be sure to get enough sleep, exercise regularly, and avoid excessive "self-medication" in the form of alcohol, caffeine, or high-sugar, high-fat comfort foods. In addition, don't spend more time than necessary on the job. Be sure to fill your outside-of-work life with rewarding activities. Wherever you can, surround yourself with the kind of loving, supportive people whose positive influence can counterbalance workplace toxins.

If You Have to Quit

Sometimes a workplace situation becomes too toxic to bear. If so, you might come to the conclusion that you have no choice—for the sake of your health and your sanity—but to leave.

If particular individuals are the problem (rather than the culture as a whole), and if your organization has transfer opportunities, consider applying for one of them. In this way you can remove yourself from the proximity of the person who is plaguing you without sacrificing your seniority, benefits, and the like. Check any job-postings within your company that list opportunities at other sites.

As a last resort, you may find that you have to leave the organization entirely. If so, try to leave on your own terms. Take the time to prepare and execute a game plan:

- Prepare an up-to-date resumé with a list of all your achievements. (Don't be afraid to toot your own horn; if you don't, no one else will!)

- Determine who at your current job can be counted on to provide you with a good reference.

- Consider a lateral move. (It might be more important to find a new position at your current level than to worry about moving up now—that can come later.)

- Look while you're still employed. (Be discreet, but it is always easier to find a job while you have a job.)

- Do a benefits inventory. (Understand clearly what's due to you when you go, including accrued retirement benefits, continued health-care coverage, and vacation pay.)

Tried and True Tactics

"I knew I could not count on my abusive boss to furnish me with a good reference. He was angry I was leaving because he would no longer have me to kick around. Instead, I lined up references from others with whom I had worked closely in team situations. I also knew I could count on references from my clients."—Ed, 34, tax accountant

When you leave you may be asked to attend an exit interview, during which you will be asked about your reasons for going. Although it's tempting to use this as an opportunity to dump your accrued anger, you are better off citing career-related goals or mentioning unspecified personal reasons. You never know when you will run into those people again—particularly if you are remaining in the same industry or a similar line of work. It's best not to burn bridges.

The Least You Need to Know

- Some people who behave acceptably outside the workplace are toxic within it. For them, it's a convenient place to dump frustrations from other areas of their lives.

- Toxic co-workers often operate by trying to undermine reputations. The best defense is to maintain a reputation so strong that it is virtually impossible to tarnish.

- Toxic bosses bully, demean, and harass because they *can*, so *do* something. If you don't feel comfortable confronting them, use your organization's formal grievance process.

- Toxic subordinates may cry foul if reprimanded and fight hard to keep jobs they don't deserve, so screen applicants carefully—it's easier not to hire than it is to fire.

- If you must quit, do so on your own terms. Try not to leave in a huff. Take the time to prepare a resumé and conduct a job search while you are still employed, because this makes you a more attractive job candidate.

18

Defending Yourself in Abusive Relationships

In This Chapter

- ◆ Saving yourself from toxic partners
- ◆ Coping with the pain of toxic parents
- ◆ Dealing with toxic siblings
- ◆ Responding when a friendship turns toxic

Our world can become a nightmare when our closest personal relationships render us victims of abuse. People who should be our sources of strength sap our energy, our joy, and our courage. Toxic partners, parents, siblings, and friends can keep us locked in a pattern of resentment, guilt, confusion, and hopelessness.

Sometimes it is possible to redefine the terms of these toxic relationships, but not always. Sometimes we have to end the relationship, let go, and move on. This chapter examines both scenarios.

The Toxic Partner

Finding a partner with whom to share our life and build a future, who will remain loyally by our side in good times and bad, is a dream most of us nurture from adolescence. Yet the sad truth is that we sometimes wind up with a partner who impoverishes our life rather than enriches it. At such times we need to rally our self-preservation instincts, but toxic partners are so good at making us lose sight of our true selves and our deepest needs that breaking free can often seem almost impossible.

Finding a Victim

You might think it would be difficult for toxic individuals to find someone with whom to be in a long-term relationship, yet many of them seem to be very successful in finding a "willing" victim. It's as if toxic people have a kind of radar that helps them zero in on potential partners who are predisposed to being abused—and when they find them, they are unashamed and unafraid to thoroughly manipulate them.

Toxic partners, consciously or unconsciously, know what they're looking for. They are searching for mates who do not think highly of themselves and tend to be dependent on others to tell them who they are and what to do. Those who wind up in toxic relationships are often people who have been mistreated or neglected by parents or grew up in an unstable family situation. No matter how desirable they are, they feel undesirable. No matter how intelligent they are, they feel incompetent. No matter how successful they are, they feel like frauds.

Toxic people know just how to exploit such self-doubts. In the context of their relationships, they perpetuate certain myths:

♦ "I am the only one who understands the real you."

♦ "I will 'cover' for you."

♦ "No one else will have you."

♦ "You're lucky to have me."

The ideal victim subscribes to these, either because no one else has ever told them differently, or because they have been unable to let themselves take in positive messages about their own capabilities.

But even someone who sees themselves as inadequate or undeserving of a healthy relationship usually has moments of clarity. These moments generally occur when they are validated by some person or event outside their toxic relationship—being praised by outsiders for a particular trait or achievement, for example. At such times, they may suspect that their partner has become the source of their distress rather than their savior.

When this occurs, they may entertain the thought of breaking away. Why don't they? Because toxic partners are adept at keeping their victims hooked.

Keeping the Victim Victimized

One secret to keeping a victim victimized is to offer occasional rewards. Toxic partners work their black magic by knowing when to stop behaving abusively for a little while. If you've ever gambled money in a slot machine, or watched anyone do so, you'll understand this principle, which is known as *intermittent positive reinforcement.*

As much as gamblers know in their hearts that the odds are stacked against them, they will often keep feeding money into a slot machine because occasionally slot machines pay off. Ironically, the longer a slot machine doesn't pay off, the more they are convinced that if they just keep on doing what they're doing, the tide will turn.

def•i•ni•tion

Intermittent positive reinforcement is a principle of behavioral psychology. It refers to eliciting certain desired behaviors by offering rewards at unpredictable and varied intervals.

If you spent your time in a casino where slot machines never, ever paid off, you would—sooner or later—stop wasting your money and your time (in the same way a mouse would stop making its way through a maze where there was never a bit of cheese waiting at the end). The promise that something may be different this time keeps you motivated.

Likewise, the victim of a toxic partner will keep trying to please an abuser if they occasionally receive small nuggets of affection and affirmation. A smile, a supposedly loving touch, a positive comment can mean so much to someone who is used to getting so little—it's enough to keep them virtually addicted to their mate.

Another way to keep a victim victimized is through the tantalizing promise that "I will change." When toxic partners feel they are truly in jeopardy of losing their victim, they may acknowledge that their mate has been mistreated and swear that they will alter their behavior. They may even take some tentative, preliminary steps in this direction, agreeing to investigate counseling options or seek spiritual guidance of some sort. Often the promise alone is enough to get a victim to abandon any plans of breaking the relationship off. The notion that "this time things will be different" is extremely appealing to a victim, especially one who is not yet convinced that they have the strength and the practical resources to make a new start.

Emotional Abusers

If you are the victim of an emotional abuser, you may find it especially hard to break away because you are not certain that the treatment you have been receiving from your partner is not normal. You may have convinced yourself that true love never runs smoothly and no one is perfect, so your relationship is pretty much the best you can expect. Yet a nagging voice inside is probably saying something else if you are willing to listen to it.

You are in a toxic, emotionally abusive partnership when your mate …

- Consistently blames you for their negative feelings.

- Frequently indicates they are disappointed in you.

- Deliberately misinterprets your words or intentions.

- Indicates there is something "wrong" with you.

- Is extremely secretive and maintains you have no right to know their business.

- Disagrees with you no matter what you say.

- Makes you feel as though you don't have the right to say no to them.

- Repeatedly says or implies that you could not survive without them.

- Often embarrasses you in front of others.

- Forbids you to have friends outside the relationship.

- Maintains that everything wrong in their life is your fault.

- Is often sarcastic toward you and ridicules you.

- Insists on making all the decisions in the relationship.

- Limits your access to money or other shared resources (the car, the phone, and so on).

- Steals from you or runs up debts for you to handle.

- Swings between being hurtful (most of the time) to being extremely loving for a short while.

Manhole Ahead

If you fear your partner's reaction to your reading this list, you should seriously consider whether you are in a toxic relationship.

Sure, everyone acts like a jerk sometimes, and a partner can be somewhat control-ling, passive-aggressive, or self-involved without being abusive overall. If the positive exchanges in your relationship significantly outweigh the negative interactions, then, although you may have some rough patches to work out, your relationship is not toxic.

To confirm that it *is* toxic, it's also important to examine your own actions and reac-tions. Do you frequently find yourself asking your partner for permission? Do you censor yourself rather than discuss issues that might make them mad? Do you feel as though you are walking on eggshells so as not to set them off? Do you ever give in to sexual demands just to keep the peace? Do you have an uneasy, sinking feeling when they're around? If so, you must look at the truth no matter how hard that can be. Only when you acknowledge your situation can you begin to do something about it.

Borderline Partners

It's worth mentioning here a particular type of abusive partner whose *modus operandi* is not as overtly sadistic, but who is nonetheless decidedly toxic. This is the sort of per-son known in psychological lingo as a *borderline*.

def•i•ni•tion

The term **borderline** was long used as a diagnostic catchall category for people who were more disturbed than the average neurotic but not as divorced from reality as psychotics. It has come to refer to those who have unstable interpersonal relationships, impulsivity, severe mood shifts, a lack of clear identity, feelings of emptiness, and extreme fears of abandonment.

If you are in a relationship with a borderline, you may be unfamiliar with this term—but you are more than familiar with a particular pattern of behavior that can take a profound emotional toll. Borderline types are like garden-variety narcissists on steroids. Their core sense of themselves is so vacant that they are frantic to find an identity by affiliating with someone else—often a romantic partner. They can cling to this partner with the tenacity of a barnacle. In fact they can practically love someone to death—until, that is, they swing in the other direction.

Borderlines are notorious for "splitting" their perceptions of people with whom they are close. One day they will view you as a white-hatted hero—their idol and savior—the next day you may be a black-hatted villain, the source of all their pain. But if you try pulling away from a borderline who suddenly hates you, they will panic and cling to you even tighter.

Borderlines are toxic partners because they are melodramatic, unpredictable, and exhausting. Their so-called love is smothering, and when they reject you, they often verbalize and act it out in the cruelest terms. There is no gray area, no room for subtlety. They are impossible to reason with most of the time because their powerful emotions hold sway over their logic. One never knows where one stands with a borderline—only that anything can happen, and usually does.

Borderlines are usually the children of borderlines, though it's not clear whether their continuation of the family pathology is the result of genetics or upbringing or both. Their family backgrounds often include psychological or physical abuse or alcoholism, as well as depression and other psychological disorders. This means that if you get involved with a borderline on a long-term basis, you might find yourself exposed to an entire clan of dysfunctional, toxic in-laws.

Yet many people get involved with borderlines before they understand that there is a flip side to the coin. Borderlines can be charming when they're "on," and it's easy to let one into your life. But it's much more difficult to get one out of your life, and you may be reluctant or even afraid to do so, because they seem so desolate or self-destructive when you threaten to sever your relationship.

Physical Abusers

Physical abuse is any use of physical force that causes injury or puts another person at risk of being injured. Physical abuse can include pushing, pinching, shaking, and holding with the attempt to restrain. It also includes extremely violent behaviors such as slapping, beating, punching, choking, and assault with a weapon. Physical abuse does not happen when someone "loses control," but rather when someone resorts to the most heinous method of controlling another person.

When someone talks of *domestic violence,* they are often referring to physical abuse of a spouse or intimate partner. Although victims of domestic violence are five to eight times more likely to be women than men, some men are physically abused by their wives or girlfriends. Both genders may be reluctant to tell others outside of the relationship the painful truth about what is happening behind closed doors. They may be frightened by what their partner may do if they tell, but the victim is also often ashamed and believes on some level that they have brought this horrible, toxic behavior on themselves.

Toxic abusers are empowered when they successfully intimidate their partners into colluding in this way. When a victim believes the violence in the relationship is their fault, that victim will actually help hide what is happening rather than take steps to put an end to it. The cycle may end, but it often takes an unfortunate situation. In some cases the violence becomes so intense that it is reported by a third party. In some cases the victim requires medical attention and thereby draws the attention of those in a position to offer counsel.

There are several reasons—not justifications, but reasons—why someone would physically harm their intimate partner. Perpetrators of domestic violence have often been victims of child abuse in their own families of origin, or they may have witnessed one of their parents abusing another. They may have psychological problems, chemical imbalances, or substance abuse problems. But if you are the victim, what your abuser's issues are should not be your immediate or your primary concern. Your immediate concern is your safety. Extricating yourself from a dangerous situation must take priority. *Do not make excuses for your assailant.*

DP Disarmer _____

Physical assault is a crime, regardless of whether it occurs inside a family. The police are there to protect you, so call 911 if you require immediate intervention. If you want to talk to someone, call the National Domestic Violence Hotline at 1-800-799-7233 (1-800-799-SAFE).

Can Toxic Partners Change?

It is within the realm of possibility that a toxic partner will change, just as anyone—at least in theory—might change. But if you are wondering whether an abusive partner will spontaneously, voluntarily change, the answer is no. *You must change your response to them and refuse to tolerate their abusiveness any longer.*

Breaking out of the dynamics that keep one bound to a toxic mate requires a willingness to …

- ◆ Take a cold, hard look at the reality of your situation.
- ◆ Stop constructing a facade of "normalcy" for friends and family.
- ◆ Seek the support of trusted confidantes.
- ◆ Seek professional help when needed.

Above all, it requires that you stop playing the victim. Realizing that you deserve more out of an intimate relationship is essential. Believing in yourself is the antidote to relationship toxicity.

Toxic Mothers and Fathers

No parent on Earth is mistake-free. But toxic parents can emotionally cripple their children. There are several types of toxic parents, but what they all have in common is that they end up committing the crime of damaging their children's sense of self-worth. Toxic styles of parenting include:

- Authoritarian
- Overprotective
- Exploitative
- Neglectful
- Rejecting
- Borderline
- Physically abusive

Children need protection and guidance, but authoritarian parents take limit-setting too far for too long. They are so strict that they prevent their children from developing sound judgment on their own. Often when a grown child has a chance to break free of parental oversight, they make extremely poor choices and rebel by abusing drugs or alcohol or by acting out sexually.

Unlike authoritarian parents, overprotective parents do not dictate outright. They cripple their offspring by disguising a pathological need to control as protection or "help." In doing everything for their children well past the time when assistance is legitimately required, they instill the belief that their children are incapable of going it alone. Their children feel powerless to master their own lives. Healthy separation and individualism become impossible—the grown children are forever dependent.

Exploitative parents are focused only on their needs. They view their children as a means of solving their problems. They wish to reverse roles with their children and to remain forever dependent on their sons and daughters. Any show of independence on their children's part is viewed as a betrayal.

Neglectful parents pay scant attention to their children at all. Sometimes these parents may view themselves as "permissive" or "free thinking," but in reality they're irresponsible and aren't thinking of their children at all. They're too wrapped up in their own lives to do any parenting. The result is often a deep sense of depression in their offspring. The children feel that if their parents don't care about them, there must be something unworthy about them.

Nothing a child can ever do is good enough for rejecting parents. They are constant critics, always citing what their child could have been done better. Often they will negatively compare their children to others—including perhaps a favored sibling.

Borderline parents vacillate between being overly attached to and overprotective of their children to rejecting and devaluing them. They are melodramatic and erratic, yet oblivious as to how their mood swings impact their family.

Physically abusive parents use physical injury or the threat of physical injury to intimidate and control their children. They often blame their children for eliciting their own deep-seated rage.

All these parenting styles can cause damage that takes years to unravel. It is no simple feat to move beyond these toxic relationship patterns and cope with the pain of toxic parenting, because children spend such a long time directly under their parents' influence. But it can be done if a grown child is determined to break the chain of toxicity.

Manhole Ahead _____

Individuals who fail to recognize toxic behavior in their parents are likely to repeat such patterns with their own children. This stems not from evil intent but from simply not knowing any other way. Toxicity will almost certainly be passed from one generation to another until someone challenges and breaks out of the family mold.

Should Toxic Parents Be Confronted?

If you have a toxic parent, you may reach a point where you feel a need to confront them. If you do, be aware that you are doing it for yourself, not for them. Be prepared for the fact that you're not very likely to substantially change your parent's attitude or behavior. The confrontation may, however, serve as a psychological dividing line between a time when you allowed your parent's nature to dominate your life and a new era when you decided to break free.

Toxic parents tend to be extremely insensitive to the pain they have caused, so it's a good idea to anticipate the reactions they may have if you do confront them. Do not let these reactions deter you from your goal of ending a toxic cycle. Say what you need to say even if they claim:

- "What you're talking about never happened."
- "It was your fault I acted that way."
- "You are an ingrate—I did everything for you."
- "I did my best—what more could I do?"
- "Stop talking to me like this—you're killing me."

Your toxic parent may have willed themselves to forget or deny that certain events happened. They may also blame you somehow in an attempt to induce extreme, irrational guilt, but a parent's toxic behavior should never be blamed on a child—parents who behave appropriately know how to respond rationally even to a child who is being provocative. And although toxic parents often play the guilt card when confronted, that is an attempt to deflect attention from their own wrongdoings.

If you do not feel you could tolerate these kinds of responses from your parent, or feel that you would be putting yourself at risk by confrontation, know that it is possible to heal without a confrontation. Becoming aware of your situation has already been a significant first step. You might find the support you need by confiding in others whom you trust and embarking on a quest for personal growth that will put you in touch with the parts of your real self your toxic parents caused you to subvert for so long.

Tried and True Tactics

"I felt that confronting my toxic father would not actually result in his listening to me and that it would not be worth the emotional toll it would take. Instead, I put all my thoughts and feelings down in a very long letter. I never sent the letter—I had never planned to—but it helped me put things in perspective and make sense of my personal history. After that I felt better equipped to move on."—Arnie, 32

The Toxic Sibling

How is it, you may wonder, that one sibling of several would develop a toxic personality? There's no clear answer, yet both nature and nurture can play a role.

Siblings share some genetic traits, but not others. And even people raised by the same mothers and fathers spend their childhoods in different environments. Parents can change as time passes, as can the dynamics of their relationship, not to mention their financial and social standing. Further, parents may treat one sibling quite differently from another. Sometimes the toxic sibling is assigned a negative role (see Chapter 14) in the family from the start, such as the "identified patient" or the "black sheep."

Sometimes everyone in the family will acknowledge that a toxic sibling is acting in a destructive manner. But sometimes a sibling might behave toxically only around or toward you. If that is the case, the underlying motivation for the toxic behavior is very likely envy.

Envy, remember, is a prime motivator of toxic people. You probably have or represent something that your sibling covets deeply. They may disparage you because of this, or tell lies about you. They might try to steal or undermine the status they think you have, or try to exploit you in some material way.

Curtailing your interactions with a toxic sibling may be the only way to prevent yourself from being the target of negativity and exploitation, but unless everyone in your family feels the same way about your sibling, there will be occasions when you'll be expected to interact with them and behave as if everything's fine. This can be tough, but so can refusing to do so—which may mean upsetting the entire family.

If you choose to maintain a relationship with a toxic sibling, you can insulate yourself by …

- ◆ Making certain there are other people around to serve as buffers.

- ◆ Spending only a limited amount of time in their company.

- ◆ Being careful not to divulge too much personal information (and requesting that other family members do not share information about you).

Whether you can tolerate limited contact or feel you need to cut off contact altogether, try not to get drawn into conflicts with other family members about your relationship with your sibling. You'll probably never be able to convince parents or other siblings that a family member is a danger to you if that person acts differently toward them; it may even lead them to question your judgment. You must do what you believe in your heart is in your best interest.

When a Friendship Turns Toxic

All of us have difficult friends we may choose to keep in our lives in some capacity, but toxic friends are by no means friends. The entire premise of friendship is invalidated when one person tries to defame, undermine, or exploit the other.

If you have a friend who is toxic to you, the relationship probably didn't begin that way. At some point you liked this person, and you treated each other well. But over time, a friend who seemed to have your best interests at heart may, usually due to envy and resentment, begin to act in an ill-spirited way toward you.

To complicate matters, a toxic friend who is consumed with feelings of being less adequate than you might begin to act out self-destructively. Perhaps you will notice them drinking too much or entering into reckless romances or spending money on things they can ill afford. When that is the case, our instinct as a friend may often compel us to help them. This rarely works, however, if they see *us* as the source of *their* problem.

Don't be surprised if your efforts to assist a toxic friend result in their behaving even more outrageously toward you. There may come a time when you simply have no choice but to sever the relationship. This can be painful, but it's not as painful as letting yourself be harmed. There is a line between loyalty and foolishness, and you must be careful not to cross it.

The Least You Need to Know

♦ Despite a toxic partner's periodic promises to change, what must actually change is your willingness to be their victim. Stop presenting a facade of normalcy to the outside world and seek help and support.

♦ If you choose to confront a toxic parent, be prepared for them to deny their culpability. They are heavily invested in believing that their behavior has been for your own good, but you must recognize this as a myth and persist in recreating your life.

♦ Toxic siblings could be toxic only to you (often due to envy) and behave differently toward other family members. In such cases it's unlikely you will change anyone else's estimation of your sibling, so just limit your contact and protect yourself.

♦ If a friendship turns toxic, you may feel compelled to "save" your friend and restore your relationship—but if they rebuff your efforts, you must move on with your life.

Chapter 19

Reacting to Dangerous Strangers

In This Chapter

- ◆ Protecting yourself from con artists
- ◆ Recognizing pick-up artists
- ◆ Evading online and telephone menaces
- ◆ Steering clear of the litigious
- ◆ Discovering whether there's hope and help for sociopaths

Call them psychopaths, sociopaths, or the personality-disordered. All these terms refer to the same thing: toxic people who are devious, thoughtless, and remorseless and have a callous disregard for their fellow human beings.

Even if you're lucky enough to be free of such types in your workplace and your personal life, we all know that toxic sociopaths are still out there, willing to prey on innocent strangers. Psychologists estimate that as many as one in four people manifest sociopathic characteristics. Who are they and how can we prevent ourselves from being taken in by them? That is the essence of this chapter.

The Con Artist

If you've ever seen movies such as *The Sting*, *The Rainmaker*, or *The Producers*, you already know something about how con artists work. They earn the *con*fidence of others before executing a scheme that will result in financial gain. Earning the trust of a potential victim (known as a "mark" in con artist lingo) is the first essential step in their plan. The successful con artist is extraordinarily skilled at this—which is something of a paradox, because deep down they are unable to relate to other people as anything other than objects to be exploited.

A neural-imaging study with a group of sociopathic criminals suggested that these subjects actually had a deficit in the brain circuitry of the area that allows us to empathize with the distress of others. Yet despite their cold-heartedness (or cold-brainedness), con artists can appear to be the warmest folks on Earth. They have an uncanny ability to surmise what others are thinking and pretend to be thinking similar thoughts and feeling similar emotions. They can, in effect, write a script and act it out to perfection—all the while being completely and utterly disingenuous.

 Manhole Ahead _____

Some toxic types, unable to manifest true empathy, practice "faking it" by reading self-help books and watching therapy-oriented TV shows. Be cautious with people who talk the talk of popular psychology but do not seem to be able to walk the walk of compassion.

Con artists are also good at intuiting other people's motives, especially any that have to do with greed or fear (two impulses to which we all succumb on occasion). When they sense that the person they've targeted for a con wants something very badly, they say what that person wants to hear: *You can have it!*

Finally, con artists tend to be charming and interesting in out-of-the-ordinary ways. They are somehow more intense than the average person, often sexy, complex, dynamic, and insightful. Because they seem like such fascinating companions, con artists have an especially easy time preying on victims who are lonely or isolated (such as the aged or the bereaved). Lonely individuals are so delighted to have a "friend" at long last that they lose any sense of objectivity where that friend is concerned.

The con artist wants some sort of material gain, of course. But they also want to win at a game they have constructed. Con artists have successfully convinced people to invest in miracle cures for cancer, in fake alternatives to gasoline, and in bogus oil and gas exploration companies. In fact, the elaborate constructions of some con artists have become legendary—and show just how inventive and intelligent some sociopaths can be:

♦ Frank Abagnale (whose escapades were documented in the movie *Catch Me If You Can*) masqueraded as an airline pilot, doctor, and professor, passing bad checks on multiple continents to sustain his lifestyle.

♦ Tino De Angelis, a commodities trader, sold rights to $175 million in soybean oil stored in tanks, which was actually a thin layer of oil floating on water.

♦ Robert Hendy-Freegard, a British bartender and car salesman, posed as a British intelligence agent, kidnapped people after convincing them they were being hunted by terrorists, and then conned them out of their hard-earned life savings.

♦ Charles Ponzi, a poor immigrant to America, concocted a vast *pyramid scheme* involving currency-trading with postal coupons, and became so closely identified with these types of ruses that they are now sometimes referred to as *Ponzi schemes*.

def•i•ni•tion

A **pyramid** or **Ponzi scheme** is a fraudulent investment operation that involves paying abnormally high returns to investors out of the money paid in by subsequent investors, rather than from net revenues generated by any real business.

If so many people of all classes and cultures could be taken in, what is your best defense against the con artist? Common sense, for one thing. If something seems too good to be true, it is. Don't let yourself be charmed into parting with your money. Ask yourself: *If this is such a good deal, why is this stranger willing to include me?*

These days it is easier than ever before to research an investment or to check someone's credentials. Be diligent. Be thorough. Take your time. Do not be pressured into believing that if you do not *act now* the opportunity will disappear. If someone is applying time pressure, that's a tip-off that something is not as it should be.

Also keep in mind that some con artists prey not on greed but on sympathy. They may ask you to help them out of a jam, assuring you that you will soon be reimbursed and that you will have earned their eternal gratitude. Ask yourself: if they are so personable and outgoing, why don't they have other friends who are willing to assist them in their time of need?

Finally, do not give in to flattery. Do not rely on a stranger to remind you about your admirable qualities. And do not feel as though you must prove your goodness to this stranger. If you feel the need to show your own compassion, do so by volunteering in your community or working with a reputable philanthropic organization.

The Pick-Up Artist

Toxic strangers can also be sexual predators. Under the guise of seeking to strike up a potential romantic relationship, their game is to see how quickly they can initiate sexual intimacy. Needless to say, they don't stick around *at all* after they have scored.

If a pick-up artist has targeted you, they will do everything they can to make you feel that they have singled you out as someone special. But rest assured that what they do to woo you has nothing to do with who you are as a person. Similar to a con artist, a pick-up artist sees others as objects only.

How can you spot a toxic and predatory pick-up artist? Watch for the following:

- They eyeball the crowd looking for a prospect, and if they are turned away by one, they start over with another within moments. To them targets are interchangeable.

- They have an opening line that seems memorized and well rehearsed (albeit clever and seductive).

- They paint a very intriguing biography of themselves, but without too many details.

- If they approach a target who is in a group, they quickly become the group's center of attention.

- After a while, they separate their target from the group, literally moving in with body language, proprietary touching, and flattery.

- They quickly suggest going off to a quiet place (most often their place, so they will be in greater control) and persistently try to talk their target out of any reluctance or reservations.

DP Disarmer

Toxic pick-up artists want instant gratification. If you're uncertain as to whether someone has anything but a one-night encounter in mind, ask for their phone number and tell them *you'll* call. See if they stick around or head straight for the hills.

You might be thinking that this kind of player is easy to spot, but people fall for such maneuvers every day. Partly it's because such pick-up artists have perfected a kind of magnetic charisma. These artists *are* confident, entertaining, and easy to talk to, even if their target knows on some level they are being "played."

But the target is also looking for outside affirmation. The con artist is selling something we all want to believe: that we are attractive, interesting, and desirable. We only need the slightest encouragement to buy that! Again, we can see how one of the best defenses against a toxic person is to be strong in our belief of who we are and what we have to offer.

The Online Menace

Toxic people and the tricks they perpetrate are as old as civilization, but lately con artists have gone high-tech, using the Internet to defraud innocent victims in a variety of clever ways. What makes the Internet such a perfect vehicle for the exploitative is that anyone can pretend to be anyone or anything online. A person trying to scam you can present themselves to you as whatever you want them to be—a lonely soul-seeking love, a mentor offering a surefire business opportunity, a physician offering to cure what ails you.

Online menaces are especially adept at trolling cyberspace for people who are lonely and need a friend or confidante. But almost anyone can be taken in. Because toxic people are only a click away, it's good practice to always be cautious when communicating with a stranger on the Internet.

Has a newfound "love" asked you to wire them money for an emergency? Ask yourself how sincere any declarations of love can be if they are from someone you've never met. And why can no one else help them out of their jam?

Has a cyberfriend offered you an incredible deal on a luxury car? See what happens when you insist on paying with a credit card rather than sending it to an online "escrow service."

Has someone offered to cut you in on an incredible business opportunity? Insist on seeing a hard copy of a prospectus and verifying the company's credentials with your accountant or attorney.

Has a very persuasive online pal clued you in on a day-trading service or other investment company that offers huge overnight returns? Check out the promoter with state and federal securities and commodities regulators.

Perhaps most important of all, no matter how well you seem to be getting along with someone you encounter in cyberspace, no matter how much you seem to have in common and no matter what they promise you in return, *never* give an online contact sensitive personal information such as your Social Security number or credit card or bank account numbers. This could easily result in identity theft.

Identity theft occurs when someone uses your personal information without your permission to make purchases or to commit fraud or other crimes. Identity theft has become so widespread and has gotten so much media attention that you might feel you are way too smart to be convinced to offer your information to anyone. But remember how persuasive toxic sociopaths can be. I have heard of very savvy people who have, for example, given their children's Social Security numbers to strangers who have an alleged lead on a generous college scholarship. These victims were thinking of their kids' futures; their clever victimizer hit them in their vulnerable spot.

Tried and True Tactics

"Although I trust myself not to be taken in by an online scam, I am concerned that others I know might not be so vigilant. So even if a friend forwards something to me that looks suspicious, I contact them to make sure it was they who sent it and, if they did, that they checked it out."—Fran, 44

To make certain you do not fall prey to identity theft, protect all your personal information and also monitor your financial accounts routinely for suspicious activity. If you think you have been the victim of identity theft:

- Contact the fraud department of any one of the three major credit consumer reporting companies (Equifax, Experian, or TransUnion).

- Close the accounts that you know or believe have been compromised or tampered with.

- File a report with the police in the community where the theft took place (you can give this to creditors who may require proof of the crime).

- File your complaint with the Federal Trade Commission (FTC), which maintains a database of these cases.

Having someone masquerade as you is more than an inconvenience. It can cost you money and take you a tremendous amount of time to unravel. Moreover, being impersonated by a toxic individual leaves one feeling personally defiled.

The Telephone Menace

Toxic people can also use the telephone to take advantage of strangers. Under the guise of calling with a "free vacation" you have won, refunding money to which you are entitled, or even reaching a wrong number, they can insinuate a personal level of conversation and slowly begin to cultivate your trust. Often it takes a number of calls over time to establish a relationship that can be the basis for a scam, but if you happen to be lonely enough to talk to a stranger repeatedly, you could be ripe for the picking.

There are many technological defenses against toxic telephone menaces. One is to screen calls via an answering machine. Another is to sign up with your phone company for a caller ID feature that lets you know who is calling and allows you discretion as to whether to pick up or not.

It's also a good idea to sign up at the National Do Not Call Registry (www.donotcall. gov), which allows you to decline to receive telemarketing calls on your home and mobile phones. After your name has been on the list for 31 days, you can file a complaint against any telemarketer who persists in calling—and you should.

DP Disarmer _____

Telephone menaces can arrange for their numbers not to show up on caller ID by initiating a "block" feature. If you see a blocked call, let your answering machine get it. If the caller hangs up, assume they had nothing to say. That's one menace you're rid of.

But as always, the best defense against toxic people lies within you. Don't let yourself be an easy mark for a telephone predator. If you need social contact (as we all do!), reach out and call a friend. If you can't think of anyone to call, that's a sign that you need to expand your social circle. Consider volunteering in your community, as this is often a wonderful start.

So Sue Me: The Litigious Personality

Some toxic people use—or rather abuse—the legal system to prey on others. In some cases they actually set in motion scenarios that result in getting "injured" so that they can claim the need for medical expenses, pain and suffering, and lost time at work. One such fake injury scenario is to abruptly stop one's car in fast-moving traffic so that the car behind has no choice but to run into the lawsuit-happy occupant ahead. Another is to "slip" on someone's property—perhaps a front walk that has a crack or that has not been completely cleared after a snowstorm—and claim harm from the fall.

But for the most part what we call litigious personalities are not pulling off a pre-meditated scam *per se*. Rather, they are perennial opportunists—always on the lookout for a situation where they can contend that they have been harmed, defamed, or discriminated against. Criticize them, even in passing, and they will claim *slander* or *libel*. Refuse to hire or to promote them, or try to terminate their employment—even for good cause—and they will claim they are the victims of some form of bias. Officiate at an activity where they or someone in their family sustains bodily harm, no matter how minor or how accidentally caused, and they will contend you have been negligent.

Litigious personalities sue, or threaten to sue, practically everyone. All are considered fair game, including their neighbors, their employers, their doctors, their dentists, their kids' teachers and coaches, and sometimes even their own lawyers (they claim *malfeasance* if their attorneys are unsuccessful at pressing their trumped-up claims). Their complaints, apart from costing their target a great deal of money, can cause needless emotional distress as well. Enduring a lawsuit, regardless of how it comes out (even if it's ultimately thrown out of court because it lacks merit) is a nightmare of paperwork, grueling depositions, and lost time.

To make matters worse, there's always the chance that a litigious personality might win their case. You never know what a jury will do, especially because toxically charismatic types often make very compelling and believable witnesses.

To protect yourself from a ruinous judgment in favor of a litigious personality, it's a good idea to carry what is known as *personal umbrella insurance*. The cost is generally very reasonable (a few hundred dollars a year) and if you have any assets at all, it's a worthwhile precaution.

def•i•ni•tion

Slander is a spoken statement that is false and that maliciously damages someone's reputation. **Libel** is a published statement that does likewise. **Malfeasance** refers to wrong or illegal conduct, particularly within the legal profession, politics, or civil service.

Personal umbrella insurance provides added liability protection above and beyond the limits on homeowners, auto, and watercraft personal insurance policies. Depending on the insurance company, one can add an additional 1 to 5 million dollars in protection that "kicks in" when liability on other policies has been exhausted.

Of course, avoiding a lawsuit is best. So be attuned to these signs of litigious personalities:

♦ They're always complaining that things are "dangerous" or "unfair."

♦ They seem to be constantly scanning their surroundings for potential threats. (*"Hey, is that diving board of yours up to code? Hey, what's the expiration date on those hamburgers?"*)

♦ They never take personal responsibility for any ill that befalls them—everything is always someone else's fault.

Perhaps your biggest tip-off to a litigious personality is their history. Steer clear of anyone whom you know has brought a frivolous lawsuit in the past. Where toxic people are concerned, history repeats itself.

Can Society Undo Sociopathy?

When it comes to the question of whether toxic sociopathy can ever be healed, it's best to consider such people in two categories. Successful sociopaths are the Teflon of toxicity. They keep doing what they're doing and, even if they come close to being found out or actually are found out by a few, nothing seems to stick to them. They move on, fancy-free, toward the next target they will exploit. Unsuccessful sociopaths, on the other hand, do get found out, and ultimately have to deal with the consequences of their actions in some fashion. If they are to alter their behavior, one thing is certain: it will not be a quick fix.

Anyone who watches the news is periodically subjected to instant and profuse public confessions and apologies from celebrities and politicians who are caught doing scandalous, sociopathic behavior. But skepticism is the right response here. These dramatic "true confessions"—often having the ring of a script written by a committee of spin doctors—are more a sign of the ability to tie in to the news cycle and to appease fans and constituents than as signs of sincere remorse or of the inner determination necessary to affect change.

Within the criminal justice system, however, there are those who are working on developing new methods for rehabilitating sociopathic personalities. And because it has been discovered that the neural circuits that generate the capacity for empathy and for impulse control are among the last parts of the brain to mature, some are especially hopeful that certain programs might be effective in "turning on these switches," especially in the younger than age 25 end of the population.

Such methods include:

- **Repayment.** In restorative justice programs, mediators arrange for some way that a criminal can repay or repair a particular harm that was done. This might involve making direct payments to a victim, but it also usually has an emotional component, such as hearing about the crime from a victim's point of view.

- **Courses.** Taking courses in social and emotional learning can teach basic interpersonal skills (managing anger and conflict) and promote the type of self-understanding that can generate understanding of others.

- **Multi-systemic therapy.** Rather than conducting formal therapy sessions, a counselor accompanies an offender in real life (school life, work life, social life) and attempts therapeutic intervention. The counselor's job is to help their charges maintain a healthy network of nurturing connections and positive role models.

DP Disarmer

Sociopathic criminals will always exist, but one way to minimize your risk at their hands is to live in a well-connected community. Studies show that crime levels are far lower in communities where neighbors know and look out for one another.

The good news, of course, is that the overwhelming majority of people are not toxic at all, but benign. In fact, many of the people you meet are quite wonderful. Even those who have their flaws and their issues usually mean well.

Yes, toxic people exist, but it would be wrong to cut yourself off from the joys of social life, romance, and community involvement just to prevent the risk of running across one of them. Live your life and be smart.

The Least You Need to Know

- The first job of any con artist is to gain a target's confidence through an uncanny ability to surmise what others are thinking and pretend to be thinking and feeling similar thoughts and emotions.

- Pick-up artists in search of intimate gratification are not only engaging but convince their target that they are engaging, too. Your best defense is not to rely on affirmation from strangers.

- The Internet and telephone are dreams come true for toxic people who wish to find strangers to exploit, because they can pretend to be anyone at all. Never reveal personal information to someone whose true identity you cannot verify.

- Litigious personalities are opportunists, so don't give them the opportunity to sue you. Steer clear of people who continually scan the environment for potential dangers, who never take responsibility, and who have a history of filing frivolous lawsuits.

Part 6

Advanced Attitude Adjustments

This concluding part invites you to hone the skills you've acquired for dealing with difficult types. It addresses the challenges of coping with "combination types," and of handling usually reasonable people who are having a difficult day. Finally, it discusses the many valuable lessons you can learn from dealing with the difficult, and ideas on how you can avoid becoming a difficult person yourself.

Chapter 20

Dealing with Combination Types

In This Chapter

- Learning some common combination types

- Responding to a person's underlying intent

- Rewarding or discouraging behavior

- Reading and sending body language signals

Some difficult people do not fit neatly into one category or another. They encompass traits from several categories at once, or they vacillate between one frustrating type of behavior and another.

These combination types can be doubly difficult to deal with. They have twice as many tricks up their sleeve, and twice as many ways to frustrate you. But look at it this way—you have twice as many strategies you can use in your own defense.

Common Combos

Difficult people, as with all people, are individuals. Each has a unique genetic palette and a unique upbringing. No two are exactly alike. So of course you will sometimes run into difficult people whose personal issues are complex and multilayered, and whose behavior frequently seems to shift gears. As often as not, these people are combining, to various degrees, the traits embodied by the types this book has previously discussed: the self-absorbed, the controlling, the obstructionist, and—to some extent—the toxic.

Possible combinations of difficult traits are infinite—such as the number of different words we can make from an alphabet with only 26 letters. Nevertheless, there are some common combinations.

The Controlling Narcissist

This combo type aims to control everyone around them so that they can always appear as the smartest and most indispensable person. If this means they have to control others in ways that make those others fail, so be it. It's all about them.

 Manhole Ahead _____

History is full of controlling narcissists. Many of them combine charisma and compulsive drive to end up in leadership positions. Sadly, the world has not been a better place for this. The controlling narcissist will send an army into battle so that their own name will be remembered—even if that army is clearly doomed and outnumbered. The controlling narcissist will rule a country and ignore its citizens' needs to promote their own glorification.

In the workplace and in your private life, the controlling narcissist will try to get you to do anything and everything for their own self-interest. But they will not let you be successful at anything that reflects directly on you. They will hijack your pet project, your romantic relationship, and any conversation or social situation of which you are the center—and because they are so manipulative, they will try to do this in such a way that you "won't know what hit you" until it's too late.

The Self-Absorbed Obstructionist

The self-absorbed obstructionist may be a perfectionist, a slow-moving tortoise, an indecisive type, or a complete slacker. But they are completely oblivious to the fact that they are engaging in any of these behaviors. They are also oblivious as to how their behaviors, or lack of them, might be hampering others.

It never occurs to the self-absorbed obstructionist that anyone else is waiting for them, or that their behavior is anything less than acceptable. They're too busy doing the only thing that really matters to them: trying to come up with ways of being noticed, admired, and praised.

In general, self-absorbed obstructionists are not as "successful" as narcissist controllers. They usually don't rise to top leadership positions. But they often get far enough ahead that they can be a perennial source of stress for a lot of hand-wringing, teeth-gnashing subordinates. They're not much fun on the home front, either.

The Toxically Envious Obstructionist

Some people have a great deal of envy but have not turned it into the urge to attack others as does the sociopath. Instead, toxically envious obstructionists turn their envy against themselves. They think only about what others have—even if they themselves have a lot. In fact, the more they have, the more they envy others who they perceive as "ahead of them." They simply can't get off what is known as the *hedonic treadmill*.

Because this type of person is constantly making negative comparisons between themselves and others, they become boring complainers, cynics, and pessimists. Strangely, continually verbalizing their state of dissatisfaction gives them a kind of perverse pleasure. But their continual cynicism demoralizes and frustrates everyone around them—which perpetuates the complainer's unhappiness.

def•i•ni•tion

The **hedonic treadmill,** a term coined by Princeton University psychologist Daniel Kahneman, refers to the phenomenon of continually adapting our expectations upward, the result being perpetual dissatisfaction.

The Swinger

Swingers are the "jack-of-all-trades" of difficult people. They just have a knack for figuring out what irritates people and then embodying those traits. Their *raison d'etre* seems to be to annoy (though some couch it as "just trying to be funny").

Why do they do it? They seem sadistic, but they are probably masochistic. They are afraid of intimacy, most likely because they feel they really are not valuable enough to deserve it or strong enough to be able to handle it. By being a thorn in everyone's side—or a self-appointed "clown"—they will not have to risk finding out.

The Combo Layer Cake: Intent vs. Content

What all combination types have in common is that they have powerful inner motivations for the outward behavior they manifest. But their inner motivation (the *intent* layer) may not always show in their outer actions (the *content* layer).

To some extent, this can be true of any difficult person—even the "straight up" types. But combos take this dynamic to extremes, which is why they often seem so paradoxical. To successfully deal with a combination type, you have to learn to respond to both *intent* and *content*:

- **Count to 10.** Try not to react instantaneously when you are provoked by a combo type. Think about what might be behind their harsh comment or seemingly irrational demand.

- **Use your "sincerity radar."** If your gut tells you that they have a hidden motive—perhaps hidden even from their own conscious mind—they probably do.

- **Ask for clarification.** Simply asking someone to be a little more specific can get them to inadvertently reveal their true intent.

DP Disarmer

If you're not sure what someone is feeling, try mirroring their facial expression. See what feelings arise in you when you position your mouth, jaw, and brow as theirs are positioned. Are you mad, sad, curious, glad, or fearful? Research shows that facial expressions expressing key emotions are virtually the same for all people throughout the world. They offer, in effect, a window into the soul.

Although the combo type's behavior may vary, their intent generally remains steady. It reflects an ongoing, unmet need. Sometimes the needs are irrational, or impossible to meet. However, if you can figure out a way to satiate that internal need to some extent—or at least to acknowledge the need's existence—their behavior might ultimately begin to stabilize.

Offering Validation

Understanding someone's underlying intent and trying to meet unexpressed needs is especially important if you have an ongoing relationship with them. For example, if they are a permanent fixture in your workplace or a member of your family from whom you do not wish to be estranged, you might be serving everyone's best interests if you can dip into your reserves of empathy and offer them a little bit of emotional sustenance.

So, underneath it all, what do most combination types really want? A new sports car? A private island in the Caribbean? Think deeper. The upper hand? Think deeper still. Flattery? You're getting closer, but you're not quite there yet.

At the very deepest level, all difficult people want the same things everyone does. They want to be understood and validated. Regardless of what their deepest feelings and desires may be, *they want to know that they are not alone.*

To validate a person's intent, you have to be able to relate to them. At first you might reject such a notion. After all, what could *you* possibly have in common with *them*? But be honest with yourself. We all share the human condition. We all have a full spectrum of thoughts and feelings, even though some of us are better than others at choosing the nobler ones to act on most of the time.

So when in doubt about how to respond to someone's intent …

◆ **Let them know you're listening.** Lean in and pay attention. Don't use the time while they are speaking to plan what you will say next. Make a genuine effort to respond thoughtfully rather than react hastily.

◆ **Let them know you understand what they are feeling.** This does not mean you have to agree or approve of the feeling, or that you would have the same one in the same circumstance. It just means you get it.

◆ **Let them know you are not above feeling as they do.** If they are feeling empty or envious or bitter or bleak, think about times when you have felt similarly. Let them know these feelings are not alien to you. If you are able to, describe to them a time when you experienced such emotions and acknowledge that you know how difficult they are to handle.

Finally, find something that you and this person can agree on, even if it is a small, seemingly insignificant thing. It's okay to agree about the weather, or the performance of a local sports team, or whether you like latte or espresso. The point is to create a sense of synchrony and resonance that translates into the beginnings of rapport.

Encouraging or Discouraging Behaviors

To successfully deal with complex difficult people, you will also have to deal with the overt content of their behavior. And indeed when it comes to people with whom you have only brief encounters, this "outer layer" may be all you have time to deal with. There is a simple golden rule when it comes to responding to other people's behavior in a constructive way: *Reward behavior you want them to repeat; do not reward behavior you want them to cease.*

Of course before you can reward good behavior, you have to notice it. If you are a parent, you may have heard of the philosophy that advises mothers and fathers to "catch your kids being good." The same philosophy can work with difficult people. Even highly difficult combo people probably do something now and then that you find appealing or commendable. The trick is to be in a mind-set that will allow you to notice it.

Be on the lookout for a flash of humor they may show, or a moment of helpfulness they may display. Let them know you recognize it. You will be amazed at the impact if you …

- Laugh at something they say when they are trying—and succeeding—to be genuinely funny.

- Thank them for a kind gesture, even one so small as holding open a door or saying "Bless you" when you sneeze.

- Reply convivially when they ask how you are doing or inquire about the well-being of your family.

- Smile back when they smile at you.

- Compliment them when they compliment you.

- Praise them when they achieve something of value, even something small.

It's important to reinforce even the most incremental positive behaviors. Don't go overboard (that will come off as insincere and condescending), but do or say something affirmative. In doing so you will encourage them to expand that repertoire.

As for undesirable behaviors, rewarding them is the last thing you want to do. Don't laugh at a sarcastic remark that they make at someone else's expense. Don't pretend to swallow a lie they tell. Don't act afraid if you sense they are trying to intimidate you.

If at all possible, however, refrain from commenting negatively on objectionable behavior. This amounts to punishment, and research shows that punishment often just eggs people on by making them irascible and vengeful. Stay neutral. Sometimes simply not responding sends a much more powerful message.

Tried and True Tactics

"Here's how I have learned to deal with yellers. When someone yells at me, I don't yell back. I just go on about my business as if they said nothing at all. When they speak in a normal tone, I try to honor their requests, or at least open up a dialogue. I learned this trick from raising my children. They soon learned to modulate their voices. Interestingly, I find most adults do the same."—Tina, 35

Reading Body Language

Another skill set comes in very handy when dealing with combination types of difficult people: knowing how to read body language. Body language can reveal underlying intent that people go to great lengths to mask with words. To become fluent in it is to gain a profound tool for deciphering innermost attitudes.

Reading body language can add an entire new dimension to the way you respond to and influence even the most seemingly inscrutable difficult people. This book has often made reference to using one's "gut." Part of doing so involves being perceptive about body language. Interestingly, many people who are innately skilled in this do not even know they are unconsciously processing others' body messages.

Anyone—from the gifted to the less naturally skilled—can get better at reading body language by achieving a conscious understanding of some common facets of body talk. Some are culturally transmitted, but many are so deep-seated that they play a role in human evolution and survival.

There have been innumerable studies on body language, and new studies are shedding light on even more subtleties as technology allows us to analyze micro-expressions and micro-movements. But there are some basics everyone interested in dealing with difficult people ought to know—especially those signals that indicate when someone is being deceitful or manipulative.

Hands

Clenched hands indicate frustration, even if the clencher is smiling and verbally agreeing with you.

Holding one's hands together behind one's back is a gesture indicating a swaggering superiority. So is putting one's hands in one's front pockets while letting the thumbs protrude.

People who are confident that they have all the answers will make a kind of steeple by holding the fingertips of both hands together.

Someone summarizing alternative solutions or plans will reveal their bias by using their favored hand (right for righties, left for lefties) to enumerate the points of the plan they prefer.

Palms

Open palms held toward you indicate honesty on the part of someone speaking to you. Someone who is being less than honest may give identical verbal responses but will conceal their hands, perhaps by putting them in pockets.

Pointing fingers from a closed palm is one of the most universally annoying gestures and indicates that the person making the gesture is trying to beat the listener into submission.

As for handshakes, someone who expects to dominate will initiate the shake with their own palm facing downward.

 DP Disarmer

To spot a disingenuous person, look for inconsistencies between their verbal and nonverbal messages. Nonverbal messages carry far more potent information (having about five times as much impact as words, studies show). So if someone says, for example, that they agree with you while their body messages say something else, it's a pretty good bet they are trying to mislead you.

Arms

Arms folded across the chest often indicate an anxious, negative, or defensive attitude. It's a "hiding" gesture. Folding the arms and gripping the upper arms with opposite hands shows heightened fear.

Someone who is consciously trying not to show anxiety may know enough to resist making a full arm-crossing gesture, but they will often give themselves away by subtly crossing one hand over the other to adjust a watch, bracelet, or sleeve cuff.

Eyes and Eyebrows

Lowering the eyebrows indicates dominance and aggression, but slightly downturned eyebrows indicate sincere concern.

Widened eyes indicate submission; however, it has also been noted that when women do this to men, it inspires the man to feel protective toward them.

Maintaining eye contact for the majority of a conversation (about two thirds of the time) is said to enhance rapport and to indicate honesty. However, most practiced con artists and liars willfully maintain eye contact as a way of avoiding detection. So gaze alone is not the best indicator of truthfulness.

Notice as well if the pupils are dilated (a sign of interest and sincerity) or narrowed (a sign of hostility, challenge, or deception). Pay attention to tone of voice as well.

Manhole Ahead

Don't make the mistake of taking one isolated gesture as a sure sign of a hidden agenda. Look for clusters of gestures—consider what someone is doing with their hands, arms, eyes, and so on as a package. Consider the context as well. Is someone hugging themselves because they're nervous or because the room is very cold?

Legs and Feet

In general, we use our legs to move toward what we want and to run away from what we don't want. So the way a person's legs and feet are positioned provides an instant clue as to whether they want to continue speaking to you or not. If their feet are pointed toward the door, their mind is already planning an exit strategy.

Open legs tend to show openness, but wide-open legs can indicate an attitude of dominance (look for the open leg/crotch display in dominant men). Crossed legs generally indicate a closed-off or defensive attitude (unless they are the legs of a woman in a miniskirt, who may be concerned with propriety).

In general, if two people are warming up to one another, they will move from crossed to uncrossed legs or feet. When people are very interested in the person to whom they're speaking, they tend to put one foot forward to shorten the distance between them.

Speaking Body Language

Even people who are reasonably adept at reading body language usually don't realize that they can also deliberately speak body language, using their own posture, gestures, and gazes to achieve a desired effect.

We all speak body language, but few of us understand what we are saying when we do. Although we give other people clues to our true feelings, we remain oblivious to the great deal of information we are handing them. When dealing with difficult people, our own "illiteracy" can put us at a real disadvantage. By learning to speak body language, we get—pardon the pun—a leg up.

In general, if you want to use body language to instigate rapport, make another person feel accepted, and create a bond, the rule of thumb (so to speak) is to mirror the body language of the person you're dealing with. This involves not only replicating their posture and gestures, but also matching their tone of voice and the pace at which they are speaking. (Speaking at a faster rate makes the other person feel pressured.)

But mirroring is not the whole story when it comes to speaking body language. In some situations, this could work to your detriment. For example, if you are negotiating with a difficult boss, you would not want to mirror their dominance-oriented gestures or they would feel threatened and be unlikely to give you what you want. If you are trying to discourage an inappropriately flirtatious person, you would not want to mirror their "moving in" behaviors. Use your common sense!

Here are some additional handy body language communications you should know about:

◆ To encourage someone to talk, and to indicate you are ready and willing to listen, keep the palms of your hands facing up and make sure your feet are facing toward them. As they get more comfortable, put your best foot forward (literally) and move it slightly in their direction.

◆ To get someone to stop talking, focus your gaze directly at the center of their forehead above their eyes. Do not drop your gaze, just keep directing it at that area. This has a disconcerting and even intimidating effect and will stop even the most verbose, self-absorbed person from prattling on.

◆ If someone initiates a palms-down handshake, which indicates their attempt to be dominant, respond with your hand palm up but then put your left hand over their right. Using this double-handed shake technique, gently but firmly straighten their grip so that their own palm faces sideways (indicating equality).

♦ When a difficult person insults or tries to intimidate you, make a concerted effort not to blink. However, do not widen your eyes. Instead, narrow your eyes as you look at your attacker.

♦ To convey—and create—sincerity and openness, keep your arms unfolded. When your arms are folded, your credibility is reduced. What's more, studies show that when you fold your arms you actually have more negative thoughts about the person to whom you are speaking!

When considering how you will speak body language, keep the principle of cause and effect in mind. When you assume certain body language positions and facial expressions, you will begin to internally experience the emotions associated with these positions and expressions. If you want to feel more confident, hold yourself in a confident manner.

DP Disarmer

To practice your body language skills, become an ardent people watcher in public places. At home, mute the television and see how well you can follow the plot.

The Least You Need to Know

♦ Dealing with combination types—such as controlling narcissists or self-absorbed obstructionists—seems daunting, but think of it this way: you have twice as many strategies as you can employ.

♦ Part of the skill of dealing with combo types is to distinguish their underlying emotional agenda (their intent) from their outward words and actions (their content).

♦ When in doubt about someone's deepest intent, try to create rapport by listening thoroughly and finding some area of common ground, no matter how seemingly small.

♦ The golden rule for dealing with outward behavior is simple: *Reward behavior that you want someone to continue; do not reward behavior you want them to discontinue.*

♦ Reading and speaking body language can add an entire new dimension to the way you respond to and influence even the most seemingly inscrutable difficult combo people—use your body language smarts to discern intent; use your own postures, gestures, and gazes to influence outcomes.

Chapter 21

When Nice People Have Difficult Days

In This Chapter

- ◆ Learning that even good people have bad moods
- ◆ Understanding extenuating circumstances
- ◆ Dealing with irritable e-mails
- ◆ Making up and moving on
- ◆ Understanding the happiness set-point

The world is a complex place. There are difficult people and easy-to-deal-with people, to be sure. But every single person on the planet can be difficult sometimes—including the nicest, kindest, most cheerful and laid-back people you know.

This chapter explains why good people behave badly once in a while, and suggests things you should and shouldn't do in response.

Who Are You and What Have You Done with So-and-So?

"I don't know what happened. I called up my girlfriend, who is the sweetest girl in the world. I asked her what she'd like to do for dinner and she blew up, asking why I assumed we'd always have dinner together."

"I feel totally sandbagged. My boss told me a few days ago he wanted to talk about future projects for me. He was, as usual, very encouraging and enthusiastic. I reminded him today about the projects and he turned cold and distant. He gruffly told me he didn't have time to worry about that kind of 'blue sky thinking' now."

"I have a professor who usually loves to chat with students after class. He really likes it when we want to keep discussing the topic of his lecture and he praises us for asking thoughtful questions. Today I approached him with a question and the look he gave me said, 'How can you be so dense?' He told me to look the answer up and write a paper on it! Now I have extra work, and I'm afraid my professor thinks I'm a jerk."

We've all been there. We have an ongoing, satisfying personal or professional relationship. We have a set of expectations around this relationship, and those expectations are consistently reinforced. These lovely people behave as we think they will, and our interactions proceed smoothly. Until they are apparently taken over by space aliens who have replicated their cell structure but don't behave like them at all!

We are dumbfounded. But, of course, they haven't actually had their body snatched by a disagreeable extraterrestrial. But that's how it feels to us. Sometimes we just need a reminder that *anyone* is capable of being in a bad mood, and people in bad moods sometimes act badly.

Manhole Ahead _____

Common expressions often contain a lot of emotional truth. When someone who generally has an appealing, agreeable manner tells you they are "not feeling like themselves" or are "beside themselves," they're not kidding. They may do things that are very out of character. You've been forewarned, so you should be forearmed.

Mood and Attitude

A person's mood is an observable affective state. It might consist of one pervasive emotion (anger or sadness) or a combination of emotions (anxiety and irritation at once). In normal functioning—that is, where a person does not have a mood disorder such as depression—moods are influenced by external events. We've all had one of those days when we've lost our wallet or gotten a traffic ticket or spilled coffee on our favorite suit. Everyone experiences strong, sometimes unpleasant, reactions to negative events. These are adaptive responses to the real world. In other words, they are perfectly normal.

If moods are as common as clouds that pass over the sun, they are also as transitory. Unlike underlying personality traits that are more or less stable—such as extroversion or introversion—moods come and go. For some naturally cheery and upbeat souls, one setback or unpleasant or discouraging event alone is not enough to set off a bad mood. But if negative events compound—as they are sometimes wont to do—just about anyone can turn cranky or glum. When they do, they may take out their frustrations on those who do not deserve it.

Sometimes bad moods feed on themselves and tend to last a bit longer than one might expect. If you think someone should just get over it and they don't seem close to doing so, be aware that they may be dredging up *mood-congruent memories*, which will cause them to stay downbeat a bit longer. But if no new events come along to upset them, this too shall pass.

def•i•ni•tion

Mood-congruent memory is a process that selectively retrieves memories that are congruent with our current mood. Thus, if we are feeling sad we may think about sad things that happened to us in our past.

Extenuating Circumstances

It's also worth noting that some life events, for some people, contribute to somewhat lengthier—but still ultimately ephemeral—bad moods. Not all people are susceptible to these events, but because many are, they are worth bearing in mind. They might give you a clue to why someone you know is acting in unexpected and unpleasant ways. Some of the events include the following:

♦ **The holiday season:** The holiday season is a time of joy for some, and a time of almost unbearable stress for many. Some feel overwhelmed by the financial pressures of gift-giving, the anticipation of spending time with difficult relatives they'd rather avoid, and even the prospect of eating too much. The holiday-time period also has the shortest days of the year. Those with a dash of *seasonal affective disorder* are doubly challenged to keep their spirits up in diminished daylight.

def•i•ni•tion

Seasonal affective disorder is characterized by feelings of sadness and lethargy caused by diminished exposure to natural light. It affects those sensitive individuals who live in temperate climates during the winter season.

♦ **Work burnout:** Burnout affects some individuals who have been working hard for extended hours during long periods of time, especially when they believe their efforts are futile or that their work lacks meaning. Symptoms include increased grumpiness, forgetfulness, fatigue, depression, and cynicism.

♦ **Physical pain or discomfort:** Any number of conditions—including arthritis, back problems, and temporo-mandibular joint syndrome (TMJ)—can cause chronic pain, which in turn causes sleep deprivation, inability to concentrate, and anxiety. These only exacerbate emotional irritability and instability.

♦ **Hormonal changes:** The word "hormone" comes from the Greek word meaning "to excite." Hormonal vacillations (such as those that occur during adolescence or midlife, for example, or on a monthly basis in connection with a woman's menses) can excite our tempers.

If you suspect someone you care about and routinely get along with is in the grips of any such life events, fasten your seatbelt. It could be a bumpy ride. Your patience might be tested, but try to keep their special circumstances in mind. Remind yourself that someday they might have to do the same for you.

Some Stabilizing Strategies

If moods pass, do we really have to do anything when someone we care for acts less than acceptably toward us as a result of a mood? Shouldn't we just ignore it?

Sure, if we can. Cutting some slack for a good person having a bad day is a compassionate act. Try taking a breather; give them some time to recover from whatever is irritating them.

However, if a cooling-off period isn't possible, or if their mood—and attendant mistreatment of you—persists, think about trying the following:

◆ **Empathize.** Remember that all people, deep down, want to feel understood. Let this person know that even though you may not be in the same mood as them, you can appreciate how they feel and have felt that way yourself.

◆ **Get them to laugh.** The old cliché about laughter being the best medicine is true. Laughter is a kind of emotional safety valve that allows us to release anxiety, aggression, and fear. It relaxes the muscles and sharpens the mind. Two people who laugh together also strengthen their emotional bond. So if you have any inkling about what makes this person chuckle, go for it.

DP Disarmer _____

Laughter releases endorphins, which are feel-good brain chemicals and also natural painkillers. Even someone who is in a bad mood due to chronic pain will respond positively to laughter. Experts believe that laughter, used as an adjunct to conventional medical care, can actually diminish the perception of pain.

◆ **Distract them.** Mention something interesting in the news or deliver a tidbit of friendly gossip. Stay away from "hot button" topics such as religion and politics!

◆ **Get them in "flow."** What does this person really like to focus on? What intrigues them or even obsesses them? It could be anything from shooting some hoops to playing the guitar to puttering in the garden. If you can tempt them to engage in that activity, they will find themselves in a state that is known as *flow*. This state is the virtual antithesis of a bad mood.

def•i•ni•tion _____

Flow is a mental state in which a person is fully immersed in what they are doing. It is characterized by feelings of energy, focus, full engagement, and self-satisfaction at the success of the activity. The state was noticed and named by psychologist Mihalyi Csikszentmihalyi.

◆ **Get them to move.** Suggest they join you for a jog, a bike ride, a swim, or a trip to the gym. Aerobic exercise is like an instant elixir for bad moods, releasing feel-good brain chemicals and boosting self-esteem.

◆ **Give them a gift.** No, you don't have to buy them a fancy car or a cashmere coat. A small token will suffice—their favorite candy bar, a paperback novel you think they'll love, even a gag gift or card that will make them smile. The idea is to say "I understand you and I still care about you."

- ◆ **Offer practical suggestions.** People in bad moods aren't always receptive to suggestions as to how to solve a practical problem, but if you have a solution that might help them out, you can float it by mentioning the positive results you or someone else had.

- ◆ **Damage control.** If this person's bad mood has caused them to say something hurtful to you, don't take the bait. Make an excuse and end the encounter before *you* get angry!

One caveat when it comes to responding to someone's bad mood: check your *own* mood before you decide the other person is cranky or out of sorts. Sometimes when we're in a bad mood and don't feel like admitting it to ourselves, we become overly sensitive to benign things that other people might say or do. Projecting your feelings onto someone else may very well end up putting you both in a bad mood.

Avoiding the E-mail Trap

Because e-mail is so pervasive, and because it's prone to misunderstandings, it's worth noting that e-mail is generally not a good way to communicate with someone whom you sense is in a bad mood. In fact, it's not a good way to judge someone's mood at all.

E-mail leaves out a lot of essential information. When we speak face to face, we receive far more information from their posture, gestures, facial expression, and tone of voice than we do from the words they are speaking. That is why body language is so helpful in dealing with difficult people (see Chapter 20 for more on reading and sending specific body language messages).

On the telephone, we are deprived of some of this critical nonverbal information, but we still get important clues about what someone really wants, and what emotional state they are in, through their tone of voice and the pace of their words. Tone of voice conveys cheerfulness and enthusiasm or irritability and impatience. The very same words can sound entirely different if one is using an "I'm just pulling your leg" tone versus a bitter, sarcastic tone.

E-mail, however, just gives us the words, without any human cues or nuances. Hence, we can easily jump to conclusions and misinterpret what someone means—and so can they. It's easy to overreact to an innocent, innocuous e-mail (albeit perhaps sent in haste and missing some social niceties) and imagine that it is a hostile missive. The next step might be to reply in a terse, defensive manner—which angers your receiver, who wasn't angry before, but sure is now! Now, a vicious cycle has been set in motion.

> **DP Disarmer** _____
>
> A well-known software company has instituted a policy of "e-mail-free Fridays." Banning e-mail on Fridays has forced people to find other ways to communicate, to think about communication more, and to better manage e-mail on other days of the week. You might want to take a page from their book.

To avoid emotional e-mail traps such as these, consider the following:

- **Sidestep the medium if you can.** If you are confused as to what the e-mail sender's frame of mind is, or about what they really want from you, pick up the phone or visit them if possible. Even if they were in a bit of snit when they sent the message, your effort could change their attitude.

- **Beware of the all-caps trap.** When you receive an e-mail with certain phrases capitalized, YOU FEEL LIKE THE SENDER IS YELLING AT YOU! Do not respond in kind, or you will start the equivalent of an electronic silent screaming match. Keep your punctuation normal if you don't want the problem to escalate. (And think about giving them the benefit of the doubt—maybe their caps key got stuck.)

- **Use emoticons (those little smiley or sad faces that you can insert in an e-mail) sparingly.** You might think they alleviate miscommunications, but lots of people are actually put off by these faux-emotional communications. They're too cutesy for most professional communications, too shallow for personal communications, and they do not have enough variety to convey complex emotions.

Finally, if you are tempted to reply to a provocative e-mail with a sarcastic or angry response, wait at least 10 minutes. Compose a draft off-line—in a word processing program, not an e-mail program. Wait another 10 minutes and re-read it imagining you are on the receiving end. If it's offensive, rework it. Many a long-term feud could have been avoided if people waited before pressing "Send."

> **Manhole Ahead** _____
>
> If you're having a testy e-mail exchange with someone, resist the temptation to copy half the world if you think you've scored a "point." This will embarrass the person you're writing, and prolong and escalate the problem between you.

Making Up and Moving On

What if the worst happens and you have an argument with a nice person who is having a bad day? There is only one thing you can do: put it behind you as quickly as possible.

The longer a misunderstanding festers, the more one or both of you will be apt to nurse a grudge. The mind can play a lot of tricks. It looks to fill silence with suppositions. As time goes on, you might convince yourself that the argument was worse than it actually was, and that the other person said things they didn't actually say.

In addition, the longer a rift is left unmended, the more reluctant each party will be to extend an olive branch. Saying "let's forget about it" 10 minutes after a spat is relatively easy. Saying it 10 days or 3 weeks or 2 months later is hard, and can make you feel as though you're "losing face."

If you're pretty sure the person you argued with was just going through a rough patch, don't wait for them to apologize. They may be embarrassed and afraid to face you. Take the first step and let them know that there are no hard feelings. You can tell them …

- ◆ "I know you didn't mean anything by it."
- ◆ "Don't worry, we all have bad days."
- ◆ "It's not that big a deal between friends."

Then move on to another topic. Lighten the mood with a joke, or suggest an activity you both enjoy.

It's not always easy to be gracious if you feel wronged or insulted by someone you can usually count on, but look at it this way: you have just made a deposit in the bank account of your relationship. Now the next time you're in a bad mood, this person will owe you one.

Returning to the Happiness Set-Point

Bad moods come and go, and healthy people tend to return pretty quickly to a baseline mood that psychological researchers call their "happiness set-point," a benchmark around which our emotions oscillate. After a bad mood, we get a "bounce." For a while we're usually in a better mood than usual; then, ultimately, we return to our baseline mood.

And here's more good news: for most of us, the happiness set-point is a little above neutral. In other words, we're pretty happy most of the time, just by default. Our happiness set-point is, to some extent, genetically coded. But our emotional thermostat is not set in stone. Our experience also has an impact in the areas of the brain that are involved in regulating emotion. Training ourselves to be less stressed-out by events such as minor tiffs with erstwhile grumpy people can actually help us readjust our own happiness set-point upward.

The Least You Need to Know

◆ Bad moods—transient emotional reactions to real-world events—are universal, and even people who are generally easy to get along with will manifest difficult behaviors when in the grips of a bad mood.

◆ If you know someone is in a bad mood, try not to personalize what they say or do to you—if appropriate, try to help them overcome their mood by empathizing with them, getting them to laugh, getting them to exercise, or distracting them.

◆ Even if you have an argument as a result of someone's bad mood, take the high road and make up sooner rather than later. By doing so you've just made a deposit in the emotional bank account of this relationship.

◆ We all have a "happiness set-point," a baseline mood around which our emotions swing slightly up and down. After a bad mood, we generally get a mood bounce and feel better.

22

Learning from Difficult People

In This Chapter

- ◆ Having difficult people instruct us
- ◆ Practicing self-control
- ◆ Accessing our compassion
- ◆ Learning constructive confrontation
- ◆ Displaying leadership
- ◆ Discovering forgiveness

Imagine that Earth is a school and your life experiences are your individual curriculum. By the time you approach your graduation, you hope to be a wiser person from all the lessons you have learned, and to leave a positive legacy behind.

Life lessons derive from countless sources, but sometimes the most profound teachings come from the most unexpected places—and the most unlikely people. In this chapter, we look at what knowledge we can gain, about ourselves and about the world, from our dealings with difficult people.

Difficult People as Teachers

When I became a new parent, I brought my infant son home from the hospital and beamed with maternal pride and joy. He was so lovable and adorable. "Why had I waited so long to become a parent?" I wondered. This was wonderful—and so easy!

Then my baby started to cry. And cry. Night after night, he would begin wailing at around dinnertime and keep going until after midnight. I was dumbfounded and upset. I felt completely inadequate because I thought my baby's behavior somehow reflected my shortcomings as a parent. "I've tried everything!" I would say in exasperation as the nightly histrionics continued. And I thought I had. When the baby cried I held him, fed him, sang to him, rocked him. Nothing helped.

In time, though, I realized I *hadn't* tried everything. One night, taking a suggestion from a pediatrician's book, I decided to stop reacting so feverishly. When the baby cried, I gently laid him in his bassinet and lay on my bed beside him. Within minutes, he was asleep, and my husband and I had our most serene evening in quite a while.

It turned out that my son didn't want to be on our schedule—he wanted to be on his. That's the superficial lesson I learned, but I learned some much deeper lessons as well. I learned that sometimes you have to stop reacting and start *responding*; that you have to try imagining what someone else might need even if it doesn't seem "logical" at first. I learned that love would endure through a lot of crying. And I learned that I had a lot to learn about being a parent—and that my child would teach me, sometimes the hard way.

If you think back on the lessons you've learned about dealing with people constructively, you probably learned some of them without even trying—perhaps simply by observing positive, kind, and upbeat role models. But I am certain you learned some of the most powerful ones from people who were being difficult. Why? Because difficult people test us—and if life is a school, we need those tests to hone our skills and to fulfill our potential as human beings.

Tried and True Tactics

"When I'm in the middle of a tough encounter with a difficult person and I can't imagine how it will turn out, I like to remember this quote from commentator Tom Bodett: 'The difference between school and life? In school, you're taught a lesson and then given a test. In life, you're given a test that teaches you a lesson.'"—Sarah, 40

We don't always pass these tests the first time. Often we react in ways that make our situation worse and our encounters with this person more unpleasant. But the universe seems to be very accommodating when it comes to making sure we get another chance. Amazingly, until we figure the lesson out, we seem to keep running into the same type of difficult person again and again!

In the school of life, difficult people make up a large part of the faculty, so we all have ample opportunities to be attentive students. Among our courses: Self-Control, Compassion, Constructive Conflict, and Healing and Forgiveness.

Learning and Practicing Self-Control

One of the big questions that have long consumed research psychologists is how we process emotions. Do we first react physically, reacting to anger with increasing heart rate or to sadness with tears? Or do we first conceptualize these emotions as states that we can label: "I am happy" or "I am sad"? Maybe, some speculated, we do both at the same time.

But recent research on neurological processes shows we definitely experience some emotions on a physical level before we have time to think about them. That's because certain brain pathways involved in emotions bypass cortical areas involved in thinking. These pathways lead straight from our eyes and ears (through which we receive stimuli) and travel via the *thalamus* to the *amygdala*.

def•i•ni•tion

The **thalamus** is the brain's sensory switchboard. Located at the top of the brainstem, it directs messages to sensory receiving areas. The **amygdala** consists of two almond-shaped clusters of neurons located deep in the temporal lobes of the brain. It plays a primary role in processing the emotions of aggression and fear.

The amygdala sends more signals up the cortex than it gets back, which means that it is easier for certain emotions to rule our thinking than it is for our thinking to rule those emotions. Because the emotions processed by the amygdala are aggression and fear, you can see how easy it would be to let fear and aggression hijack our logic.

Patience

Difficult people make us angry, and sometimes they make us afraid. But one of the things they teach us is that letting anger and fear rule our dealing with them *simply doesn't work*. The more we give in to primal impulses, the more we see how doing so actually disempowers us. Only when we consciously counteract the primal brain by deliberately taking the time to think through how we respond can we de-escalate hostile situations, boost our self-confidence, and improve our outcomes.

In short, difficult people teach us patience. They teach us to buy the time we need to consider our options. Will we ignore them? Will we make nice? Will we negotiate? Will we exit the situation? At times, we might still decide to fight fire with fire—but when we do, it will be a conscious, considered response—not a knee-jerk reaction.

Opportunities to develop patience and self-control begin early in life. There are invariably "schoolyard lessons" of which we can take advantage—learning how to control the angry or fearful emotions we might wish to display toward bullies and teases. Not all of us develop our skills at the same time, but fortunately, if we lag behind, life presents us with similar circumstances until we get the idea.

Tolerance

Just as difficult people teach us that if we are mindful and patient, a solution will arise, they teach us to be more patient with other people. Having patience with others is essentially what tolerance is all about.

Regardless of how skillfully we develop our emotional intelligence, we will always find some people irritating or unpleasant, or have views with which we strongly disagree. As we make our way through the school of life, we come to accept this reality.

Another lesson of tolerance is that the more we expose ourselves to people we once might have considered intolerable, the more we come to see that many of them have positive traits along with the traits we consider difficult. And the more we expose ourselves to points of view with which we disagree, the more we learn that we and those who espouse those viewpoints may indeed share some common ground. With practice, we usually find that there is *something* we can agree on, and this seed of agreement may blossom into new possibilities.

DP Disarmer

Brain-imaging research shows that when people talk or even think about their tolerant attitudes, the amygdala—seat of fear and anger—quiets and the prefrontal cortex (our "higher mind," if you will) activates. In other words, the more you practice tolerance, the more tolerant you will become.

Self-Respect

Decreasing our impulsivity and practicing patience and tolerance offers us a kind of bonus. The more we do so, the better we feel about ourselves.

It's erroneous to think that self-esteem is something we can apply to ourselves from the outside, similar to a bandage or moisturizing cream, by mouthing platitudes such as "I feel good about me!" Real feelings of self-worth can only come from inside, and can only grow out of genuine accomplishments. Learning to deal well with difficult people is a very significant accomplishment.

Learning and Practicing Compassion

We are all born with a capacity for empathy, because we are all born with the neural networks needed for attachment and caregiving behaviors. Our species simply could not survive if this were not the case. But it's relatively easy to feel empathy—that is, the ability to understand and relate to what another person is feeling—toward a person whom we value and depend on. It's less easy to do so with someone whom we think of as "the other": someone who is alien to us and who we may even feel is thwarting us in some way.

With the assistance of difficult people, we can enhance our empathy, kindness, and generosity with *universality* and *impartiality*. If we do, the result is compassion—an underlying attitude of loving kindness toward everyone we meet.

Compassion in its purest form—the sort that encompasses an attitude of loving kindness toward one's "enemies"—is not easy to manifest. For most of us, it's more of an ideal than a daily reality. Nevertheless, if we can find it within ourselves—even for a moment—to experience loving kindness toward a difficult person, especially while they are actually acting in a manner we deplore, we are that much closer to achieving what some call grace and others call enlightenment.

Manhole Ahead _____

Do not confuse having compassion for someone with obsessing on how you can "help" them. Some kinds of help are more about control than compassion. And some help is not even that helpful. Practicing compassion means cultivating an attitude of alertness to the kinds of struggles everyone shares. It requires understanding that all beings are interconnected.

In Buddhist imagery, compassion has been illustrated as a moon shining in the night sky, its light reflected in hundreds of bowls full of water. In essence, this moon offers its light to all, indiscriminately. It doesn't ask or expect anything in return. It just shines serenely on. Each time you are able to behold a difficult person in a nonjudgmental way, each time you sincerely wish a difficult person well, you will be a shade closer to achieving this compassionate ideal.

Yes, manifesting compassion toward the most difficult people is a challenge. But think of it this way: your compassion benefits everyone, _including_ you. That is not idle philosophy, but—as research is beginning to show—verifiable fact. In a fascinating series of experiments where subjects meditating on compassion were given MRIs, they showed intense, consistently identifiable activity in the prefrontal area of the brain, which is associated with generating joyous mental states. The lesson: _To think compassionate thoughts is to be compassionate to yourself._

From Conflict to Cooperation

Most of us dread conflict, yet difficult people bring conflict to the fore. When we have ongoing relationships with difficult people, we have to learn how to handle conflict. If we don't, situations deteriorate.

Non-Aggressive Confrontation

If we continually sidestep confrontation with someone every time there is conflict, the same dynamics play out over and over again:

- We never get what we want.

- We never feel good about giving the other person what they want.

- We feel bad about ourselves.

In the end, we learn that there are times when *non-aggressive* confrontation is warranted. Actually, it's sometimes necessary to lay ground-rules, build some degree of trust, and make progress toward workable solutions.

Before we master certain skills, the idea of non-aggressive confrontation can seem like an oxymoron. After all, our primal brain equates confrontation with the impulse to fight. And sometimes we're more afraid of our own primal impulse to fight than we are of the person we have to face.

But, given enough schooling, the higher brain ultimately figures out that by actively listening to the other person's point of view, by expressing our empathic understanding of how they see things, by clarifying misunderstandings, and by noting points of agreement—no matter how seemingly small—we can begin to resolve issues. We don't have to become best friends with someone to resolve conflict; we just have to establish a framework of mutual tolerance.

 **DP Disarmer** _____

What people remember about a conversation is the thing they talked about the most. Communication researchers call this "the duration effect." When you have a non-aggressive confrontation with a difficult person, be sure to linger on the things about which you agree, regardless of how minor they might seem.

Being Open to Criticism

Another reason confrontation is so nerve-wracking is that it often involves allowing someone else to criticize us. No one enjoys being criticized, but, interestingly enough, if we allow ourselves to tolerate it, we might actually learn something about ourselves. After all, no one is perfect. As incredible as it may seem, even a difficult person might have some insight into how we might improve.

Difficult people can train us to respond to criticism nondefensively. As we learn to let them have their say, we begin to recognize things we might have known about ourselves but haven't wanted to admit:

♦ They might point out times when we have cut people off even though they had a good idea.

♦ They might point out times we have been inflexible in our views of others—and have refused to "catch them being good."

♦ They might notice when we let our pride rule our decision-making, act out of habit, and refuse to consider new information.

If there is even a germ of truth in the grievance of a difficult person, we must learn to consider it as dispassionately as possible. Rather than trying to one-up their criticism of us with retaliatory criticism of them, we must learn to press them for specific details as to how we could be doing better.

Is this easy? No! But it *is* necessary if you are open to becoming a better person.

Tried and True Tactics

"If I thought of someone as a perfectionist nitpicker, I tended to brush off any suggestion they made. I assumed they were just trying to goad me. Then a co-worker at my engineering firm who was just this sort of person found an egregious error I had made in some calculations. My mistake would have caused disastrous results in a critical project. At first I disregarded what they told me, but I actually woke up in the middle of the night realizing they were right. I corrected my mistake in time, but after that I was not so quick to brush off this person's comments. I still did not like their manner or appreciate their style of communication, but the important thing was that I gained a new respect for their competence."—Jack, 38

Learning About Leadership

If we have leadership as a goal, we can especially learn a lot from difficult people. For one thing, we can learn from observing difficult people how *not* to behave if we want to positively motivate others and bring the best out in them.

Consider the people in your life whom you have felt good about following. Then consider those who had the opposite effect. If you were to note each of their traits, your list might look something such as this:

Effective Leaders	Ineffective Leaders
Listen well	Listen poorly
Display empathy	Act insensitively
Accept responsibility	Blame others
Speak straightforwardly	Equivocate
Make decisions	Waffle indecisively
Remain flexible	Remain rigid
Share power	Horde power
Share information	Horde information

Encourage others	Belittle others
Use inspiration	Use intimidation
Are good-humored	Are ill-tempered
Display calm	Display volatility
Consider the good of all	Consider themselves first

As we observe what really goes on in life, we notice that ineffective leaders may seem effective in the short-term. Their aggressive stance and provocative manner can be temporarily confused with efficiency and drive. And because they are leading through coercion, no one wants to be the first to point out that the emperor has no clothes.

But in the long-term, leaders who lack emotional intelligence can lead only toward failure. Leaders who lead through fear foster insecurity, which diverts energy away from creativity because their followers decide it is better to play it safe. Moreover, leaders who display a negative attitude will find that their attitude spreads through the ranks in a top-down flow of emotional contagion. Soon their followers will be steeped in cynicism, and hence unmotivated to do anything more than the bare minimum.

Of course, being an effective leader is a challenge because—wait for it—*some people are difficult*. But if we have learned the lessons of leadership well, we will use our emotional intelligence even with those people. In fact, they're the ones we learned those lessons for because they're the ones who require it most.

It's not that an emotionally and socially intelligent leader will never voice displeasure nor criticize a follower who has been counterproductive or even destructive. On the contrary, they will—and they will do so very effectively because they have emotional leverage. Because their day-to-day attitude is consistently one of warmth, concern, and positive regard, an irascible moment will have real impact. It resonates—and motivates—precisely because it is rare, in the way that the disciplinary tone of a usually calm parent resonates with a child more than the hollers of a high-strung parent who is a perennial yeller.

Forgiveness and Self-Healing

Finally we come to the topic of forgiveness. Sometimes, in the school of life, we will be harmed by difficult people. There is just no getting around this part of the curriculum, so to speak. In the end, the lesson here is about forgiveness, but this lesson can take a long time to learn. And some of us will never learn it in this lifetime unless we take a closer look at what forgiveness is—and isn't.

Forgiving does not have to mean excusing behavior. We fear that if we forgive someone, we will let them off the hook. Not so. First and foremost, forgiveness means we have made an active choice not to let ourselves continue to be injured by harm that was done to us in the past. It is our refusal to forgive that keeps us irreparably wounded.

Forgiving and forgetting do not have to go hand in hand. It is not advisable that we forget history. When we do, history tends to repeat itself. Understanding how we were hurt in the past and objectively examining any role we might have unwittingly played in allowing that hurt to take place is an essential part of our emotional education. Nevertheless, it is possible to remember the past without clinging to it. The first path results in wisdom, the second results in stagnation.

Forgiving helps us most of all. Research shows that people who suffered hostile actions at the hands of another and who dwell on their hatred suffer physically and emotionally. Their body goes into stress-response mode. Stress hormones such as adrenaline and cortisol flood their system, raising their blood pressure and heart rate and diverting resources from the immune system.

On the other hand, forgiving those against whom they held grudges has the reverse effect. Actively manifesting thoughts of forgiveness lowers blood pressure, heart rate, and stress hormone level. Levels of depression also rise in conjunction with nursing grudges and drop in conjunction with forgiveness.

Some people help themselves forgive by comforting themselves with a belief in divine justice. They feel they can let go of their resentment because "judgment day" or "karma" will make things right in the end. If your belief system encompasses such concepts, it may help you defer to a greater power and relinquish your own role as judge and jury during your time in Earth's school. But however you do it, consider learning the lesson of forgiveness. In the end, it means being willing to move on. The alternative—staying stuck—is simply not an appealing option.

The Least You Need to Know

◆ The primal emotions of aggression and fear can hijack our higher thinking functions, but difficult people—by training us in patience and tolerance—teach us how to keep our impulses subservient to thought, as opposed to the other way around.

◆ We are all born with the capacity for empathy, but difficult people can train us to widen that capacity and develop compassion even for those with whom we might not always agree or get along.

◆ Difficult people teach us that conflict is sometimes unavoidable, and sometimes healthy and necessary. As we let them have their say and even encourage them to air their grievances, we learn that no one is perfect (not even us!).

◆ Through observing the results of different leadership styles, including the leadership of difficult people, we learn what qualities truly inspire and motivate others—in the long run, the emotionally intelligent leader creates more positive outcomes and wields more leverage with even the most difficult followers.

◆ It is hard for many of us to learn the lesson of forgiveness, but forgiving is easier to do when we realize it does not mean excusing someone's actions and does not necessitate forgetting—in the end forgiveness helps *us* most of all, as it allows us to move on.

Chapter 23

Don't Be Difficult

In This Chapter

- Being likeable
- Caring for yourself
- Keeping things in perspective
- Drawing wonderful people to you

There are days when each of us looks in the mirror and encounters a difficult person. Yes, it's true. At times we're all perfectly capable of being giant pains in the neck.

This is no reason to get down on ourselves. After all, we're only human. The goal of this chapter, however, is to help you get to a point where your pain-in-the-neck days are fewer and farther between. This is not so you can achieve sainthood. It's because, in the end, the nicer you are to other people—and to yourself—the happier and more successful you will be.

Winning Ways: The Art of Likeability

People who are liked do well in life. Research shows that dealing well with people and being perceived as agreeable are critical factors when it comes to being hired or promoted. Likeability helps us to lead. It helps us inspire confidence. It helps us gain a supportive circle of friends and maintain strong personal bonds over time.

A number of attempts have been made to statistically isolate factors that contribute to likeability. (Interestingly, marketers are behind as many of these as social psychologists, because they like to know what kinds of celebrities can sell what kinds of brands to consumers.) But in the end, being likeable boils down to a few essential attitudes. If we embody them, our personal "brand" is in demand.

Connectiveness

We humans very quickly get a gut feeling about whether we like someone, we meet. Astonishingly, that first decision takes place in about one-twentieth of a second. After that, we consciously look for evidence to support what we, in some sense, have already decided.

First impressions, therefore, are crucial. When we encounter someone, we want to feel that in some way we share a connection. Likeable people create that first connection by smiling, by making eye contact, and by speaking in a warm tone of voice. If this is your natural manner, you will have a huge head start on creating a positive relationship.

But don't stop there. Corroborating evidence for that first impression is important. If you fail to follow up initial friendliness with something more substantial, you run the risk of putting people off nearly as quickly as you turned them on in the first place.

People feel connected to you when they sense you are interested in them as individuals and that you are concerned about the same things they are concerned about. A large part of connectiveness, therefore, is curiosity. People are pretty interesting creatures, and it's a smart idea to try to learn something from and about everyone you meet. Ask someone a question about themselves and they are generally pleased. Dwell on yourself and your needs, and they generally shut down.

What connectiveness comes down to is giving people the message that you value them. When you value them, they tend to value you.

DP Disarmer _____

People like it when you remember their name. Doing so says "You're important to me." If you are not naturally good at this, make a conscious effort to improve your name recall. When you meet someone, look directly at them and repeat their name aloud. At the same time, create a mental picture of this person in association with another image that will jog your memory. If you can, make liberal use of puns (words or phrases that have humorous dual meanings). For example, see Phil "filling" a bucket; see Stan "standing" tall. Break long names into syllables and do the same.

Optimism

People appreciate upbeat people who embrace positive attitudes. Optimists are consistently rated as more likeable than pessimists. That could be because optimists tend to make other people feel more optimistic themselves. Their frame of mind is "catchy."

Being an optimist doesn't mean being inappropriate. It's boorish and insensitive to react to someone's bad news or bad mood with an exclamation of joy. But even if someone is rightfully sad or angry, a bit of encouragement tends to ease their woe. Sometimes being optimistic simply means expressing your faith that adversity can be handled with courage and grace.

Tried and True Tactics _____

"When someone I know is feeling down, I don't tell them what I would do in their situation. I remind them of what they have done in the past to triumph under negative conditions. I find that people want and often need to be reminded of their own strengths and capabilities."—Carol, 40

Genuineness

Remember how important that first one-twentieth of a second is in establishing likeability? One thing that will work against you is if you are "faking it." Most people have pretty good radar for "phoney baloney." If they think you are only pretending to connect to them, and pretending to care about what concerns them, they will always be a little uneasy around you, no matter how hard you try to cover up your true feelings.

The solution is to be authentic. Find something you actually share with someone and make that your focal point. Think of a question you actually do want to know the answer to, and ask it.

Being genuine means being self-aware. Understand what drives you and what excites you, and be able to gauge your own moods.

If you need to interact with someone when you are genuinely preoccupied, it is better to indicate that than to pretend they have your full attention and be less than fully present. People will like and respect you more if you say, "Forgive me, I'm so distracted by a problem at work today," than if they observe you nodding and absent-mindedly yes-ing them along while your mind is clearly elsewhere.

Calm

People who are anxious make us anxious. People who are insecure and self-pitying frustrate us and tax our patience. On the other hand, people who radiate calm have a salutary effect on our own emotions. They are similar to human tranquilizers. No wonder we like being around them!

Calm people do not overreact, even in crisis. In fact, they are often at their best in crises, because they trust their own effectiveness. At the same time, they understand the difference between events that they can influence and those they cannot. They are philosophical about the latter, and so help us put things into perspective.

Perhaps most important in terms of calmness and likeability, calm people tend not to take the bait dangled before them by others who are being difficult. Unwilling to be provoked into doing something thoughtless or overly defensive, they are able to maintain positive relationships even when the going gets rough.

 Manhole Ahead

Being calm doesn't rule out being enthusiastic, wholehearted, or even passionate. On the contrary, an underlying equanimity enables calm people to access their passions because they are not preoccupied with worrying.

Self-Care and Self-Calming

In addition to being good to other people, being a nondifficult person involves being good to someone you might have forgotten: yourself. Unless you take good care of yourself—especially with regard to managing your stress level—you simply won't have the energy or the patience to consistently interact positively with others.

Doing the things you need to do to keep yourself healthy and balanced is neither self-centered nor selfish. Look at it this way: if you burn your candle at both ends, you will soon lose the ability to give off any light.

Move It

Everyone knows that exercise is good for the body. Fewer people are aware of how profoundly beneficial it is for one's mental state. If you want an instant boost in mood and energy, engaging in moderate aerobic activity—such as jogging, brisk walking, swimming, bicycling, or simply putting on your favorite music and dancing—for as little as 30 minutes ought to get you there.

Back in the 1970s when running first became a national craze, devotees routinely reported feeling a phenomenon known as "runner's high." Researchers began to investigate and discovered that prolonged bouts of aerobic exercise do, in fact, result in the release of mood-enhancing serotonin and beta-endorphins. These brain chemicals are released in exercisers at up to five times the levels found in resting subjects.

Exercise also has impressive long-term effects. More than 150 studies support the fact that exercise reduces depression and anxiety—and increases self-confidence. As if that's not enough, it also promotes the growth of new brain cells and raises our cognitive abilities.

No one really knows if the many long-term mental and emotional benefits of exercise are a side effect of increased body arousal and warmth, of the muscle relaxation and sound sleep that occur after exercise, or of the sense of accomplishment that accompanies an improved physique. Nor does it matter. The point is that exercise is a good way to both take care of yourself and improve your ability to relate to others with a positive attitude.

DP Disarmer _____

Exercise is also a wonderful means of catharsis. It helps you blow off steam. If you're mad at someone, but don't want to risk acting on that anger inappropriately, try pounding a treadmill or taking a kickboxing class instead. You will absolutely feel better.

Play Every Day

To further decrease stress and enhance your mood and manner, it's a good idea to allot some time almost every day to an activity that is fun for you and about which you are very enthusiastic. It doesn't matter what it is—drawing or gardening, writing or singing, or puttering with carpentry or car repair.

Ideally, this activity should help you transcend daily mundanities. When you do it, time should fly. In other words, you should be so completely focused and engaged in what you are doing that you enter the psychological state known as "flow."

Flow feels as good as it sounds. It reminds us of how interesting life is and how much positive energy we can bring to an endeavor. It allows us to surprise ourselves with new thoughts, new ideas, and stimulating sensory input. It also makes us more creative, able to generate multiple solutions to problems that arise (which certainly comes in handy for acquiring people skills as well).

Be Still

If you can devote 20, 15, or even 5 minutes a day to a quiet meditative practice, you will soon see the results manifest themselves in a newfound sense of calm. The restorative benefits of simple meditation, visualization, progressive relaxation, or prayer simply cannot be overstated.

Many people say they have "tried" to meditate, but that they were too easily distracted. They believe they have failed and so give up. But the whole idea of undertaking such daily practices is to notice how anxious and distracted you usually are. Within a short time you will learn that, although thoughts and worries may come and go, you can access a wellspring of tranquility that underlies them.

People who engage in some form of daily meditation or centering prayer are more focused and more composed in the rest of their lives. Intriguingly, research shows they are also better at "reading" nonverbal interpersonal signals (such as fleeting facial expressions) given off by others. By honing their attentiveness, they become more sensitive to others.

DP Disarmer _____

There are many styles of meditation, and many guides to meditating. It's worth casting about to find a style that suits you. Until then, you might try this simple breath counting meditation:

Inhale fully, filling the lungs and diaphragm, then expel the air slowly through the nose. That's breath number one. Now repeat the process, counting four breaths. Then start over. In the beginning you will lose count on your way from one to four as random, uninvited thoughts divert your attention. This is perfectly normal. Just start over at the first breath.

Sleep on It

Meditating in the evening has the additional advantage of calming your mind and body down before sleep. But even if you don't care to meditate, you should find other means of ensuring that you routinely get a good night's sleep.

You know how much more difficult it is to deal with any frustration when you have slept poorly the night before. That's because sleep deprivation increases stress hormones and keeps us from replenishing stores of energy in our brain.

Within the last century, the average American has eliminated an hour and a half of sleep from their regimen each day. Maybe that's why so many of us are so cranky! But we don't just need more sleep—we need more sound, uninterrupted sleep.

To increase the quantity and quality of your sleep. Try ...

- **Unwinding before bedtime by a means other than TV.** Television is too stimulating and sometimes even disturbing. Instead of watching the tube, take a warm bath or listen to soothing music.

- **Declutter your bedroom.** Piles of newspapers and magazines are distracting. Make your bed as inviting as possible, with pillows and comforters you relish. Keep the lighting low before bedtime, and crack open a window for ventilation.

- **Consider a white noise machine.** If sleep still eludes you, think about getting a gadget designed to relax you by simulating sounds of waves breaking or rain falling. They are easily found on the Internet, but if you can shop for one in person you can discover which sounds work best for you.

Manhole Ahead _____

You are sleep-deprived if you yawn frequently and have a tendency to nod off when you are inactive for a little while. Your lack of rest can contribute to moodiness and a tendency to explode emotionally at the slightest provocation.

You probably know you shouldn't drink caffeine in the hours before bedtime. But you might not know that alcohol right before bedtime can also keep you up or—even more likely—cause you to wake up in the middle of the night. If you're a milk drinker, that's a great pre-bedtime beverage. It contains calcium and the amino acid L-tryptophan, both of which help you relax.

Eat Smart

Speaking of caffeine, it won't help you in your efforts to stay calm and agreeable when dealing with people. If you spend much of your day imbibing it in any form, you'll only assure that your nerves will be jangled and your fuse will be shorter.

Sugary foods—exactly the sort we tend to reach for when stressed—won't help either. Your burst of energy will be followed by a crash—and woe unto the person who interacts with you while you're on the way down.

If you think alcohol improves your ability to relate to all kinds of people, think again. Alcohol is a "disinhibitor." It loosens the tongue, and you might just find yourself saying something you'll regret.

There are no magic foods that will make you more personable, but you will feel more stable overall if you are not enslaved to food and drink that keeps you on a mood pendulum. A balanced diet that includes lots of protein and complex carbohydrates (whole grains, fruits, and vegetables) is best for body and brain.

Keeping Things in Perspective

Another way to bring out the best in yourself is to keep things in perspective. Often we exaggerate and exacerbate minor frustrations and dwell on worries, forgetting to notice the good things—and good people—around us.

People and events have the potential to frustrate us every day. But we can control how we let them affect us if we …

♦ **Get past the past.** We cannot change what has already happened. If we hold on to a grudge, it won't change anything and will just make us feel worse.

♦ **Stop anticipating the worst.** Although it's wise to take prudent precautions for the future, we have to keep in mind that worst-case scenarios rarely unfold. Admit it: most of the time, things actually seem to work out.

♦ **Ask "Will it ultimately matter?"** When something is bothering me, I play a little game with myself called "Will It Matter?" Will this person or event that is really getting under my skin matter in a month? A year? Five years? If I can think of a time in the future when it will not matter—and I usually can—then I can let it go *now*.

♦ **Tell yourself it will all make sense—later.** When we are in the midst of a frustrating situation, we can't imagine the outcome. Nor can we imagine why we have been sent this particular "test." But if you think back to the darkest, most confusing times in your life, you have to acknowledge that you came out stronger on the other side. You just can't know what strength or insight you'll gain from adversity while the latest plot line of your life is still unfolding. Trust that one day you will see how all the pieces fit together.

♦ **Know that everything changes.** Change is the law of the universe. Everything, even each cell in our own body, is metamorphosing all the time. So don't get too attached to one way of being or of doing things. Stay flexible and you will work with the universal law instead of fighting against it.

♦ **Go easy on yourself when you feel you make a "mistake."** If you have trouble forgiving people, perhaps you should try starting with yourself. Sometimes blunders are blessings in disguise. You just have to wait and see.

Perhaps the most important perspective shift of all comes when we begin to acknowledge the fact that we who share this planet are all connected. We share a home, we share the essential building blocks of life, and we share a global fate. We often think we have nothing in common with someone, but at this very basic level we have everything in common with everyone. We may as well be good to them if we can.

Attracting Wonderful People

When we are likeable, when we treat ourselves and others well, and when we try to maintain a philosophical perspective about life's ups and downs—in short, when we act as our best selves—an amazing thing happens. We become a magnet, attracting all sorts of interesting, wonderful, and positive people toward us.

This phenomenon, in turn, makes us even more secure and content. That's because having a strong network of social support increases our ability to navigate life with increased stamina and resilience.

Having warm, caring people in our lives is a blessing of inestimable benefit. They offer us moral support by being in our corner. They offer us shoulders to cry on and hands to hold when we need them. Beyond these things, they add to our lives an abundance of opportunities for variety and fun. They introduce us to different interests and different points of view. They give our life bounce.

Be sure not to take these wonderful people for granted. Each of these relationships will require nurturing. That means an investment of time, effort, and attention on your part. And although it's often a pleasure to bestow time and attention on people we care about, we also have to be cognizant of maintaining relationships during those times when we become preoccupied.

Sure, good friends and loved ones understand when we're busy—to a point. But there's also a tipping point beyond which it gets more difficult to reconnect. Even a brief check-in to say what's going on with you and when you'll have more time will be much appreciated—and, face it, you would want them to do the same for you.

In addition, if you want to keep wonderful people in your life, it's a good idea to periodically express the gratitude you feel for having them there. Thanking people is one of those things we so often forget to do, but the currency of gratitude holds tremendous value.

Acknowledging people for the comfort and joy they bring to our life will ...

- ◆ Reinforce their positive, supportive behavior.
- ◆ Build up a reservoir of good feelings to draw on in the event that a conflict occurs.
- ◆ Make them feel smart and proud that they chose you to hang around with!

Besides, they'll probably thank you right back for being in their life.

Many of us are shy about saying thank you. That's kind of ironic when you think about it, because we're often not shy when it comes to complaining. We're also shy about receiving thanks, and we sometimes wave an expression of gratitude away with a flick of the hand and a dismissive statement such as "Hey, no problem."

It's time to get over it. Giving and accepting thanks are similar to any skill. It takes practice, so start today.

The Least You Need to Know

◆ Likeable people are successful at love and at work—and much of what we call likeability boils down to being connected, optimistic, genuine, and calm.

◆ You can't treat others well unless you know how to treat yourself well—managing your stress level through proper self-care is critical, so take the time to relax and restore yourself through exercise, play, meditation, and good sleeping and eating habits.

◆ Many things have the potential to bring out our worst, but we can bring out our best by keeping things in perspective. Try not to dwell on past grudges or on future worst-case scenarios, and remind yourself that things tend to work out and make sense in time.

◆ The more you act as your best self, the more wonderful people you will attract—they'll increase your confidence and your resilience and make your life more interesting, so don't forget to thank them for being there.

Appendix A

Glossary

amygdala   Consisting of two almond-shaped clusters of neurons located deep in the temporal lobes of the brain, the amygdala plays a primary role in processing the emotions of aggression and fear.

anal-retentive   The term Freud used to describe people whose obstinate and obsessive behaviors originated as a result of toilet-training struggles. Nowadays, without dwelling on its roots, we often use "anal" as shorthand for implying that someone is controlling.

approximations   A term from behavioral psychology that refers to rewarding the small steps that occur en route to a new behavior.

borderline   Long used as a catchall category for people who were more disturbed than the average neurotic but not as divorced from reality as psychotics, this term has come to refer to those who have unstable interpersonal relationships, impulsivity, severe mood shifts, a lack of clear identity, feelings of emptiness, and fears of abandonment.

crowding stress   A type of psychosocial stress induced by an increased density of population. It can induce complex behavior changes, including an increase in aggression and a decrease in the ability to learn and adapt.

disinhibitor   Any stimulus—such as a drug or alcohol—that incites someone to relax their usual reticence or reservations and, often, to act inappropriately as a result.

domestic violence   Use of physical force against a family member in a way that causes injury or puts the person at risk of being injured. Domestic violence can include pushing, pinching, shaking, and holding with the attempt to restrain someone. It also includes extremely violent behaviors such as slapping, beating, punching, choking, and assault with a deadly weapon.

echoing   A communication skill that involves understanding a speaker's emotional intent, paraphrasing it, and then repeating it back to them. It indicates: *I understand your feelings.*

emotional intelligence   Abilities involved in understanding and appropriately expressing one's emotions, and in understanding and responding appropriately to the emotions of others.

empathy   The ability to understand and relate to the feelings and perceptions of others; to imagine how circumstances appear from their point of view.

EQ   An abbreviation for emotional intelligence quotient, often compared to or contrasted with IQ (intelligence quotient), which measures cognitive abilities.

false self   A contrived, grandiose construct that narcissists project as their persona, but which actually masks an underlying feeling of inadequacy.

fight-or-flight response   The term coined by physiologist Walter Cannon to describe a reflexive sequence of internal reactions that prepare an organism to seek escape from or do battle with a stimulus that it considers a threat.

flow   A mental state in which a person is fully immersed in what they are doing. It is characterized by feelings of energy, focus, full engagement, and self-satisfaction at the success of the activity. The state was noticed and named by psychologist Mihalyi Csikszentmihalyi.

gaslighting   The practice of getting someone else to doubt themselves, dismiss their own reactions, and perhaps even feel they're mentally unbalanced. The term comes from the movie *Gaslight*, in which Charles Boyer played a scheming husband bent on inheriting his wife's fortune.

gravitas   A serious or solemn attitude. When it is said one speaks with *gravitas*, the implication is that one's words carry weight.

hedonic treadmill   A term coined by Princeton University psychologist Daniel Kahneman, it refers to the phenomenon of continually adapting our expectations upward, the result being perpetual dissatisfaction.

helicopter parent   A popular term for parents who hover too closely over their children and who rush in to help with every situation—whether their help is actually needed or not.

hypochondriac   A person who is excessively preoccupied with their health and who consistently searches for reasons to believe that they are seriously ill or becoming seriously ill. Such a person usually spends an inordinate amount of time detailing real or imagined symptoms to others.

incompatible behavior   A behavioral modification technique based on the simple idea that it is impossible to do two things at once. (Instead of teaching someone to stop what they are doing, you give them something else to do that precludes doing the first thing.)

instinct   This term can refer to a fixed, inborn behavior, but in a species as complex as humans, it is usually meant to signify a predisposition to learn a certain behavior or set of behaviors.

intermittent positive reinforcement   A principle of behavioral psychology, the term refers to eliciting certain desired behaviors by offering rewards at unpredictable and varied intervals.

Kafkaesque   An adjective used to describe situations that involve trying to navigate a baffling, illogical, even nightmarish bureaucratic system. It alludes to situations often described in the works of the novelist Franz Kafka.

libel   A published statement that is false and that maliciously damages someone's reputation.

likeability   The ability to induce positive emotional experiences in those whom we encounter.

Machiavellian   A term sometimes used to describe a person with a tendency to deceive and manipulate others for gain. It refers to the writings of Niccolò Machiavelli, a sixteenth-century political philosopher from Florence, especially as set forth in the treatise *The Prince*.

magical thinking   The confusion of wishes and fantasies with reality.

malfeasance   Wrong or illegal conduct, particularly within the legal profession, politics, or civil service.

managing up   The practice of influencing those above you in the workplace to recognize and reward your abilities. (Sometimes overdone by self-centered types who overstate their accomplishments and who also tend to fawn.)

masochism   This term initially referred to sexual gratification achieved via humiliation and physical pain, but has also taken on a more general psychological meaning as the tendency to enjoy misery of various kinds, especially to be pitied by others. The word comes from the name of the nineteenth-century novelist Leopold von Sacher-Masoch, whose writings centered on self-abusive predilections.

micromanager   Someone who manages a business or organization via painstaking attention to small details.

mind-body system   A conceptual understanding of the human essence as an inter-related psychic and physical self. In practical terms, this concept informs contemporary medical and psychological thinking with regard to such matters as stress-related illness.

mirroring   A communication skill that involves acknowledging to the speaker that you are capable of feelings similar to the ones they are having. It signifies: *I am capable of feelings not unlike yours*.

mood-congruent memory   A process that selectively retrieves memories that are congruent with our current mood. (Thus, if we are feeling sad we may think about sad things that happened to us in our past.)

mouse potato   A popular term for someone who is more or less permanently affixed to their computer screen, in the way a couch potato is affixed to a television screen.

narcissistic injury   A blow to the pride of an extremely self-centered person. Because it represents a challenge to their grandiose yet fragile self-perceptions, it can unleash a response of rage and revenge.

narcissistic supplies   Material objects (such as branded displays of wealth) or interpersonal reinforcements (including attention and adulation) that keep the narcissist's false self from deflating.

organizational culture   The collection of values and norms that are shared by people and groups in an organization. The culture determines the ways in which employees interact with each other and with stakeholders outside the organization. They guide standards of behavior and ideas about what is and is not acceptable.

passive-aggressive   This seeming contradiction in terms refers to a style of exerting control by indirect means, for example by intentional failure. The term was coined during World War II by a U.S. military psychiatrist who noticed certain soldiers subtly rebelling against authority by ignoring orders, feigning illness, or pretending to be incompetent.

personal umbrella insurance   A policy that provides added liability protection above and beyond the limits on homeowners, auto, and watercraft personal insurance policies. Depending on the insurance company, one can add an additional 1 to 5 million dollars in protection that kicks in when liability on other policies has been exhausted.

personality disorder   A mental disorder signaled by an enduring and inflexible pattern of maladaptive behavior and inner experience (thoughts, feelings, perceptions) that results in dysfunction and subjective distress.

pyramid scheme   Sometimes called a Ponzi scheme, the term refers to a fraudulent investment operation that involves paying abnormally high returns to investors out of the money paid by subsequent investors, rather than from net revenues generated by any real business.

reaction formation   An unconscious psychological defense mechanism that switches unacceptable feelings into their opposites. For example, if someone feels a sense of inner anxiety, they might devise a way to maintain outward calm.

red tape   A derisive term for excessive regulations or rigid conformity to formal rules that are considered redundant and that hinder or prevent action or decision-making. The origins of the term allude to the seventeenth- and eighteenth-century English practice of binding documents and official papers with red tape.

road rage   Also known as road violence, this is the informal name for deliberately dangerous and/or violent behavior under the influence of heightened negative emotions—such as anger and frustration—involving an automobile in use.

seasonal affective disorder   A syndrome characterized by feelings of sadness and lethargy caused by diminished exposure to natural light. It affects those sensitive individuals who live in temperate climates during the winter season.

Schadenfreude   Pleasure taken at the misfortunes of others. This is a German word used as a "loaner" not only by English, but by many other languages as well.

sense of entitlement   A feeling of supremacy leading to assumptions that one deserves subservience, leniency, special treatment and favors, and special outcomes and concessions.

sexual harassment   As defined by the U.S. Equal Employment Opportunity Commission, this can consist of unwelcome sexual advances, requests for sexual favors, and other verbal or physical conduct. The sexual nature of it is when submission to or rejection of this conduct explicitly or implicitly affects an individual's employment; unreasonably interferes with an individual's work performance; or creates an intimidating, hostile, or offensive work environment.

Simon Legree   A character, a vicious plantation owner, in Harriet Beecher Stowe's famous American novel *Uncle Tom's Cabin*. The name has come to be associated with someone who is overtly cruel to those who work for them.

sixth sense   The ability to perceive something using more than the five senses of sight, hearing, smell, touch, and taste.

slander   A false spoken statement that maliciously damages someone's reputation.

thalamus   The brain's sensory switchboard. Located at the top of the brainstem, it directs messages to sensory receiving areas.

transference   A psychological phenomenon that involves the unconscious redirection of feelings for one person toward another. Transference was first described by Sigmund Freud, pioneer of psychoanalysis, who saw the phenomenon as a way of better understanding patients' conflicts.

Appendix B

Further Reading

Allen, Marvin. *Angry Men, Passive Men: Understanding the Roots of Men's Anger and How to Move Beyond It.* New York: Ballantine, 1993.

Babiak, Paul, and Robert D. Hare. *Snakes in Suits: When Psychopaths Go to Work.* New York: Regan, 2006.

Badowski, Roseanne. *Managing Up: How to Forge an Effective Relationship with Those Above You.* New York: Currency, 2003.

Berkowitz, Leonard. *Aggression: Its Causes, Consequences and Control.* New York: McGraw Hill, 1992.

Bok, Sissela. *Lying: Moral Choice in Public and Private Life.* New York: Vintage, 1979.

Caldwell, Mark. *A Short History of Rudeness: Manners, Morals and Misbehavior in Modern America.* London: Picador, 2000.

Carnegie, Dale. *How to Win Friends and Influence People.* New York: Pocket, 1990 (reissue).

Elgin, Suzette Hayden, Ph.D. *The Gentle Art of Verbal Self-Defense.* Hoboken, NJ: John Wiley & Sons, 1997.

Fisher, Roger, and William Ury. *Getting to Yes: Negotiating Agreement Without Giving In.* New York: Penguin, 1991.

Ford, Charles. *Lies, Lies, Lies! The Psychology of Deceit.* Danvers, MA: American Psychiatric Publishing, 1999.

Forward, Susan. *Toxic Parents: Overcoming Their Hurtful Legacy and Reclaiming Your Life.* New York: Bantam, 2002 (reprint).

Gabor, Don. *Speaking Your Mind in 101 Difficult Situations.* New York: Fireside, 1994.

Glaser, Susan and Peter. *Be Quiet, Be Heard: The Paradox of Persuasion.* Eugene, OR: Communications Solutions Publishing, 2006.

Goleman, Daniel. *Emotional Intelligence: Why It Can Matter More Than IQ.* New York: Bantam, 1997 (reprint).

Hotchkiss, Sandy. *Why Is It Always About You? The Seven Deadly Sins of Narcissism.* New York: Free Press, 2002.

Kantor, Martin. *Passive Aggression: A Guide for the Therapist, the Patient, and the Victim.* New York: Praeger, 2002.

Kreisman, Jerold, M.D., and Hal Straus. *I Hate You: Don't Leave Me.* New York: Avon, 1991.

Lasch, Christopher. *The Culture of Narcissism: American Life in an Age of Diminishing Expectations.* New York: Norton, 1991 (revised edition).

Lloyd, Ken, Ph.D. *Jerks at Work: How to Deal with People Problems and Problem People.* Franklin Lakes, NJ: Career Press, 1999.

Lorenz, Konrad. *On Aggression.* New York: Harcourt, 1966.

Lundin, William. *When Smart People Work for Dumb Bosses: How to Survive in a Crazy and Dysfunctional Workplace.* New York: McGraw Hill, 1999.

Masterson, James F., M.D. *The Search for the Real Self: Unmasking the Personality Disorders of Our Age.* New York: The Free Press, 1988.

Millon, Theodore. *Personality Disorders in Modern Life*. Hoboken, NJ: John Wiley & Sons, 2000.

Reisman, David, Nathan Glazer, and Reuel Denney. *The Lonely Crowd, revised edition: A Study of the Changing American Character*. New Haven, CT: Yale University Press, 2001.

Ridley, Matt. *The Origins of Virtue: Human Instincts and the Evolution of Cooperation*. New York: Viking, 1996.

Robinson, David. *The Personality Disorders Explained*. Port Huron, MI: Rapid Psychler Press, 2003.

Seligman, Martin, Ph.D. *Learned Optimism*. New York: Knopf, 1981.

Simon, George K., Ph.D. *In Sheep's Clothing: Understanding and Dealing with Manipulative People*. Little Rock, AR: A. J. Christopher & Co, 1996.

Stout, Martha. *The Sociopath Next Door*. New York: Broadway, 2005.

Strauss, Neil. *The Game: Penetrating the Secret Society of Pickup Artists*. New York: HarperCollins, 2005.

Tavris, Carol. *Anger: The Misunderstood Emotion*. New York: Touchstone, 1989 (reprint).

Truss, Lynne. *Talk to the Hand: The Utter Bloody Rudeness of the World Today, or Six Good Reasons to Stay Home and Bar the Door*. New York: Gotham Books, 2005.

Urbina, Ian. *Life's Little Annoyances: True Tales of People Who Just Can't Take It Anymore*. New York: Times Books, 2005.

Weiner, David. *Power Freaks: Dealing with Them in the Workplace or Anyplace*. New York: Prometheus Books, 2002.

Web Resources for Coping Assistance

General Sites

http://inconsiderate.net   Read contributor stories of problems and solutions regarding difficult people in all areas of life. You can even contribute your own by e-mailing stories@inconsiderate.net.

http://messageboards.ivillage.com/iv-cadifficult   At the iVillage site you have an opportunity to read and contribute to message boards that address problems with all manner of difficult folk.

www.negotiationskills.com/articles.html   Articles on skills for negotiating with difficult people in all areas of life, including advice about health-care–related negotiations.

www.cartoonstock.com/directory/r/rude_people_gifts.asp   Because humor is essential, this site offers the opportunity to purchase cartoons featuring rude behaviors (for example, cell phones in church). The cartoons can be emblazoned on mugs, plaques, and T-shirts.

www.revengelady.com/index.html   Blow off steam by submitting stories about boyfriends/girlfriends/bosses/neighbors "from hell." Maybe they'll make the top 10 lists. Hint: don't use real names.

www.myroommateisdrivingmecrazy.com   Survival tips for college students who have difficult relationships with roommates.

www.apa.org/topics/controlanger.html   The American Psychological Association offers advice and information on the topic of anger management.

www.angries.out.com   This award-winning site offers constructive anger management techniques for children, parents, couples, adults, and teachers.

www.angereducation.com   Online anger management courses for the general public as well as for those who have been court mandated.

Work-Related Sites

www.itstime.com/game.htm   Visitors to this site can play *The Personality Game*, a fun way to learn about personality types and their quirky traits. This personality system focuses on improving teamwork and increasing productivity in the workplace. It's adapted from the work of psychotherapist Dr. Jose Stevens.

www.badbossology.com   Provides the latest news on difficult bosses along with resources to assist people in understanding and analyzing their boss to develop an action plan, protect themselves, and achieve career success in spite of their boss.

www.managementmalpractice.com   Tales and advice from the front—those who have been "demeaned, manipulated, deceived, oppressed, abused, or injured by management."

www.employeeterminationguidebook.com   Advice on firing difficult employees.

www.impactfactory.com   Sign up for "difficult people skills" courses that offer training in areas such as communication and assertiveness. Most of the content is work-oriented, but much can be applied to other life areas as well.

Assistance with Dangerous Situations

www.now.org/issues/violence   This NOW (National Organization for Women) site offers valuable information—such as research articles and legal rulings—on domestic violence, sexual assault, and sexual harassment.

www.naesv.org/index.html   This site of the National Alliance to End Sexual Violence has a good resource center and useful fact sheets.

www.ncadv.org   The National Coalition Against Domestic Violence site has an excellent section on protecting oneself and creating and implementing a safety plan.

www.al-anon.alateen.org   This is the go-to site for anyone whose life is impacted by the drinking of a family member or friend.

www.ojp.usdoj.gov/ovc   This is the site for the Office for Victims of Crime, a division of the U.S. Department of Justice. It offers numerous resources for victim assistance.

www.crimes-of-persuasion.com   This site exposes various investment, telemarketing, and consumer fraud scams.

www.wiredsafety.org   WiredSafety provides help, information, and education to Internet and mobile device users of all ages who want to protect themselves against cyberabuse—ranging from identity and credential theft, to online fraud and cyberstalking, to hacking and malicious code attacks.

www.cyberangels.org   Offers advice for preventing and fighting cyberabuse and Internet crime, such as fraud and identity theft.

www.metlife.com/Lifeadvice/Money/Docs/fraud3.html   Information for victims of fraud including identity theft, insurance fraud, and telemarketing fraud.

www.cdc.gov/niosh/violcont.html   The National Institute for Occupational Safety and Health publication discusses risk factors and prevention strategies of workplace violence.

www.workplaceviolence911.com   The National Institute for the Prevention of Workplace Violence offers research and training in the area of workplace violence prevention.

www.roadragers.com   At this organization's website you can post a report on rude and reckless drivers that will remain online for anyone to access for research purposes.

Index

P-Q

R

S

Check Out These
Best-Sellers

Grammar and Style
SECOND EDITION
978-1-59257-115-4
$16.95

Buying & Selling a Home
FIFTH EDITION
978-1-59257-458-2
$19.95

Being a Groom
THIRD EDITION
978-1-59257-451-3
$9.95

Learning Spanish
FOURTH EDITION
978-1-59257-485-8
$24.95

Investing
THIRD EDITION
978-1-59257-480-3
$19.95

Baby Sign Language
978-1-59257-469-8
$14.95

Total Nutrition
FOURTH EDITION
978-1-59257-439-1
$18.95

Positive Dog Training
SECOND EDITION
978-1-59257-483-4
$14.95

The Bible
THIRD EDITION
978-1-59257-389-9
$18.95

Calculus
SECOND EDITION
978-1-59257-471-1
$18.95

Music Theory
SECOND EDITION
978-1-59257-437-7
$19.95

The Perfect Resume
FOURTH EDITION
978-1-59257-463-6
$14.95

Playing the Guitar
SECOND EDITION
978-0-02864244-4
$21.95

Manga Illustrated
978-1-59257-335-6
$19.95

Knitting & Crocheting
THIRD EDITION
Illustrated
978-1-59257-491-9
$19.95

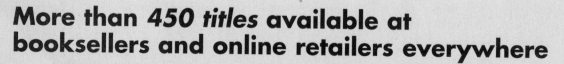

More than *450 titles* available at booksellers and online retailers everywhere

www.idiotsguides.com

ALPHA